Stalin's Cold War

In the first analysis of the start of the Cold War from a Soviet viewpoint, Caroline Kennedy-Pipe draws on Russian source material to reach some startling conclusions. She challenges the prevailing orthodoxy of Western historians to show how Moscow saw the presence of US troops in Europe in the 1940s and early 1950s as advantageous rather than as a check on Soviet ambitions.

The author points to a complex web of concerns that fuelled Moscow's actions, and explores how the Soviet leadership, and Stalin in particular, responded to American policy. She shows how the Soviet experience of the United States and Europe, both before, during and after the Second World War, led Moscow to a policy that was not simply fuelled by anti-Americanism. Six chapters cover events from the wartime conferences of 1943 until the death of Stalin. A final chapter places the book in the context of the current debate over the causes of the Cold War.

Stalin's Cold War combines the best traditions of narrative international history with the latest insights offered by access to previously hidden Russian sources. It should become a standard narrative history of Soviet–European relations in the formative years of the Cold War.

Caroline Kennedy-Pipe is Deputy Director of the Institute for International Studies at the University of Leeds.

For Gregory and Alexander

Stalin's Cold War

Soviet strategies in Europe, 1943 to 1956

Caroline Kennedy-Pipe

Manchester University Press
Manchester and New York

Distributed exclusively in the USA and Canada by St. Martin's Press

Copyright © Caroline Kennedy-Pipe 1995

Published by Manchester University Press
Oxford Road, Manchester M13 9NR, UK
and Room 400, 175 Fifth Avenue, New York, NY 10010, USA

Distributed exclusively in the USA and Canada
by St. Martin's Press, Inc., 175 Fifth Avenue, New York,
NY 10010, USA

British Library Cataloguing-in-Publication Data
A catalogue record for this book is available from the British Library

Library of Congress Cataloging-in-Publication Data
Kennedy-Pipe, Caroline, 1961 –
    Stalin's cold war : Soviety strategies in Europe, 1943 to 1956 /
Caroline Kennedy-Pipe.
        p.   cm.
    ISBN 0–7190–4201–1 (hardback). — ISBN 0–7190–4202–X (pbk.)
    1. Soviet Union—Foreign relations—Europe.   2. Europe—Foreign
relations—Soviet Union.   3. Soviet Union—Foreign relations—United
States.   4. United States—Foreign relations—Soviet Union.
5. World politics—1945–1955.   I. Title.
D1065.S65K46   1995
327.47′009′044—dc20   94–36785

ISBN 0 7190 4201 1 *hardback*
     0 7190 4202 X *paperback*

Photoset in Linotron Sabon
by Northern Phototypesetting Co. Ltd, Bolton

Printed in Great Britain
by Bell & Bain Ltd, Glasgow

Contents

Acknowledgements

I would like to thank the following for their advice, inspiration and friendship during the writing of this book. First, my husband Gregory who now knows more about the Cold War than any lawyer could ever want to. For his patience I am very grateful. My parents and brothers have supported me over many long years. To John Kennedy in particular I owe much. I have the following to thank. In Oxford, Adam Roberts and Richard Kindersley for believing in the original project, Jackie Wilcox and Archie Brown of St Antony's Russian Centre for their continued encouragement; June Currie, Diane Reddish, Daniel Calingaert and Julie Newton all provided invaluable support. Steve Smith, Clive Jones, Colin McInnes and Nick Rengger have all provided help in more ways than I could list. In particular, Len Scott and Jim Piscatori have commented at length on the project. I would like to thank my colleagues in the Institute for International Studies, Robin Brown, Hugh Dyer, Owen Hartley, Stephen Griffiths and John Gooch for their friendship during recent difficult times. A debt of gratitude is also owed to the ESRC for sponsoring my work at Oxford University. My MUP editor, Richard Purslow, also deserves thanks for his patience! Above all, however, I have to thank Professor Harry Hearder of Cardiff University, who started me on the academic path with his enthusiasm for history and Professor Robert O'Neill of All Saints College, Oxford, not only for supervising my doctoral work but for his unstinting encouragement, friendship and advice over the last few years. My final debt is to Professor Ken Booth of Aberystwyth, who has remained a valued source of continued academic wisdom and friendship. To all the above I owe many debts. Needless to say, any shortcomings in the text are mine.

C.K.-P.

Introduction

With the end of the Cold War, questions are once more being asked about the origins and nature of the antagonism which dominated the Russian–American relationship during the period 1945–90. My work began at the height of the second Cold War in 1985 and attempted to add to the debate over Soviet–European policies in an age of almost universal anti-Soviet sentiment in the West. It was and remains an attempt to understand Moscow's policies in Europe and to point to certain complexities and ambiguities which characterised Soviet aims on the continent. It seeks to do this by examining one of the most fundamental arguments that frequently pervade academic works about the Cold War: the idea that the Soviet leadership was absolutely opposed to a US military presence in Europe.[1] This study challenges that view. It shows that the historical evolution of Soviet perceptions of, and objectives in relation to, US forces in Europe between 1943 and 1956 does not sustain the standard view. It attempts to fill a gap in the Western literature by examining Moscow's inconsistent policies towards the US presence. In particular, it investigates whether Moscow perceived any benefits to arise from a continued, direct, US military involvement in Europe.

The emergence of the Cold War has been discussed without consideration of this issue. Historians have, by and large, concentrated primarily on the question of who was responsible for the division of Europe and the subsequent Cold War. The so-called 'traditionalist' school blamed Moscow. It pointed to an ideologically inspired foreign policy and assumed that Soviet leaders regarded the American military involvement in Europe as the primary obstacle to a predetermined strategy of territorial expansion.[2] Other scholars think Stalin pursued a more *ad hoc*, opportunist strategy which was

similarly impeded by the American military presence. The subsequent and reactive 'revisionist' school has portrayed Soviet policy
as predominantly defensive and reactive to America's assertion of
economic, atomic and military power in Europe. At its core, the
revisionist argument holds that the Cold War might have been
avoided if the United States had not alienated the Soviet Union.[3] In
particular, some revisionists (who might be termed 'hard
revisionists') point to the primacy of economic considerations for
Washington, and the subsequent domestic constraints under which
Truman operated in pursuit of these policies. The 'revisionists'
tended to assume that the US military presence was perceived by the
USSR as exclusively adverse to Soviet interests in Europe. The 'neo-
revisionists', who currently dominate the debate, sought to strike a
balance between these two major interpretations. They extensively
analysed the making of American foreign policy and portrayed the
Cold War as having arisen from an unfortunate but understandable
series of mistakes and misunderstandings.[4] At the moment, however, this line of thinking is being challenged by what may be termed
the 'post-neo-revisionists', who affirm that actually Stalin was guilty
as charged by the traditionalists.[5]

The debate still begs the question of Soviet motivations and
ambitions in relation to the American military presence in Europe.
Scholars, myself included, are, of course, working in the dark to a
considerable extent because of the lack of access to source materials
on the Soviet side.[6] It is clear though, from what is known, and from
what can be pieced together from existing sources, that Soviet
behaviour in this period was far more complex than any of the
existing major works on the Cold War suggest. Through an examination of Soviet policy towards US troops in Europe, this book
argues that, at certain points, Moscow was not wholly hostile
towards a US presence on the continent and even perceived certain
benefits to accrue from it. In terms of the debate over the Cold War
several new questions are asked about Soviet policy. What benefits
did Soviet leaders believe could be derived from the American military presence in Europe? Did these benefits outweigh the limitations
on Soviet power and influence in Europe which the American presence necessarily entailed? And what were the key moments for Soviet
thinking on this issue? In the midst of the break-up of the USSR,
other analysts have also posed important questions, not least
whether, in fact, there were missed opportunities for accom-

modation with Stalin and to what extent the Soviet leadership understood Western motives.[7]

This book outlines the development of the USSR's political and military interests in Europe after the Second World War. It considers the effects of the consistent Soviet preoccupation with Germany and its potential influence on the political and military composition of Europe. In particular, the question is asked whether the ability of the United States to exert military control in varying degrees over Germany endowed the American presence in Europe with a certain utility in Soviet eyes. One major theme is the Stalinist preoccupation that a defeated Germany would rise again. It is of some interest to scholars of the Cold War to note that whilst analysts do admit the Soviet preoccupation with Germany they do not necessarily link these Soviet motives in the post-war world. This book attempts to make that linkage explicit.

The willingness of the Soviet leadership to acknowledge the pre-eminent military and political influence of the United States in Western Europe, in return for the recognition of a similar pre-eminent Soviet influence in most of Eastern Europe, is examined. Of course, much has made in textbooks of the so-called Percentages Agreement of 1944 between Churchill and Stalin. The book looks at the obvious benefits to be derived from dividing the continent but it also looks at Soviet initiatives for joint occupation. Whilst most historians have dismissed out of hand Soviet proposals for joint security arrangements in Europe, such as the offer to join NATO, this work evaluates Soviet initiatives more seriously and asks whether they reflected a genuine attempt to reshape security arrangements.

One major issue addressed is the extent to which Moscow, through its American policy, attempted to manipulate the Western bloc as a whole. Initiatives designed to appeal to Washington are shown as designed at certain stages to manipulate bloc cohesion in the West. Moscow believed itself able to manoeuvre between what it perceived as tensions in the West to its own advantage. This work identifies at what stages in the Cold War it succeeded and failed.

The book also attempts to distinguish between divergent views within the Soviet leadership on the role it should assume in Europe. Again, questions which have received little attention in the Cold War literature are asked about Soviet policy. What influence, for example, did apparent differences between Soviet leaders have on

Soviet policies in Europe? This work indicates the influence of contrary strains in Soviet policy towards the American military presence
in Europe. This theme has been addressed only recently by Western
historians, many of whom have taken for granted the absolute
control of Stalin over foreign policy for the whole period.[8] Hence,
the claim made for this work is that it asks rather different questions
about a much studied period of history and attempts to shed new
light on the making of Soviet foreign policy towards Western
Europe.

Historians have argued not only over the nature of the Cold War
but over the very date at which it started. It has been dated variously
by historians as starting as early as 1917 with the establishment of
Bolshevik rule in Moscow, at Yalta in 1945 when the division of
Europe was agreed upon, and in 1948 with the blockade of Berlin.
This work takes as its starting point 1917. This date is critical, not
necessarily because it was the starting point of the Cold War, but
because the roots of Moscow's relationship with the West are to be
found in the events of the 1920s and 1930s. The factors which bore
upon the formulation of Soviet foreign policy in this period are
examined. The failure of the West European powers seriously to
pursue collective security arrangements against the contingency of a
rebirth of German militarism is shown as a formative experience for
Soviet leaders. Indeed, the preference of the West European powers
to act with Nazi Germany against Soviet communism was central to
Soviet thinking about post-war arrangements.[9]

One of the key features of the early post-war period is that the
Soviet leaders did not view Western policy-making in the period as
monolithic. Soviet notions of a Western bloc come later; during the
inter-war period Moscow differentiated quite clearly between the
Western capitalist states and sought to gain advantage from their
policy differences. This book argues that this view persisted into the
post-war period.

Historians have rarely doubted that the post-war political and
military division of Europe originated in the broad agreements on
spheres of influence tacitly negotiated by the Allies in the period
1943–45.[10] This work puts forward the view that these agreements
essentially followed, and in many cases formalised, the disposition of
military forces in East and West Europe. Soviet strategy is viewed as
operating on two levels at the end of the war. First, Stalin expected
that, where Soviet troops were in occupation when the war ended,

Soviet influence would thereafter predominate. He therefore exercised a policy of military denial to exclude US forces from those territories that he regarded as vital to Soviet interests, hence the military concentration of Soviet military forces in East European countries such as Czechoslovakia and the Eastern parts of Germany. In this sense, the book agrees with the work of those historians who have pointed to Soviet military manoeuvres in trying to push as far West as possible in the closing stages of the war.[11] However, there was a second more sophisticated level on which Soviet strategy operated: Stalin seized territory in the closing phase of the war as a bargaining counter and to ensure American respect for Soviet strategic interests in Eastern Europe. If the Western powers chose to be obstructive about Soviet post-war aims, Stalin would have something with which to negotiate. But in addition to this competition with the West, this section also points to Stalin's desire for cooperation with the United States. A major theme of this section of the book is to examine his tacit acceptance of US troops' presence, and, indeed, despite the obvious element of territorial competition, his approval of US troops in Germany for a longer period.

The military presence of the United States in Europe became established in 1945–47. Soviet attitudes to this process form the core of Chapter 3. The American possession of atomic power is examined as an influence on the making of Soviet foreign policy. Again, work currently under way in the wake of the demise of the USSR is adding considerably to our knowledge of this issue. The extent to which the US monopoly of atomic power affected the origins of the Cold War has been one of the most important issues of the Cold War. Did US atomic power make a difference to Stalin? The book puts forward the view that US possession of the atomic bomb did make a difference not least because, in the summer of 1945 after victory over Germany, Stalin was now faced with technological inferiority *vis-à-vis* an emerging great power.[12]

The chapter also considers Soviet perceptions of the occupation policies pursued and implemented by the United States in the Western zones of Germany.[13] The influence of Western military coordination in Western Europe on Soviet occupation policies in Eastern Europe is also examined. The consolidation of the lines defined at the end of the war is one theme in this chapter. The actual operation of joint Western and Soviet occupation policy in Germany and Austria is described, and the idea postulated that Soviet policy, rather than appearing designed to lever the United States out of these occupied zones, was far more ambivalent. The cases of joint military withdrawal which confounded Western expectations, such as in Czechoslovakia in November 1945 and Iran in early 1946,[14] are shown as designed to maintain a good relationship with Washington, not to jeopardise it. This discussion does not intend to support the revisionist assertion that the United States was to blame for the Cold War but, rather, is designed to point to a complex set of priorities on the Soviet side, which was to maintain a working relationship with the United States, particularly in view of the atomic bomb, whilst not conceding post-war gains.

A fourth chapter focuses on the confrontations of 1948. The central crises which accelerated the formation of opposing military blocs were the Czech coup and the Berlin blockade. This work suggests that Stalin did not initiate the Berlin blockade as a mechanism to reopen the broader issue of the legitimacy of American occupation rights in Germany as a whole.[15] Stalin's provocation of the crisis was obviously intended to challenge Western rights in Berlin, but it was also intended to encourage a more formalised division of Germany. In this crucial period, the Soviet debate over the future of Germany is shown to have different and contradictory strands that resulted in a Soviet policy of reclaiming Berlin but also of accepting a divided state.

The next section deals with the Soviet response to the creation of NATO in 1949. The formalisation of the US presence in Europe is shown to have had two distinct results in Moscow. The first is that Stalin used Western military integration in 1949–53 to justify the military and political consolidation of the east European territories controlled by the Red Army.[16] But, more critically, Western rearmament reinforced the traditional Soviet doubts about German militarism. At this stage, it is argued, Moscow began to regard the US presence more obviously with alarm, particularly because of its nuclear superiority. A section deals with the Soviet initiatives designed to counter bloc cohesion on the Western side. In particular the Soviet suggestions for pan-European security arrangements are depicted as the moment at which the Soviet leadership might seriously have attempted to 'dilute' or 'deny' American military influence in Europe.

The death of Stalin is portrayed as a turning point for Soviet foreign policy in many ways. The book examines the Soviet reaction to the formal incorporation of the Federal Republic of Germany into NATO, and the creation of the WTO, and puts forward the idea that, actually, this was in many ways a satisfactory outcome for dealing with Moscow's historic enemy – Germany.

Overall, the book, by examining some hitherto neglected issues relating to Moscow and American military forces in Europe and by asking different questions, provides a different view of Soviet behaviour during the early Cold War period. This work argues that Moscow had a far less rigid strategy for Europe than has been assumed, and that it did not have a wholly negative view of the US troop presence in Western Europe. Even when the West rearmed, in the wake of the Berlin crisis, US troops provided, in the Soviet leadership's eyes, a useful counterweight to German remilitarisation. In all, the book points to a more variegated, a less monolithic and a more complex set of policy objectives on the Soviet side than has so far been assumed.

Notes

1   For Soviet views on the US role in the Western alliance, see Robbin F. Laird and Susan L. Clark, *The USSR and the Western Alliance* (London: Unwin Hyman Ltd, 1990). This book analyses the view that Soviet foreign policy in Europe was designed to 'decouple' the United States from its Western allies and ultimately to weaken, if not destroy, the alliance. On this issue see also T. Wolfe, *Soviet Power and Europe 1945–1970* (Baltimore: The Johns Hopkins University Press, 1970).

2   See, for example, G. F. Kennan, ('X'), 'The Sources of Soviet Conduct', *Foreign Affairs*, July 1947.

3   William A. Williams, *The Tragedy of American Diplomacy*, Revised Edition (New York: World Publishing, 1962), and G. Alperovitz, *Atomic Diplomacy: Hiroshima and Potsdam* (New York: Simon and Schuster, 1965).

4   The leading proponent of this school is J. L. Gaddis. See *The United States and the Origins of the Cold War 1941–1947*. (New York: Columbia University Press, 1972).

5   See, for example, Alexander Dallin and Gail W. Lapidus, eds., *The Soviet System in Crisis, A Reader of Western and Soviet Views* (Boulder, Colorodo: Westview Press, 1991) pp. 481–530.

6   With the collapse of the USSR, we have seen a gradual opening of the Soviet archives. The archives of the Foreign Ministry began to declassify its files in 1989–1990, while after the demise of the CPSU, its archives were reorganised into two centres; the Russian Centre for the Preservation and

Study of Contemporary Documentation (RTSKhIDNI) in September 1991 and the Storage Centre for Contemporary Documentation (TSKhSD) in February 1992.

7   See, for example, Vladislav Zubok and Constantine Pleshakov, 'The Soviet Union' in D. Reynolds, ed., *The Origins of the Cold War in Europe* (New Haven and London: Yale University Press, 1994), pp. 53–77.

8   These issues do, however, appear in specialist studies of Soviet decision-making. See, for example, W. O. McCagg, *Stalin Embattled 1943–1948* (Detroit: Wayne State University Press, 1978), and G. D. Ra'anon, *International Policy Formation in the USSR, Factional Debates during the Zhdnaovshine* (Hamden, Conn.: Archon Books, 1983), and Anthony D'Agnostino, *Soviet Succession Struggles, Kreminology and the Russian Question from Lenin to Gorbachev* (Winchester, Mass.: Unwin Hyman, 1988).

9   See J. Haslam, *The Soviet Union and the Struggle for Collective Security in Europe 1933–1939* (New York: St Martin's, 1984).

10   V. Mastny, *Russia's Road to the Cold War; Diplomacy, Warfare and the Politics of Communism* (New York: Columbia University Press, 1979).

11   See, for example, T. Sharpe, *The Western Alliance and the Zonal Division of Germany* (London: OUP, 1975).

12   See D. A. Holloway, *The Soviet Union and the Arms Race* (New Haven and London, 1983).

13   The US military presence in Germany was not a seamless web of commitment. Withdrawal of US troops from the continent became a major source of discussion on the American side. See Gaddis, *The United States and the Origins of the Cold War*.

14   Louise Fawcett, *Iran and the Cold War* (Cambridge: Cambridge University Press, 1992).

15   A. Shailm, *The United States and the Berlin Blockade 1948–1949. A Study in Crisis Decision-making* (Berkeley: University of California Press, 1983).

16   W. Loth, *The Division of the World 1941–1955* (London: Routledge, 1988).

Chapter 1

Strategies of survival

The requirements of the victorious Soviet Union after World War II were critically shaped by the inter-war years. Some of the major themes of Soviet thinking about security were established, at an early stage, by the experiences of revolution, isolation and war. The history of the Soviet Union before 1941 was dominated not only by the internal demands of state-building by the new Bolshevik leadership but also by a fight for survival in a hostile world.

The revolutionary heritage

Soviet external relations between 1918 and 1921 centred on three issues: civil war, foreign intervention, and the attempt to export revolution to the rest of Europe. The Bolsheviks' hold on power was precarious. They were continually challenged by rival groupings such as the Mensheviks and the Socialist Revolutionaries,[1] and were riven by factionalism over the course of revolution.[2] In addition to the problems caused by its tenuous grip on domestic affairs, the new leadership was besieged by the threat from external powers. The invaders of Russia in the last 800 years have been described as like a *Who's Who* of military aggression. Moscow had been regularly besieged by hostile forces.[3] The early Soviet experience was little different, though this was not what the Bolsheviks had expected. Trotsky, the Commissar for Foreign Affairs, perceived his function to be 'to issue a few revolutionary proclamations to the peoples of the world and then shut up shop'.[4]

The Bolshevik leaders believed that Europe was composed of peoples waiting to abolish traditional state mechanisms and that the state itself was an instrument of class oppression. They saw the world divided, not by traditional state boundaries, but by class division. In line with these beliefs, the Bolsheviks shunned the normal apparatus of state power. Before the October Revolution, there was, for example, no preparation for raising an army.[5] However, the Bolshevik leadership was forced by the Civil War and foreign intervention to construct military forces. In the spring of 1918, Lenin called for an army of one million men.[6]

In line with the belief that revolution was imminent, in December 1917, Trotsky appealed to the 'peoples' of those states at war with Russia to rebel against their governments and to join the revolution. The Bolsheviks pinned their hopes on revolution in Germany. Czarist Russia had entered the war against Germany in August 1914, but the Bolshevik leadership expected that the German people would rise up against the Kaiser in support of the revolution. The uprising failed to materialise and the German army advanced deep into Russian territory. It met with little resistance from dispirited Bolshevik forces whose numbers had been depleted by the desertion of the Muzhiks, who were rushing home to share in the break-up of the estates. The Bolsheviks had, on seizing power, committed themselves to ending the war only when a new revolutionary group was in power in Germany, but in early 1918 they were forced to consider a humiliating armistice with a Germany in which the revolution had never materialised.

The prospect of an armistice with Imperial Germany provoked considerable controversy amongst the Bolshevik leadership.[7] Lenin argued that in the short term a pragmatic course should be adopted. He believed that, if necessary, peace should be accepted on German terms, so that at least the revolution in Russia itself could survive.[8] He was opposed by a group led by Bukharin who argued that the revolution could only be continued through war, and that a peace with Imperial Germany would be an utter humiliation.[9] Stalin, at this point an increasingly important member of the ruling group, seemed hesitant on the issues and took little part in the debates over policy. However, he eventually sided with Lenin in advocating peace.[10] Stalin reasoned that the German people were not going to support revolutionary aims and that war was weakening the Bolshevik position at home. He argued that

There is no revolutionary movement in the West; there are no facts of a revolutionary movement; and we cannot base ourselves on a mere potentiality. If the Germans begin to advance this will strengthen the counter-revolution in this country.[11]

Trotsky, a representative at the peace talks, disagreed and pro-longed the discussions in the erroneous but optimistic belief that the proletariat would rise against the Kaiser. The working classes did not rise, and German military power proved irresistible by the Bolsheviks. On 3 March 1918, Sokolnilov, head of the Bolshevik delegation, signed the armistice at Brest-Litovsk.[12] It represented a considerable defeat for the Bolsheviks. They lost a third of their population, conceded thirty-two per cent of Russia's cultivable land, twenty-seven per cent of its railways, fifty-four per cent of industry and eighty-nine per cent of its coal mines.[13] Brest-Litovsk was of great significance in future thinking about security. The considerable losses underlined the importance for the Soviet leadership of being able to negotiate from a position of strength.

This agreement sparked the fragmentation of the ruling coalition. The left-wing Socialist Revolutionaries resigned from the govern-ment and encouraged uprisings against the Bolsheviks. By the sum-mer of 1918, civil war raged. Lenin responded by outlawing both the Socialist Revolutionaries and the Mensheviks, and engaged in a ruthless campaign to eliminate them.[14] At the same time the Bolsheviks faced foreign intervention on their already embattled soil by the British and French. Admiral Kolchak, one of the leaders of the White armies, proclaimed himself ruler of Russia upon taking power in Omsk on 18 November 1918. This claim was recognised by the Allied Control Council in Paris.[15] French troops occupied Odessa, while the British Royal Navy assisted White commanders in the Bay of Finland. By the autumn, White forces had practically reached both Moscow and St Petersburg. By the end of 1919, however, the White forces had been repelled, mainly through the ability of the Bolsheviks to exploit a lack of military coordination on the White side.[16] By the end of the year, the Red Army, under Trotsky, had claimed victory.

Even while facing the peril of intervention by the Great Powers, the Bolsheviks were still actively contemplating the export of com-munism. With the end of World War I and the defeat of the Austro-German armies by the Western allies, 'soviets' sprang into existence in Berlin, Munich, Warsaw and Riga. In March 1919, the Comintern (Communist International) was established in Moscow.[17] Its pri-mary function was to serve as the guiding force for revolutionary movements throughout the world. The Comintern targeted Germany as having potential for revolution. Yet again, however, the hopes of revolution proved illusory. The uprising of 1919 proved to be a rather dismal and short-lived affair. In Hungary, a communist leadership actually emerged, but by the end of the year, that government, led by Bela Kun, had collapsed.[18] Zinoviev admitted that 'Perhaps we were carried away by our enthusiasm; perhaps it is true that not one year, but two or three years, will be necessary before all Europe becomes Soviet'.[19] The failure of revolution abroad was compounded in 1920 when the Bolsheviks attempted to inspire revolution in Poland. The Poles launched an invasion of Ukraine. Bolshevik forces managed to repel the attack and, still encouraged by a belief in the revolutionary potential in Europe, proceeded to follow the retreating soldiers on to Polish soil. As the army marched to Warsaw, the Bolsheviks confidently refused to consider an armistice, proposed by the British, based on the so-called Curzon line.[20] Nationalism superseded any native revolutionary fervour, and the Poles, with help from their friends in the West, forced the Red Army back. The Peace of Riga, agreed in 1921 between the two sides, actually established the border to the east of the Curzon line.[21]

These failures brought home to the Bolshevik leaders that there was little if any immediate revolutionary potential abroad. The priority became to secure a period of peace to strengthen the new regime at home and to stave off intervention by the other powers. In the minds of the new Bolshevik leadership this did not mean the abandonment of the revolution abroad but merely a tactical postponement. In concrete terms this meant, in the short term, acceptance of traditional European state diplomacy: recognition of borders and non-intervention in the affairs of other states. Indeed, and somewhat ironically, the Bolshevik leaders now had a vested interest in these norms, not least to protect their own state. But, and this was critical, the revolution abroad was still to be fostered by the Comintern.[22] It is here that we see the origins of what, for the West, was to be the major paradox of Soviet foreign policy in the post-war period – a pragmatic acceptance of the norms of diplomacy but a commitment to revolution abroad through the activities of foreign communist parties. There was no doubt, though, that the prospect of world revolution had been pushed far into the unforeseeable future.

To justify the postponement of revolution, the Bolshevik leadership developed the idea of 'peaceful coexistence'. In essence this meant that Moscow accepted that, at least in the shorter term, capitalist states would continue to exist and that some form of accommodation was possible with them. The announcement of peaceful coexistence would, Lenin hoped, reassure the Western states that Russia was essentially peaceful, and would stave off the inevitable conflict between the revolutionary state and the capitalist West.[23] The Bolsheviks would then, in the period of peace, be able to reconstruct their economy and assert their grip upon the state. One crucial aspect of this formulation of coexistence with the West was the expectation that peace would enable Moscow to acquire the Western technical assistance necessary for modernising the new Soviet state.[24]

For the Bolsheviks there was no obvious contradiction in pursuing such a course of action. For example, the Comintern, at its fifth Congress in 1924, proclaimed the right of all 'oppressed minorities' in Poland, Czechoslovakia, Romania, Yugoslavia and Greece to struggle for freedom; yet within five years, Maxim Litvinov, the Soviet Foreign Minister, concluded friendship treaties with some of these very states.[25] This ability to distinguish between the traditional demands of state-to-state intercourse and the need to inspire revolution across state boundaries became a hallmark of Soviet foreign policy in the subsequent decades.[26] While a policy of ideology, tempered by *Realpolitik*, provided flexibility for the Soviet leadership in some ways, in others it became counter-productive, leading Western states to regard Moscow with enormous suspicion.

The hostility of the Western states was especially counter-productive for the Bolsheviks as they embarked upon the modernisation of the state. In December 1924, Stalin, who had succeeded Lenin, announced that the energies of the Soviet state would henceforth be devoted to a programme of 'Socialism in one Country'.[27] Building on ideas that Lenin had espoused,[28] Stalin argued that the Soviet state could achieve socialism without the help of a Western revolutionary movement.

> The basic and new feature, the decisive feature that has affected all the events in the sphere of foreign relations during this period, is the fact that a certain temporary equilibrium of forces has been established between our country, which is building socialism, and the countries of the capitalist world, an equilibrium which has determined the present period of 'peaceful coexistence' between the land of soviets and the

capitalist countries. What we at one time regarded as brief respite after the war has become a whole period of respite. Hence there was a certain equilibrium of forces and a certain period of 'peaceful coexistence' between the bourgeois world and the proletarian world.[29]

The revolution would arrive in the West – but not yet. In the meantime, Stalin proposed the construction of a strong state at home. Peaceful coexistence was still the order of the day, but the crucial change was that Russia no longer needed revolutions abroad. Rather, other states needed the revolution in Russia: the consolidation of the revolution at home would aid other revolutions abroad. Stalin adapted the meaning of peaceful coexistence to justify not only postponement of revolution abroad but also the building of the Soviet state.[30]

Peaceful coexistence did not, however, mean that the Soviet state was reconciled to capitalism. War was still inevitable but, in the shorter term, the Kremlin believed, it could be postponed by buying off the capitalists and manipulating the 'contradictions' between the capitalist states.[31] As Stalin said:

> The basic facts are that in spite of the existence of a bloc between America and Britain against the annulment of Allied debts, in spite of this bloc . . . the conflicts of interests between Britain and America is not being allayed, on the contrary, it is becoming more intense.[32]

The relationship with Germany was central to Soviet foreign policy in the 1920s and 1930s. A pragmatic and tenuous alliance was codified in the 1922 Treaty of Rapallo. It was born out of the isolation of the two states from the norms of European diplomacy after the Versailles agreement. The Treaty of Rapallo provided Moscow with access to the technology needed for modernisation at home. In a subsequent and secret protocol, it was agreed that the Reichswehr and the Red Army would collaborate.[33] The Germans were able to build and test military equipment, forbidden under the Versailles agreement, on Soviet soil.[34] The Germans erected arms factories and Moscow shared in the output. The Soviet Union benefited from military instruction by German specialists.[35] In 1926, the Berlin Treaty of Friendship and Neutrality was signed, reinforcing the relationship. Germany, on which the Bolshevik Party had pinned its revolutionary hopes, became its main trading partner. But the idea of revolution did not go away. Despite the Treaty of Rapallo, the Soviet leadership still attempted, albeit in a rather limited and half-hearted manner, to support a communist coup in Germany during 1923.[36] The attempt failed and Moscow and Berlin maintained a pragmatic relationship through which the Soviet leadership primarily obtained technical and military aid.[37]

In 1925, Stalin predicted the inevitability of war in Europe. He specifically pointed to the rebirth of German militarism and the potential for conflict between the capitalist states. He made clear what the position of the Soviet Union would be if such a situation arose:

> We shall have to come out, but we ought to be the last to come out. And we should come out in order to throw the decisive weight on the scales, the weight that should tilt the scales.[38]

Soviet foreign policy was premised on a belief that differences existed amongst the Western powers, particularly over economic issues, that could be exploited to Moscow's advantage.[39] This balancing act remained a major theme of Soviet foreign policy.

The late 1920s were dominated in Soviet politics by two domestic issues. The first was the complete 'Stalinisation' of the state, and the second was the drive for collectivisation. Between 1925 and 1928, Stalin consolidated his almost complete control of the institutions and political life, eradicating rivals such as Trotsky. The massive drive for collectivisation and industrialisation imposed a draconian regime on the peoples of the Soviet Union. Some analysts have claimed that these internal demands of the economy fed directly into the making of Soviet foreign policy. Stalin, it is claimed, deliberately inflated the threat of war with the capitalist states in an attempt to justify the regime at home. In particular, in the late 1920s, he blamed the Conservative government in Britain for conspiring against the Soviet state.[40] It is certainly true that the rhetoric of the period continually castigated the capitalist states for their actions.[41] The official Soviet line was still the one developed by Lenin that imperialism necessarily generated conflict, which would lead to world war.[42] Nevertheless, Soviet external policies were actually designed to maintain a period of peace. While collectivisation and consolidation dominated domestic politics, external forces threatened to destroy the Soviet experiment.

The search for collective security, 1933–38

Moscow's security problems increased seriously when Germany left the League of Nations in October 1933. *Izvestiya* commented that 'Germany's exit from the League of Nations is for the supporters of peace an alarming warning of the need to be on guard'.[43] Already, with Hitler's take-over of power, Moscow had begun to feel uneasy, but Soviet leaders declared that the established Soviet–German relationship would not change. In September 1933, Soviet military leaders declared their commitment to the Rapallo Treaty. Tukhachevsky, in November, stated that the Red Army would never betray its cooperation with the Reichswehr.[44] Despite these pronouncements, Moscow decided to close down all the German military stations in the USSR, indicating unease with the relationship.[45]

In December 1933, Maxim Litvinov, in a speech to the Central Executive Committee of the Congress of Soviets, divided the states of Europe into two camps. He distinguished not between socialist and capitalist states but rather divided Europe between revisionist powers, such as Germany, and those who wished to maintain the *status quo*. The Soviet Foreign Minister emphasised Hitler's ambition, outlined in *Mein Kampf*, to 'enslave the Soviet People'. To avert this threat, he proposed that the USSR seek collaboration with other anti-revisionist states.[46] On 12 December, the Politburo passed a resolution in favour of collective security, which was subsequently approved on 19 December.[47] The Soviet leadership sought a multilateral assistance pact between the USSR, France, Poland, Belgium, Czechoslovakia, the Baltic states and Finland.

Litvinov targeted France as a possible ally against Hitler. In 1933, he embarked upon discussions with Barthou, the French Foreign Minister, on arrangements for a security agreement which would guarantee the eastern frontiers of Germany. In April, Litvinov and Barthou tried to create an 'Eastern Locarno', that is, some form of eastern security system which included the USSR, Germany, the Baltic states, Poland and Czechoslovakia. As part of the deal, Moscow would join the League of Nations, and the French would recognise the rearmament of Germany.[48] The two Foreign Ministers also agreed a separate Franco-Soviet pact under which Paris would aid Moscow in the event of an attack. In return, Moscow would guarantee the western frontiers of Germany.[49] This plan was rejected by the Germans, and then by the Poles, leaving the scheme in

tatters. It is questionable as to how seriously the French were prepared to take the arrangement, as ratification of the treaty was
obstructed in Paris, and French Ministers were simultaneously
negotiating with Hitler.[50]

That Moscow saw some utility in collective security can be seen
from the development of a positive attitude towards the League of
Nations. The founders of the League had been scathing about the
Bolsheviks, and had left them out.[51] Prior to 1933, Soviet statesmen
had been derogatory about the organisation. In January 1934 Stalin
had, in an interview in *Izvestiya*, apparently signalled a definite
change in Soviet thinking.[52] He commented that 'despite the withdrawal of Germany and Japan from the League of Nations, or
perhaps just because of this, the League may act as something of a
brake to retard the outbreak of military actions or to hinder them'.
He reiterated this positive view again in September when the USSR
was admitted to membership:

> Given the current world situation, with Japan having turned Man-
> churia into a springboard against the Soviet Union, day after day
> provoking the outbreak of war, and with a German–Japanese
> rapprochement on the subject of war a fact, one does not have to rack
> one's brains for an answer to the question as to what prompted the
> Soviet Union to accept the invitation to enter the League of Nations.[53]

Stalin probably placed little faith in the willingness or ability of the
West European nations to act with the Soviet Union, but he saw
alliances as a possible deterrent to Hitler and therefore acted to
promote them. Stalin recognised the antagonism that the activities of
the Comintern aroused within Western governments. Accordingly, it
appears that Moscow instructed the Western communists to calm
their activities during this period. At this time, for example, the
French Communist Party changed its aim from class warfare to one
of 'popular fronts'. Support for this move was confirmed by Laval,
the new French Foreign Minister. After a meeting with Stalin in
Moscow, in May 1935, he described how encouraging the Soviet
leader had been about the new programme of rearmament in
France.[54] Subsequently, at the Seventh Congress of the Comintern,
which was held in Moscow during July and August 1935, it was
decided that the primary function of the organisation was to defeat
fascism, through 'popular fronts' which were organised along
national lines.[55]

Despite the apparent willingness of Moscow to cooperate, the West European states, and Britain in particular, were reluctant to reciprocate. In March 1935, Anthony Eden, at this point junior Foreign Office Minister in the British government, undertook a trip to Moscow for talks with Stalin. During these discussions, the Soviet leader attempted to impress upon Eden Moscow's desire for a rapprochement with the West against Germany. According to Eden's memoirs, the Soviet leader wanted Hitler to realise that if he attacked any other nation he would have the rest of Europe against him.[56] Little came of the discussions, which, indeed, seemed merely to reinforce Stalin's scepticism about the prospect of British support against Hitler.

This scepticism about the British was compounded in early 1936. On 7 March, German units entered the area of the Rhineland which had been demilitarised under the Versailles agreement. Through this action, Hitler could now fortify the western frontiers of Germany; thus Polish and Czech soil would become increasingly vulnerable, as would, ultimately, the Soviet Union itself. Moscow hoped that Hitler's breach of Versailles would galvanise the Western powers into action. Litvinov, in a speech to the Council of the League of Nations called to discuss the question, expressed willingness to join in any or all actions that the council might take against Hitler.[57] Litvinov's bid for a collective security arrangement was premised on the belief that the Western powers, like Moscow, had a vested interest in propping up the system established at Versailles for as long as possible.

There appears, however, to have been division within the Kremlin about the policy of searching for agreement with the Western powers. Some Soviet officials openly advocated a strategy of self-sufficiency. In January 1936, Molotov stated that 'we toilers of the Soviet Union must count on our own efforts in defending our affairs and above all, on our Red Army in the defence of our country'.[58]

This became increasingly likely as Hitler continued to press German territorial claims and Britain and France proved little disposed to challenge him. After the occupation of Austria in March 1938, Hitler focused his attention on the Sudetan Germans in Czechoslovakia. At the height of this crisis, on 17 March, Litvinov stressed again the willingness of his government to act with other states against Hitler. He also informed the Czechs that the USSR was prepared to go to war, if the French carried out their obligations.[59] It is difficult to tell whether Stalin was serious, because he was careful to tie Soviet behaviour to that of the French. The British and French did not take up the Soviet offer. Indeed, during September, they exerted pressure on Prague to give in to Hitler's demands. The subsequent Munich agreement, in which the Western powers agreed to Hitler's demand for the division of Czechoslovakia, has been taken by some historians as dramatically changing the course of Stalin's foreign policy towards alliance with Hitler.[60]

This is a moot point. There is little doubt that Munich, as the agreement through which the Western powers attempted to turn Hitler east, had enormous significance for Soviet security thinking. Stalin had placed little faith in the ability or willingness of the French and British to act with Moscow, and had never ruled out any option that would have averted a war involving the Soviet Union. But for the purposes of this chapter what was crucial to Soviet perceptions was the unwillingness of the British to ally with Moscow.

The Western countries, in particular Britain, preferred not to have to fight Hitler at this juncture, and some members of the British government would have been quite satisfied if Hitler could have been turned east.[61] It is an interesting question why the British preferred not to deal with Moscow against Germany. There are several possible explanations. The first is that ideological antagonisms, arising from the Russian Revolution, had not been forgotten. It did not really matter that the Comintern had, from 1935 onwards, changed its 'mission' to one of fighting fascism. Only fifteen years earlier it had been the vanguard of communism into Europe. In the mid-1930s, in Western Europe, particularly in France, there had been waves of social upheaval, with strikes and factory sit-ins. These trends appeared to some in the West to have been orchestrated by Moscow.[62] Indeed, Moscow's involvement in the Spanish Civil War led some to the conclusion that Stalin was seeking to undermine Western Europe.[63] A second explanation of why the British and the French wished to avoid alliance with Stalin was the very nature of the Stalinist regime. Some historians argue that the purges of 1936–38, with the show trials and executions, created an unwillingness to act in concert with such a government.[64] A third explanation is that the British and the French doubted the military ability of the Red Army to carry out Soviet promises of support. With the devastating purges of the high command, Stalin had effectively wiped out his senior and experienced officer corps. Men such as Marshal Tukhachevsky, who had fought in the Civil War and been responsible for the modernisation of the Soviet military throughout the early 1930s, had been executed in large numbers.[65]

The British and French appeasement of Hitler at Munich effectively ended the Soviet bid to formulate collective security alliances with the West European states. Deutscher writes: 'It must have been shortly after Munich that the idea of a new attempt at rapprochement with Germany took shape in Stalin's mind.'[66] But an approach to Germany had been suggested by some in the Soviet leadership at a much earlier stage. Molotov had been sceptical about the policy of relying on an alliance against Hitler.

At the Eighteenth Party Congress on 10 March 1939, Stalin declared that the British and French had given Germany parts of Czechoslovakia in payment for Hitler to go to war with the Soviet Union. This reasoning remained the official Soviet justification for the conclusion of a pact with Nazi Germany. Soviet spokesmen claimed that the British and the French had not wanted to deal with the Soviet Union. As Gromyko remarks in his memoirs:

> For its part the Soviet Union has shown with the utmost clarity that the pact was the result of the policy of a number of Western powers which did not wish to join the USSR in blocking Hitler's path to aggression and the unleashing of war.[67]

Early in 1939, Hitler invaded Bohemia-Moravia, a predominantly Czech territory with an ethnic German minority. The British and French performed a considerable volte-face and began to seek alliances to stop Hitler. Again, the British preferred not to rely on the Soviet Union but rather sought to form a coalition with Poland. The British guarantee to Poland was given on 31 March, and consisted of a promise that the British and French would act if Polish interests were threatened. Litvinov read this as meaning that 'Anglo-Soviet co-operation had been summarily dropped.'[68] It was generally expected in Moscow that, with this final exclusion of Moscow from collective security arrangements, Litvinov would be dismissed from his post as Stalin adapted a foreign policy to fit the alliance with Hitler.

The Nazi–Soviet Pact

Litvinov was indeed dismissed as Soviet Foreign Minister on 3 May

1939. This act has been pointed to as the signal for the opening of negotiations over the Nazi–Soviet pact. Litvinov was not only of Jewish origin but had also been closely identified with the policies of collective security and was regarded as pro-Western. He records in his memoirs that he had been, for some time, aware that power was gradually being taken from him. After the Eighteenth Party Congress, following Stalin's instructions, Potemkin published foreign policy articles in the journal *Bolshevik* and other mass media. Litvinov had learned about them only after they actually appeared in print. He also discovered that not all Soviet ambassadors were sending him important information. Many of them were sending their reports over his head to Molotov.[69]

The Nazi–Soviet pact was signed on 23 August 1939, and Stalin seemed to have achieved his primary goal – the deflection of Hitler's aggression (at least for the time being). He also gained territorially. Having failed in his attempt in 1935 to achieve an eastern security pact, Stalin now managed to buttress Soviet security by annexing Polish territory and by obtaining the German dictator's recognition of Moscow's predominant influence in Finland, Estonia, Latvia and Bessarabia. These gains provided Stalin with greater space on the periphery to use as a militarily defensive buffer, should it become necessary. This deal was reinforced by an additional protocol, signed after the defeat of Poland, which enabled the Soviet sphere of influence to be extended to Lithuania.[70]

Stalin also had territorial ambitions to the north, in Finland. Khrushchev writes in his memoirs that the Soviet leader had always intended to annex Finland.[71] Stalin's aims in 1939 for Finland appear more limited. It is true that he wanted to control parts of Finland, especially the area of Karelia. This would have achieved much greater protection for Leningrad. Stalin attempted to 'persuade' the Finnish President to allow for the provision of Soviet naval and military facilities. Stalin believed that a settlement could be reached through negotiations. The Finns, however, rejected Soviet demands for bases. Soviet hopes that security could be achieved on their north-western borders by agreement were undermined.[72] Stalin attempted to install a puppet government under the communist, Otto Kuusinen. This went badly wrong. The Winter War began on 30 November. It defied Soviet expectations. Strong resistance by Finland led to a costly war that Stalin could ill afford. Eventually he accepted peace terms which gave less than outright domination.

Finland had to cede a tenth of its territory in the west and a base in the south, at Hango. It is clear that Stalin had wanted to settle the war quickly, not least because the performance of the Red Army revealed military weakness.[73]

During 1939 and 1940, Stalin indicated the geographical requirements for Soviet security, namely, buffer states on its periphery. He imposed conditions upon the Baltic states, providing for bases in preparation for the war with Germany, and he occupied Finland to give greater defensive depth. He calculated upon the war between the Western imperialists lasting long enough for them to severely weaken each other before attention could be directed against the Soviet front. In so doing, he overestimated the military strength and resolve of France. Khrushchev later revealed that 'Stalin's nerve cracked when he learned about the fall of France'.[74] The Nazi–Soviet pact had been a gamble and there had been intimations from the first that it could not be sustained for long. Despite this, Stalin did not expect the German invasion in June 1941, or was not willing to prepare for it. The dictator's behaviour in the wake of the initial German attack has been well documented. Khrushchev writes that 'Stalin was so afraid of war that even when the Germans tried to take us by surprise and wipe out our resistance, Stalin convinced himself that Hitler would keep his word and wouldn't really attack us'.[75]

Perhaps Stalin's desire not to provoke Hitler accounts for his reluctance to listen to warnings of impending invasion. He rejected messages from Soviet field commanders that they could hear and see German preparations for attack. Under the terms of the pact, Moscow could carry out aerial reconnaissance flights over German territory, and Germany had the same privilege of over-flying the Soviet front lines.[76] Requests by Soviet front-line commanders for permission to dig defensive fortifications were rejected.[77] Khrushchev's view is reinforced by other sources which also tell of Stalin's shock at the timing of the German betrayal.[78]

On the day of the Nazi invasion, the British offered unsolicited aid to Moscow. A few days later, Washington proffered similar help.[79] On 27 June, Molotov proposed to the British 'a political agreement to define the basis of cooperation between the two countries'.[80] As Hitler threatened the very survival of the Soviet state, Stalin began negotiating with the British and the Americans to forge an anti-fascist alliance to destroy Germany for ever and to secure the future of the Soviet Union.

Soviet thinking about the United States

Moscow's approach to Washington was different from its approach to the West European powers. The United States was 'outside' Europe for a good deal of the inter-war period. This fact had a crucial effect on Moscow's perceptions of the Western powers.

President Wilson was acutely hostile towards the Bolsheviks.[81] The ideology of the regime that took power in Russia in 1917 was a cause of fundamental concern to Washington.[82] The ideas of Marx and Lenin represented a direct threat to the US commitment to liberalism, capitalism and democracy. This challenge had drawn anxious US attention.[83] In the period after the revolution, there was ideological conflict between Russia and the United States.

Despite this ideological hostility, the Bolshevik leadership had sought to develop an economic relationship with the United States almost immediately after the revolution. In May 1918, Lenin attempted to secure an agreement which would allow Moscow access to US credits. During the Paris Peace Conference, Bolshevik Ministers tried to cultivate economic ties with the United States. The Bolsheviks were at this time pursuing economic ties with any state that would trade with them, but Lenin emphasised the importance of a relationship with the United States: 'America is strong, everybody is now in its debt, everything depends on it.'[84] In 1921, the Soviet newspaper *Izvestiya* recognised that 'the US is the principal force in the world . . . all possible means will have to be employed somehow or other to come to an understanding with the US'.[85] Lenin also argued that, because of its industrial strength, 'everybody hates America more and more . . . everything indicates that America cannot come to terms with other countries, because the most profound economic differences divide them, because America is richer than the others'.[86] Lenin also believed that the very strength of the United States would lead to schisms between the capitalist states and that it would be possible to 'exploit' these economic rivalries.

Lenin and Stalin both perceived the most profound cleavage in the capitalist world to be between the United States and Britain. Moscow attempted to establish a closer relationship with the United States by offering economic inducements to US companies which, it was believed, needed Soviet resources and markets. The prevailing view held that Washington would be forced by economic necessity to recognise the Soviet regime. This view remained popular throughout the 1920s and early 1930s, particularly after the Wall Street Crash of 1929 and the ensuing economic depression. In 1930, Boris Skvivskii, the head of the Soviet Information Bureau in Washington, reported to Moscow that the importance of Soviet markets was felt in the United States and that Moscow could therefore pressurise Washington. This appears to have happened: in 1932, American exports to the Soviet Union came down to only $12.6 million, compared with $103.7 million the year before.[87]

Moscow was, however, not only interested in closer economic relationships with Washington. The United States was perceived as critical to the struggle against Japan in the Far East. In 1931, Japanese forces had moved into Manchuria and created a puppet state. The Soviet Union, in an attempt to stave off conflict with Japan, offered Tokyo the opportunity to conclude a non-aggression treaty. At the same time, Stalin strengthened his Far Eastern army and attempted to find new allies to act with Moscow against Japan. Moscow tried to use the Chinese communists to pressurise Chiang Kai-Shek into opposing Japan. By December 1931, Molotov had characterised the Japanese threat in the Far East and the emerging crisis in Manchuria as 'the most important problem of our foreign policy'.[88] From 1932 onwards, Moscow felt its security threatened on two fronts: in Europe and in the Far East. While it sought alliances with the French and the British in the West, it saw the United States as a potential ally in the East.

Soviet spokesmen began to refer to a history of Soviet–American collaboration in the Far East. Indeed, accounts of the US intervention in Siberia during the Civil War period were now explained as intended not to hurt the new Soviet state, but to halt Japanese expansionism.[89] This benign view of US actions was designed to signal Soviet willingness to cooperate with the US. Washington reciprocated with encouraging signs.

In January 1932, the US Secretary of State, Stimson, announced that the United States would not tolerate a situation resulting from a negation of the Pact of Paris. It was also reported that the US fleet would conduct extensive manoeuvres in the Pacific.[90] Encouraged by this action, Litvinov proposed that the two states conclude a bilateral non-aggression pact and attempt to form a series of interlocking agreements to include Japan and China. Voroshilov, the

Commissar of War, requested, in a conversation with the American ambassador to Moscow, that Washington send military and naval attaches to Moscow to conduct talks. He declared the hope that this would lead to 'a relationship of the utmost intimacy with the military authorities of the Soviet Union'.[91]

In 1933, the new Roosevelt administration established formal relations with Moscow. Recognition of the Soviet regime appeared to promise joint Soviet–United States action. Secretary of State Hull explained that recognition by the United States would be a factor in preventing a Japanese attack on the maritime provinces. *Krasnaya Zvezda* commented that 'recognition would subdue the Japanese and that American power would tilt the correlation of forces if not in favour of the Soviet Union then at least in favour of the *status quo*'.[92]

Moscow's expectation that the establishment of diplomatic relations with the United States would deter the Japanese and lead to concerted action against Tokyo was soon disappointed. There were considerable reservations in Washington about acting in the Far East, let alone in concert with the Soviet Union. There was concern about the repayment of Czarist debts and the activities of the Communist Party in the United States. Before formal recognition had taken place, Roosevelt had made clear his anxieties over these issues during a meeting with Litvinov. He required the Soviet Foreign Minister to sign a statement pledging that Moscow would not encourage or permit the formation of any organisation which aimed to disrupt the political and social system of the United States. In his memoirs, Litvinov wrote that this caused few problems, and instead emphasised what he described as Roosevelt's agreement to act against Japan.[93] Yet again, Soviet spokesmen showed a willingness to downgrade the Comintern to achieve important security objectives.

Washington expected that recognition would provide it with political leverage over Moscow. Specifically, some of Roosevelt's advisers believed that, in return for words of encouragement against Japan, Moscow should both resolve the issue of the debts and moderate the activities of the Comintern. This linkage failed to tempt Moscow. When the negotiations began on debts and future credits in early 1934, Moscow linked payment of debt with open support against Japan.

This support was not forthcoming in the mid-1930s for two reasons. The first was that the United States still laboured under the influence of isolationism and was reluctant to become involved in overseas commitments. The second was the antipathy of some of Roosevelt's advisers to the Stalinist regime. Historians have pointed to the views held in the 1930s by George Kennan[94] and Charles Bohlen, both of whom served on the embassy staff in Moscow, who warned against the dangers of international communism.[95] Kennan pointed to Soviet pressure on the Chinese communists to act with Chiang Kai-Shek as an attempt by Moscow to take over China, rather than as an attempt to bolster Chinese opposition to Japan. The scruples against acting with Moscow were strengthened by the bloody Stalinist purges which confirmed for many in Washington the brutality of an undemocratic system.[96]

Roosevelt never ruled out the possibility of pragmatic cooperation with Stalin if it became necessary to subdue both Japan and Germany, and, following his re-election in 1936, he took steps to rebuild a positive relationship. In November 1936, Joseph Davies was appointed ambassador to Moscow.[97] This was significant because Davies had continually espoused the value of working with the Soviet Union (despite his reservations about the nature of the regime). In January 1938, Roosevelt authorised Davies to examine the possibilities of cooperation. In the discussions which followed, Litvinov sought the clear promise of a definite pact with the United States against aggression. The President refused to go that far.

Roosevelt adopted a strategy of trying to put pressure on the alliance between Hitler and Stalin. He chose to maintain relations with the Kremlin while isolating Germany. To this end, he quite deliberately distinguished between the behaviour of the USSR and that of Nazi Germany. The Soviet assault on Finland had come close to undermining Roosevelt's strategy, but while Washington condemned Stalin's actions, it did nothing to aid the Finnish resistance.[98] After the fall of France in 1940, the US State Department began a lengthy series of negotiations to improve relations with Moscow and to keep open the option of cooperation. For example, the option of providing Lend–Lease credits was not ruled out. Washington actually alerted Stalin to evidence of the impending Nazi attack, but this was ignored.[99]

Hitler's invasion of the USSR changed the relationship between Moscow and Washington. While remaining suspicious of the Soviet state and the motives of its leaders, Roosevelt saw that if Germany's military attentions were diverted to the east, Britain might survive.

Roosevelt observed late in June that if Hitler was serious about turning east, 'it will mean the liberation of Europe from Nazi domination'.[100] The American leadership had already deemed that British survival was vital and determined that it would at this point do everything it could to supply the Soviet effort. In the autumn of 1941, Roosevelt ordered that Lend–Lease be made available to Moscow. The German declaration of war on the United States, four days after the Japanese onslaught on Pearl Harbour, made the communist Soviet Union and the United States of America allies.

The Grand Alliance between London, Moscow and Washington was founded in the desperate days of 1941. Stalin asked the West for both economic and military aid to fight Hitler. His primary request was, however, that his allies should open a second front in Europe to relieve pressure on the Eastern front. The British and American inability to commit themselves to such a vast military undertaking in the immediate future immediately raised suspicions in Stalin's mind that his allies were seeking to destroy him. The Grand Alliance was forged from desperation, not trust. It was based only on the common good of destroying Hitler and did not dispel the legacy of mutual suspicion which had characterised the inter-war years.

Conclusion

This brief history has shown the evolution of Soviet thinking about security and the 'West' in the 1917–43 period in order to bring out themes that will resurface in the post-World War II period. These may be identified as follows.

The first theme is the primacy of state security over external revolution. The revolutionary Bolshevik experiment had been replaced, some would argue usurped, by a security-minded Stalinist regime. Russia's geography, with its lack of natural boundaries, had been a major influential factor. There was an enduring fear of invasion which led to a preoccupation with secure borders and a desire to push those borders westwards. There was acute concern over the resurgence of German military power. The experience of the Nazi invasion was traumatic; it marked a generation of Soviet leaders.[101] How to subdue Germany, especially after the devastation wreaked by war, was the key Soviet concern that straddled the pre- and post-World War II eras.

A second theme is the perceived and actual technological

inferiority of the Soviet state. Much of Soviet foreign policy in the post-World War II period may be explained, at least in part, by Moscow's comparative economic and technological backwardness. Russia had been, for a long period, a predominantly agricultural state, relying on copying, borrowing or trading for technologies. Until Stalin, the mass of Russians were still peasants who distrusted innovation and were ill-equipped to assimilate and utilise Western technology.[102] This technological weakness was grafted on to existing feelings of geographical insecurity.

A third factor which characterised the inter-war period was the ideological antipathy which separated Bolshevik Russia from the other European states and from the United States. The very *raison d'être* of the Soviet state – its desire to actively propagate the revolution both at home and abroad – threatened the West and made its statesmen initially reluctant even to recognise the regime in Moscow. Marxism–Leninism was regarded as a fundamental challenge by many in the West. G. F. Kennan writing in 1960 described Moscow's attitudes during the inter-war period as a threat to the entire Western theory of international relationships. He wrote that the Soviet leadership challenged the West in the following terms:

> By the universality of their own ideological pretensions—by the claim, that is, to the unlimited universal validity of their own ideas as to how society ought to be socially and politically organised. They challenged it by their insistence that the laws governing the operation of human society demanded the violent overthrow everywhere of governments which did not accept the ideological tenets of Russian communism and the replacements of these governments of ones that did . . . It was this which was irreconcilable with the theory of international relations that had grown up in the West.[103]

For both the Soviet leadership and the Western states, ideological differences did not preclude pragmatic dealings, but they did provide the basis for mistrust.

A fourth theme arises from the nature of Marxist–Leninist thinking. Although socialist and capitalist states were bound to clash, so too were capitalist states themselves. Indeed, it was through the exploitation of these perceived antagonisms that Stalin hoped to pursue security for the Soviet state. Thus, for most of the 1930s, he sought alliances against one capitalist state, Germany, with other capitalist states, France and Britain. Stalin and the Soviet leadership distinguished between the Western states. The concept of 'the West' or of a 'Western alliance' is not really apparent in this period. Although Stalin perceived the United States to be naturally aligned with Britain, he saw that there were irreconcilable differences which would affect their respective attitudes towards the post-war world.

A fifth factor which had a profound effect upon Moscow was the failure of the British and French to act against Hitler. The appeasement at Munich left a legacy of enormous suspicion in Moscow. The United States, having entered Europe at a late stage, was relatively untainted, in the Soviet perception, by the struggles of the 1920s and 1930s.

On to these experiences was grafted the trauma of World War II with its immense devastation of the Russian homelands and peoples. The survival of the Soviet state was bought at a huge human cost. These experiences of revolution, war and alienation from the European state system combined to produce by 1943 what some analysts have described as a unique 'strategic culture' for the Soviet leadership. That is that, from their history, Soviet leaders developed specific security requirements. This did not mean that Soviet leaders were provided with a blueprint for foreign policy behaviour but that they developed certain expectations. This became clear in 1943. As the tide of war in Europe began to turn against Hitler, Stalin began to outline Soviet requirements for the post-war world.

He did this in two ways: first, by seeking political agreements with the British and Americans which would grant him control in East and Central Europe and, second, by using Soviet troops to underwrite those agreements through occupation.

This strategy of denial was developed, first, to 'deny' Germany any future; Stalin sought American and British compliance in this endeavour. Second, this strategy was devised to 'deny' Stalin's Western allies influence in Eastern Europe.

Notes

1 E. H. Carr, *The Bolshevik Revolution 1917–1923* Vol. 1 (London: Macmillan, 1950), pp. 58–75, 192–3.

2 E. H. Carr, *The Bolshevik Revolution*, pp. 195–9.

3 K. Booth, 'Soviet Defence Policy', in J. Baylis, K. Booth, J. Garnett, P. Williams, *Contemporary Strategy, Theories and Policies* (Beckenham, Kent: Croom Helm, 1975), p. 218.

4 L. Trotsky, *My Life* (New York: Scribner, 1930), p. 341.

5   Report to the Eighth Party Congress: See V. I. Lenin, *Pol'noe Sochinenii*, Vol. 38 (Moscow: Polizdat, 1963), pp. 139–40. See D. A. Holloway *The Soviet Union and the Arms Race* (New Haven: Yale, 1983), p. 3.

6   J. Erickson, 'The Origins of the Red Army', in R. P. Pipes, ed. *Russian Revolution* (Cambridge, Mass: Harvard University Press, 1968), pp. 224–5.

7   For a history of the CPSU see L. Schapiro, *The Communist Party of the Soviet Union* (London: Eyre and Spottiswoode, 1962).

8   V. I. Lenin, 'On the History of the Question of the Unfortunate Peace', *Collected Works*, Vol. 26 (Moscow: Progress Publishers, 1964), pp. 442–6.

9   R. Conquest, *Stalin: Breaker of Nations* (London: Weidenfeld and Nicolson, 1991), p. 75. For a depiction of Stalin's realism in this period, see D. Volkogonov, *Triumf i tragediya poletechkiy portret*, kniga 1, chast 1 (Moscow: Izdatel'stvo agenstva politicki, novostii, 1989), pp. 193–5.

10   R. Tucker, *Stalin as Revolutionary 1879–1929, A Study in History and Personality* (London: Chatto and Windus, 1974), p. 50.

11   *The Bolsheviks and the October Revolution Central Committee Minutes of the RSDLP, 1917–1918* (London: Penguin, 1966), p. 195.

12   I. Deutscher, *Stalin* (London: Penguin, 1966), p. 195.

13   A. Bullock, *Hitler and Stalin: Parallel Lives* (London: Harper Collins, 1991) p. 69.

14   R. Conquest, *Stalin*, pp. 83–4.

15   J. L. Gaddis, *Russia, the Soviet Union and the United States* (New York: McGraw-Hill, 1990), Second Edition, pp. 82–4.

16   Ibid.

17   J. W. Hulse, *The Forming of the Communist International* (Stanford: Stanford University Press, 1959), pp. 3–4.

18   V. Mastny, *Russia's Road to the Cold War* (New York: Columbia Press, 1979), p. 13.

19   Speech by Zinoviev, 19 July 1920, in *Vtoroi Kongress Kommunisticheskogo Internatsionala*, p. 11. cited in R. Goodman, *The Soviet Design for a World State* (New York: Columbia University Press, 1960), p. 33.

20   W. Lerner, 'Attempting a Revolution from Without: Poland in 1920', in T. T. Hammond and R. Farrell, *The Anatomy of Communist Takeovers* (New Haven: Yale University Press, 1975), pp. 94–106.

21   See V. Mastny, *Russia's Road to the Cold War*, p. 16.

22   For a discussion of the origins of the Comintern and its mission see M. Light, *The Soviet Theory of International Relations* (Brighton: Wheatsheaf, 1988), pp. 86–7, p. 156.

23   V. I. Lenin, Speech delivered at a Meeting of Activists of the Moscow Organisation of the RCP, *Collected Works*, Vol. 31, (Moscow: Progress Publishers, 1966), pp. 438–59.

24   M. Light, *The Soviet Theory of International Relations*, p. 28.

25 V. Mastny, *Russia's Road to the Cold War*, p. 10.

26 For a discussion of the debate over revolutionary aims abroad see M. Light, *The Soviet Theory of International Relations*, pp. 156–7

27 J. V. Stalin, 'Political Report of the CC', 18 December, *Works*, Vol. 7 1925 (Moscow: Foreign Languages Publishing House: 1954), pp. 267–8.

28 E. H. Carr, *The Bolshevik Revolution 1917–1923* Vol. 3 (London: Macmillan, 1953), pp. 436–7.

29 J. V. Stalin, 'Political Report of the CC', 18 December, pp. 267–8.

30 E. H. Carr, *The Bolshevik Revolution*, pp. 436–7.

31 J. V Stalin, 'Political Report of the CC', p. 284.

32 Ibid.

33 See H. W. Gatzke, 'Russo-German Military Collaboration during the Weimar Republic', *American Historical Review* 63 1957–58, pp. 565–97.

34 E. H. Carr, *The Bolshevik Revolution*, pp. 436–7.

35 Malcolm Mackintosh, *Juggernaut. A History of the Soviet Armed Forces* (London: Secker and Warburg, 1967), p. 61.

36 R. Fischer, *Stalin and German Communism* (Cambridge, Mass: Harvard University Press, 1948), p. 342.

37 I. Deutscher, *Stalin*, pp. 320–21.

38 Quoted in I. Deutscher, *Stalin*, p. 405.

39 J. Degras, ed., *The Communist International 1919–1943. Documents: 1919–22* (London and New York: Oxford University Press, 1956), p. 233.

40 See A. Ulam, *Expansion and Coexistence Soviet Foreign Policy 1917–73*, Second Edition (New York: Praeger, 1974), p. 164.

41 Ibid.

42 For a discussion of the Leninist theory of imperialism, see Allen Lynch, *The Soviet Study of International Relations* (Cambridge: Cambridge University Press, 1987), pp. 15–16.

43 'Vykhod Germanii iz ligi natsii', *Izvestiya* 16 October 1933.

44 W. Lacqueur, *Russia and Germany. A Century of Conflict* (New Brunswick, N.J.: Transaction Publishers, 1990).

45 Ibid. See also M. Mackintosh, op. cit. p. 75.

46 For Litvinov's views on collective security see Litvinov, Speech to the Central Committee, 29 December 1933, *Dokumenty Vneshnei Politiki SSSR* (Moscow: Politizdat, 1974)

47 Ibid.

48 See A. Bullock, *Hitler and Stalin*, p. 577, and Z. Sheinis, *Maxim Litvinov* (Moscow: Progress Publishers, 1988), p. 259.

49 Ibid.

50 The Soviet leadership were desperate to persuade the French not to appease Hitler. J. Degras, *The Communist International*, Vol. 3, p. 79.

51 For an assessment of the Western reaction to the Bolsheviks, see G. F.

Kennan, *Russia and the West under Lenin and Stalin* (Toronto: Little Brown, 1960), See Chapter 2.

52   *Izvestiya*, 24 January 1934.

53   'SSSR, Liga Natsii', *Kommunisticheski Internatsional* no. 26–7, 20 September 1934, pp. 3–11.

54   See *Pravda*, 16 May 1935, Quoted in R. Tucker, *Stalin in Power*, p. 347, and I. Deutscher, *Stalin*, pp. 411–15.

55   A. Ulam, *Expansion and Coexistence*, pp. 229–30.

56   The Earl of Avon, *The Eden Memoirs* Vol. 1, *Facing the Dictators* (London: Cassell, 1962), p. 148.

57   J. Degras, *The Communist International*, Vol. 3, p. 177.

58   E. Gnedin, *Iz Istorii Otnosheniy mezhdu SSSR i fashistkoy Germaniey* (New York: Khronika, 1977) pp. 21–3.

59   Press statement by Litvinov, 17 March 1938, in J. Degras, *The Communist International*, p. 272.

60   A. Ulam, *Expansion and Coexistence*, p. 267.

61   See Lord Cranbourne, Minute, 17 March 1936, in L. Woodward and R. Butler *Documents on British Foreign Policy 1919–1939*, Vol. 1, (London: HMSO, 1949), Document 122.

62   J. L. Gaddis, *Russia, the Soviet Union*, pp. 107–9.

63   Ibid.

64   I. Deutscher, *Stalin*, pp. 368–9.

65   Malcolm Mackintosh, *Juggernaut*, p. 93.

66   I. Deutscher, *Stalin*, p. 419.

67   A. Gromyko, *Memoirs* (London: Hutchinson, 1989), p. 37. This view has been endorsed by some Western historians. See J. Haslam, *The Soviet Union and the Struggle for Collective Security in Europe 1933–1939*. (New York: St Martin's, 1984). Haslam writes that 'Molotov had apparently wrung from the Germans in a matter of months what Litvinov had over six years failed to win from the Entente, ' p. 232.

68   Z. Sheinis, *Litvinov*, p. 293.

69   Ibid.

70   A. Ulam, *Expansion and Coexistence*, pp. 277–9.

71   S. Talbot, ed., *Khrushchev Remembers* (Boston: Little Brown, 1970), pp. 127–8.

72   D. W. Spring, 'The Soviet Decision for War against Finland, 30 November 1939', *Soviet Studies*, Vol. XXXVIII, no. 2, April 1986.

73   M. Mackintosh, *Juggernaut*, p. 124.

74   S. Talbot, *Khruschchev Remembers*, pp. 127–8.

75   I. M. Maiskii, 'Drii ispytanii', *Novyi Mir* 40, (12), 1964.

76   R. H. S. Stolf, 'Barbarossa: German Grand Deception and the Achievement of Strategic and Tactical Surprise against the Soviet Union, 1940–1941', chapter 9 in D. C. Daniel and K. L. Herbig, *Strategic Military Deception* (New York: Pergamon Press, 1982), pp. 195–223.

77   J. Erickson, 'The Soviet Response to Surprise Attack: Three Directives, June 22, 1941', *Soviet Studies*, XXIII, 4, April 1972.

78   See A. Gromyko, *Memoirs*, p. 38.

79   W. S. Churchill, *The Grand Alliance* (London: Cassell, 1950), p. 372.

80   A. Ulam, *Expansion and Coexistence*, p. 318.

81   See G. F. Kennan, *Russia and the West*, chapter 2.

82   M. P. Gehlen, *The Politics of Coexistence – Soviet Methods and Motives*, (Bloomington, Indiana University Press, 1967).

83   See G. F. Kennan, *Russia and the West*. For an analysis of the British efforts to persuade the Americans to intevene in the Russian Civil War, see M. Kettle, *The Road to Intervention. Russia and the Allies 1917–1920, March–November 1918*, (London and New York: Routledge, 1988).

84   V. I. Lenin, *The Essentials of Lenin*, Vol. 11 (London, 1947), pp. 690–700.

85   *Izvestiya*, 6 December 1921.

86   V. I. Lenin, *Polnoe Sobranie Sochinenii* (Moscow: Politizdat, 1958–65), XXXIX, 209, XL, 152.

87   Skriviskii to Soviet Foreign Ministry, 13 August 1930, 'Dokumenty Vneshnei politiki SSSR', XIII, 458. Quoted in J. L. Gaddis, *Russia, the Soviet Union and the United States*, (New York: McGraw–Hill, 1978), pp. 114–15.

88   For the Soviet view of the situation in the Far East, see G. Voitinskii, E. Iolk and N. Nasonov, 'Sovytiia na Dalnem vostoke i opasnost voiny', *Bolshevik*, 31 March 1932, pp. 42–55. See also V. Voronshov, *Tixookianska Politika SShA 1941–50*, (Moscow: Nauka, 1967), pp. 3–6.

89   *Pravda*, 24 December 1931.

90   J. L. Gaddis, *Russia, the Soviet Union*, pp. 115–16.

91   Dokumenty Vneshnei Politiki SSSR (USSR Foreign Policy Archives), folio 48. 0. 24. b. d. 1. p. 8. See also US National Archives, Records of the Department of State, relating to Internal affairs of Russia and the Soviet Union 1910–1929. Vol. 19.10.281, 0/2976–3220, both quoted in V. L. Mal'Kov, 'Soviet–American relations 1917–1940', paper prepared for seminar on the origins of the Cold War, sponsored by the United States Institute for Peace and the Research Coordination Centre. Ministry of Foreign Affairs, USSR, Moscow, June 1990.

92   *Krasnaya Zvezda*, 20 November 1933.

93   Z. Sheinis, *Litinov*, p. 249.

94   See, for example, G. F. Kennan, *Russia and the West*, chapter 1.

95   See J. L. Gaddis, *Russia, the Soviet Union*, pp. 128–9.

96   See J. L. Gaddis, *Russia, the Soviet Union*, pp. 107–9.

97   J. E. Davies, *Mission to Moscow* (New York: Welles-Harper, 1941).

98   See J. L. Gaddis, *Russia, the Soviet Union*, p. 142. Gaddis argues in an earlier work that actually the Americans were hard pushed to distinguish

between Hitler's Germany and Stalin's Russia. He writes 'Stalin's decision to sign a non-aggression pact with Japan in April 1941 simply confirmed the prevailing view: that the Soviet Union was a cruel and rapacious dictatorship only slightly less repulsive than Nazi Germany'. See John Lewis Gaddis, *The United States and the Origins of the Cold War 1941–1947* (New York: Columbia University Press, 1972).

99   S. Welles, *The Time for Decision* (New York: Harper, 1944), p. 171.

100   Roosevelt to William D. Leahy, 26 June 1941, FDR, Personal Letters, II, 1177, quoted in John Lewis Gaddis, *The United States and the Origins of the Cold War*, p. 4.

101   R. L. Garthoff, *Perspectives on the Strategic Balance* (Washington D.C.: The Brookings Institution, 1983), p. 27

102   See David R. Jones, 'Strategic Culture', in Carl J. Jacobsen, ed., *Strategic Power: USA/USSR* (Basingstoke: Macmillan Press, 1990), pp. 35–50.

103   G. F. Kennan, *Russia and the West*, pp. 188–9.

Chapter 2

Strategies of denial

This chapter looks at the way Moscow attempted to demarcate future lines of influence in Europe. It did this in two ways: first, through political agreements and, second, through the use of military force. This chapter addresses two key issues for the development of the Cold War: how did Moscow perceive its future role in Europe, and how did the presence of US forces affect that view?

The political dimension

In 1943, as the war progressed, London and Washington agreed that there was a need to hold a meeting with Stalin.[1] The Soviet leader was reluctant to leave Moscow and eventually agreed to hold a conference in the Soviet capital in October.[2] The three allies had different expectations and aims. Both the British and American delegations approached the meeting with some confidence that victory over Germany would be secured, and hoped to reach agreement on aspects of the future peace.[3] The Soviet delegation, on the other hand, was far more concerned with actually ending the war as soon as possible. Visitors to the Soviet Union in 1943 had remarked upon the desperate poverty and suffering of the ordinary citizens. The country was obviously war-weary; the Red Army had suffered massive casualties on the eastern front.[4] These different conditions were reflected in the agendas that the three states had prepared for the meeting.

The British were eager to secure some allocation of responsibility for liberated areas in post-war Europe. They wanted specific agreements on the future conduct of the Great Powers; in particular, on whether the Great Powers should be jointly responsible for the future of Europe or whether there would be separate areas of interest. They also wanted agreement on the treatment of territories liberated by the advance of Allied forces.[5] The American delegation agreed in principle with the aim of trying to construct a framework for post-war relations but was not concerned, at this juncture, with the details of the arrangement. It preferred to try to reach agreement to act under the auspices of a general security organisation.[6] The Americans believed that, unless agreements in principle were secured, the Great Powers would be dogged by future disputes.[7]

In stark contrast, Moscow put forward a very limited agenda. Its major proposal was that the Allies should find some way of shortening the war, preferably by naming the date of the second front in Europe.[8] This demand caused some consternation among the British and Americans, who had not expected to need to take military advisers with them.[9] The Soviet delegation was insistent that the issue of the second front should be the first matter to be discussed. The USSR wanted an absolute guarantee that the second front would be created during the next year. General Shtemenko wrote that 'The primary political aim of the Soviet Army was to liberate our country completely from the Nazi invaders'.[10] While this was undoubtedly true, Moscow demonstrated that it too was interested in future lines of demarcation. This secondary interest became apparent when the Soviet delegation responded to the British and American proposals.

The first British proposal was that the Great Powers should refrain from concluding bilateral treaties with European states.[11] The second was that the Allies should encourage regional associations.[12] Eden wanted to reinforce an informal understanding, reached in 1942,[13] that no agreements would be entered into by Moscow.[14] The Soviet delegation rejected the proposal, proclaiming the right to conclude agreements on post-war questions with bordering states.[15]

The British proposals seemed to fail completely. The British, for example, wanted to stop Moscow entering into a bilateral treaty with Czechoslovakia.[16] During the discussions, Eden agreed to withdraw his objections and excluded such a pact from the original proposal. Molotov was surprised by the British attitude; he revealed later that he had expected strong opposition.[17] The second British proposal, to secure a commitment to the development of regional associations, which was designed to break down a Soviet sphere of interest, also failed. Yet again, Eden conceded Moscow's special interests by expressly excluding Finland, Hungary and Bulgaria from the arrangement, and by conceding that Moscow alone was responsible for what armistice terms should be imposed on those countries.[18] Indeed, the British even supported Molotov's memorandum against regional confederations.[19]

The American delegation, led by Hull, suggested a set of principles designed to delineate activity after the defeat of Nazi Germany. Moscow objected, in particular, to clause 2, which read:

> That those at war with the common enemy will act together in all matters relating to the surrender and disarmament of that enemy and to any occupation of enemy territory and territory of other states held by that enemy.[20]

According to the Soviet interpretation of this clause, Soviet forces would be allowed to take part in the occupation of territory liberated by Western forces, such as Holland, Belgium and France, and Anglo-American forces would be permitted to occupy areas bordering the USSR.[21] Moscow did not want Western political influence so close to its border and was quite prepared to forgo future opportunities offered by the prospect of occupation rights in West Europe.

Molotov objected to a second clause in Hull's proposal that would have required Allied consultation and agreement *before* the employment of military forces within the territory of other countries.[22] This would, effectively, have permitted a Western veto over Soviet activity in Eastern Europe. Molotov was insistent that he would not permit the British and the Americans a veto power over Soviet troop movements into neighbouring countries, like Poland and Czechoslovakia, which were, as he pointed out, in the path of the advancing Red Army. Hull accepted Molotov's point: the Americans had put much the same argument in fending off earlier Soviet demands for joint consultation and agreement in the case of Italy.[23]

The trade-off of interests at the Moscow conference was apparent during the talks on Italy. The Italian surrender had been negotiated only a month before the beginning of the conference and Italy's status as a co-belligerent had been accepted by the Allies on 13 October.[24] Stalin had routinely expressed unease over what he perceived as his exclusion from those negotiations.[25] To remedy this, he proposed the creation of an Allied Military Political Commission consisting of representatives of the three powers to supervise the Italian situation.[26] It was the nature of this commission that threatened Allied harmony. The Soviet delegation believed the Military Political Commission should coordinate and direct not only all civil matters in Italy, but also military organisation, thus rendering the creation of a new Allied Control Commission unnecessary.[27] Had these proposals been accepted, Moscow would have played a substantial role in the shaping of post-war Italy. The suggestions were opposed by the British and the Americans, whose own proposals were geared to limiting Soviet influence in Italy. They envisaged that the Military Political Commission should merely play an advisory role, and that real power should be entrusted to the Allied Control Commission.[28] Molotov eventually acquiesced and did not even insist on equal representation.[29]

Soviet acceptance of effective exclusion from Italy may be explained in several ways. First, it was actually little more than recognition of existing reality. British and American troops already controlled large areas of Italy.[30] Second, as Italy was the first country to surrender, Moscow recognised that a precedent would be set for the future treatment of the liberated territories. Soviet acceptance of a merely representative role in Italy established an important principle that the countries that occupied a territory at the surrender would take the predominant role in the settlement, with other Allies acquiring only a representative interest.[31] Indeed, Molotov did in fact use the Italian example as just such a precedent in the years which followed.[32] Moscow had not relinquished all hope of influence in Italy, but Stalin expected that it would be through future Italian party politics rather than more direct involvement.[33]

The issue of the post-war settlement revolved mainly around the question of what to do about Germany. The Allies were committed to the principle of unconditional surrender and the imposition of a harsh settlement, but Soviet initiatives seemed to many in the West to undermine this position.[34] In a speech on 1 May, Stalin had distinguished between the German army and people,[35] and suggested that Moscow would hold only the German officer corps accountable for the war. Soviet propaganda also urged the German people to rid themselves of their leaders.[36] The Americans and the British were worried that if they advocated dismemberment, Moscow could and would pose as the legitimate supporter of a united Germany. At this point, no actual consensus existed between the British and the Americans over the future of Germany;[37] however, the Americans did suggest guidelines. They envisaged the elimination of all Nazis, the destruction of the German political system, and *joint* occupation by the three Allied powers, to be effected and maintained by contingents of British, Soviet and American forces.[38] These proposals were greeted enthusiastically by Molotov, who described them as stating 'Russia's thoughts about Germany as if we had expressed them'.[39] The significant feature of this response was that it foresaw, accepted and even welcomed US military involvement in Central Europe.

Throughout the conference, Molotov appeared concerned to discover the exact nature of American views on Germany; on several occasions he referred such questions to Hull.[40] The Soviet strategic obsession was that Germany would recover once again to dominate the European continent. Stalin referred constantly to his belief that a resurgence of German militarism would be difficult to suppress.[41] He suggested no definite plans and the matter was referred to a new commission formed by the Allies – the European Advisory Commission. The principle was established that all three powers would take responsibility for both Germany and Austria. It was agreed that Austria's union with Germany should be declared void;[42] determination was expressed that Austria should not escape war guilt.[43] A commitment to joint Allied action in Austria and Germany was expressed.

At the conference, there was an obvious desire to avoid subjects that might prove controversial enough to splinter the alliance. This applied to areas where all three powers felt they had an interest, most obviously Poland. Hull described this issue as a 'Pandora's box'.[44] The British and Americans did not want to discuss Poland at this critical juncture in the war, although Eden urged Moscow to re-establish relations with the Polish government in exile,[45] which had been severed as a result of Red Army involvement in the deaths of thousands of Polish officers in the Katyn Forest[46] and Soviet claims to the eastern provinces of Poland.[47] The Polish Prime Minister, Mikolajczyk, had tried to put pressure on the Americans and the British to provide guarantees against Soviet territorial demands, and had asked that, if necessary, British and American troops should be involved in the occupation of Poland alongside the Red Army.[48] Both Hull and Eden made it clear to Mikolajczyk that they were not prepared at this stage to sacrifice Allied unity to satisfy the demands of the Polish government in exile.[49] When Eden raised the issue, Molotov summarily dismissed the demands.[50] With the British and

Americans unwilling to antagonise Moscow, discussion was deferred, but Soviet interests in Poland had been clearly demarcated.

The Teheran conference

Broader Soviet interests were further clarified the following month at the Teheran conference. A major part of the discussions at Teheran, again, concerned the issue of the second front. On this subject an Anglo-American dispute was quickly apparent. The Americans advocated that the new offensive should take place in the spring of 1944, by a cross-Channel invasion of France. Churchill, however, wanted Western forces to be used for operations in the Mediterranean and the Adriatic. The Soviet delegation, urging speed, supported the American approach.[51] They had long urged the Western Allies to launch an offensive in France, although Stalin had indicated at the Moscow conference that he had not actively ruled out the possibility of a landing at some point in the Mediterranean or the Adriatic.[52] Within the space of a month he appeared to refute this possibility and become more insistent on an invasion of France. Some analysts claim that Stalin now realised that Churchill's military plans would have resulted in Western domination of the southern parts of Europe.[53] There is something to this, but a far more plausible explanation relates to the military situation in the east. In the month before the Teheran conference, the Red Army had encountered fierce resistance in the Ukraine and wanted the Western powers to open an operation to divert attention.[54] Stalin seemed to realise that Churchill could hardly resist concerted Soviet–American pressure to open the offensive in France. Indeed, Churchill eventually conceded the point, and May 1944 was set as the date for the invasion of France.[55]

Moscow still suspected that the British would try to delay the launch of the second front. Voroshilov, the Soviet military representative at the conference, accused Western representatives of prevarication when they tried to explain the operational difficulties of a cross-Channel operation.[56] He stated that what was needed was more will power, not more planning.[57] The Americans interpreted this as indicating that the Soviet general staff had no conception of the difficulties of planning such an operation.[58]

Stalin's endorsement of the American preference at Teheran was also illustrative of his recognition that Washington was beginning to exert more influence on strategic planning, and that the British were beginning to become the relatively junior partner in the Anglo-American coalition. This impression was reinforced by Roosevelt's behaviour at the conference. The US President believed that it was important that Stalin did not receive the impression that the Western states were ganging up on him. For that reason, he refused to hold a meeting with Churchill before the conference itself.[59] The British Prime Minister was also excluded from informal Soviet–American meetings at which the President confided his thoughts about the post-war world. Roosevelt made clear his objections to the British or the French maintaining their imperial possessions.[60] At the end of the conference, Stalin once again showed his recognition of US power by toasting its great economic and industrial strength, which was, he said, the most important factor on the Allied side.[61]

It was at Teheran that Roosevelt made clear a vision of a post-war settlement. Hull had, the month before, outlined the idea of a world organisation. Roosevelt elaborated on this proposal. He put forward a suggestion for a three-tiered organisation consisting of, first, an association with a membership of thirty-five to forty countries; second, an executive committee of the four major powers – China, Britain, the Soviet Union and the United States – alongside six minor countries; third, a group of states which had the task of maintaining and enforcing the peace.[62]

Stalin approved of the scheme in general, but disapproved of China's inclusion as a major power, preferring that the three Allies should retain responsibility for enforcing the peace. Stalin suggested that two security organisations should be created, one of which would take responsibility for the post-war order in Europe and the other responsibility for the Far East. The idea was rejected by Roosevelt on the grounds that 'Congress and United States public opinion would not support any arrangement which involved America in a purely European organisation'.[63]

Roosevelt's real objection was that he believed that such an arrangement would lead to a sphere of influence agreement.[64] Stalin questioned the logic of supposing an American public opinion that would tolerate a global commitment but not a European one. He pointed out that, if the American scheme was acted upon, US troops might have to go anywhere in the world.[65] Roosevelt envisaged Great Britain and the USSR taking responsibility for ground forces in Europe, with the United States providing naval and air support.[66]

It is difficult to assess Stalin's reaction to Roosevelt's declaration that the United States would not support a long-term ground commitment to Europe. One interpretation is that it signalled to Moscow that only a weakened Britain would be left in Europe to restrain its ambition.[67] However, this theory ignores the German factor. It is possible to speculate that Roosevelt's assertion caused not glee but anxiety in Stalin's mind. Every Soviet proposal for the post-war treatment of Germany so far envisaged involved an American presence as an integral feature. Indeed, at the Teheran conference the Soviet delegation sought guarantees to this effect.

The Americans put forward proposals for the dismemberment of Germany and suggested that the country should be split into regions: Prussia, much reduced in size; a north-western area surrounding Hanover; Saxony and Leipzig; an area south of the Rhine; and a fifth region constituted from Bavaria, Baden and Württemberg. It was envisaged that Hamburg and the Ruhr would be controlled by the United Nations.[68] The British proposal was not so radical: it suggested that Prussia and the southern states should be linked in a Danubian confederation.[69] Like the Americans, the British saw Prussia as the root of German militarism. Stalin, although favouring the American plan, declared that both were inadequate and stated his belief that Germany would revive within twenty years unless it was dealt with very severely.[70]

Stalin justified this harshness; speaking bitterly of the attitude of the Germans, he suggested that there was no hope of reforming their national character.[71] He suggested that the Allies create a series of military strongpoints both within Germany and outside it. These would act as military checks upon the German people. He proposed that the three Allies should permanently occupy these points and be ready to act against any rebirth of German hostility.[72] Stalin also suggested this scheme for post-war Japan. This is quite revealing. First, the proposal for joint occupation demonstrates that Moscow envisaged all three powers assuming responsibility for post-war Germany. Despite the fact that Roosevelt had voiced doubts over a long-term political and military commitment to Europe, Stalin saw it as an integral part of his scheme for Germany. Second, it also shows that Stalin foresaw the German question as requiring long-term political and military cooperation between East and West. No decision was taken on the proposals at Teheran, and the matter was referred to the European Advisory Commission.

The Americans asked Molotov to elaborate this idea of creating military strongpoints.[73] Indeed, the American delegation mentioned Belgium as a possible future site for Allied air bases.[74] Molotov defined the scheme more clearly, stating that, as the occupation points would obviously affect the countries in which they were located, the power responsible for securing the posts should provide the occupation forces.[75] So, for example, in countries liberated by the Red Army, Moscow would be responsible, while Western states would be responsible in Italy. The American delegation reinforced this point by making clear that it had no intention of permitting any other power to hold American bases in the Philippines.[76] Logically this meant that in countries such as Germany, liberated by all the Allies, the strongpoints would be jointly occupied. This principle was approved.[77]

It is apparent, then, that in 1943 Moscow saw a US military presence as important in Germany. Nevertheless, it wanted to exclude US troops from Eastern Europe, particularly from Poland. At Teheran, Stalin outlined Soviet plans for Poland. He wanted a revision of frontiers. The 'new' Poland would be created between the Curzon line and the river Oder in the west, and would include East Prussia and Oppeln. The Soviet–Polish frontier would be the Curzon line, but Moscow would acquire the Prussian cities of Tilsit and Königsberg, giving Moscow an ice-free port on the Baltic and a piece of German territory.[78] These proposals meant that Poland would be shifted significantly to the west.

From a Soviet perspective, this represented an essential security arrangement.[79] Churchill, despite initial reservations, eventually agreed to present these terms to the Polish government in exile, for two reasons. First, the Red Army was approaching the Polish frontier and rumours were rife that Moscow intended to foster a communist-dominated government.[80] Churchill considered it essential to obtain some agreement. Second, the British had received no support from the Americans on the Polish question. Roosevelt effectively abdicated responsibility for the post-war future of Poland. In private conversations with Stalin, he confided that he would prefer not to discuss the matter, as, during the next year, he had to face an election and there were six or seven million US voters of Polish extraction.[81]

The military dimension

Immediately after the Teheran conference, Charles Bohlen, who had been present, wrote an assessment of what he considered to be Stalin's plan for the domination of Europe.

> Germany is to be broken up and kept broken up. The states of Eastern, South Eastern and Central Europe will not be permitted to group themselves into any federation or association. France is to be stripped of her colonies and strategic bases beyond her borders and will not be permitted to maintain any appreciable military establishment. Poland and Italy will remain approximately their present territorial size, but it is doubtful if either will be permitted to maintain any appreciable armed force. The result would be that the Soviet Union would be the only important military and political force on the continent of Europe. The rest of Europe would be reduced to military and political impotence.[82]

This assessment ignores several important factors in Soviet perceptions of the situation in 1943. First, Moscow did not see itself as the lone military force in Europe. Every Soviet proposal for post-war Europe, and specifically the plans for Germany and Austria, envisaged a US or British military presence. Indeed, from Stalin's comments during the conference, the Americans and British were viewed as indispensable for subduing any resurgence of German militarism. Second, Bohlen's assessment credits Stalin with having a master plan which, given the military situation in 1943, he could not realistically have counted upon.

Until he received confirmation from the British and the US military mission in Moscow that the second front would actually take place, Stalin acted with great caution. It was only when he received confirmation, on 7 April 1944, that he made explicit plans for the Red Army to move.[83] This caution is illustrated by the Soviet attitude to the situation in Czechoslovakia. The Czech government, in anticipation of the Red Army's entry into that country, submitted a proposal to Moscow that would establish the procedure for transferring power to local authorities. Moscow changed the wording of the proposal concerning entry on to Czech soil, so that it read 'Allied troops', not 'Soviet troops', signalling concern not to move before a second front had been created.[84]

Once the second front had begun, Stalin moved quickly to assert Soviet influence and to demarcate the areas of interest outlined at Teheran. The Red Army first turned its attention to Poland, and, despite the objections of the British, and ignoring the Polish government in exile in London, recognised the so-called Lublin government.[85]

Romania was taken by the Red Army in late July and August 1944. The Romanians then joined the Allied side and fought the Germans until the end of the war. Throughout the war, Moscow had been plotting to oust the Romanian leader, Antonescu.[86] In the spring of 1944, the Soviet Union sent a former Romanian army officer and trusted 'agent', Emil Bodnaras, to organise the underground communist movement in Romania. After a purge in the party, the communists attempted to stage a *coup d'état*.[87] However, they were overtaken by the actions of the king, who, along with some dissident generals, had also been planning a bid for power. Shortly after the communist coup, the king managed to overthrow Antonescu. On his orders, the Romanian forces relinquished their arms and the Red Army was able to sweep through the country. The king accepted armistice terms which included acceptance of the Soviet–Romanian border of 1940 and also provided for occupation.[88] Although not the *coup d'état* envisaged by either Moscow or the communist underground, it enabled the Red Army to assume control of the country.

On 5 September, Moscow declared war on Bulgaria. This represented a drastic change of policy and was inspired by a British demand that Moscow should do something in response to the Bulgarian declaration of neutrality.[89] There is evidence that, throughout the war, Moscow had sought to increase its influence in traditionally pro-Russian Bulgaria, both through negotiations with Bagrianov and through the Communist Party.[90] Moscow had countered Anglo-American influence by blocking discussion of armistice terms for Bulgaria in EAC meetings.[91] But it was the British request that gave Moscow the chance to invade and occupy Bulgaria. The move was made quickly and without much planning. It received the approval of both the British and the American ambassadors, although they had not been given prior notification.[92] Both the British and the Americans were very shortly to express misgivings over the Soviet invasion.

In October, the Red Army invaded Hungary and met with fierce resistance from the Germans and the Hungarians. The Soviet Union insisted that Hungary should turn its armies against the Germans and revert to its pre-war frontiers. The Red Army threatened to continue the war against Hungary if Horthy, the Hungarian leader, failed to comply with Soviet demands.[93] Horthy eventually agreed to the Soviet terms, one of which was to set up a Hungarian Provisional National Assembly under the auspices of the Red Army.

Churchill was concerned to clarify Soviet intentions towards Western Europe. To that end, in October, Churchill, whilst visiting Moscow, presented Stalin with a proposal for the post-war treatment of Europe.[94] This proposal concerned the amount of 'influence' that Moscow, on the one hand, and the British and the Americans, on the other, would exercise in certain areas of post-war world. Churchill suggested the ratios as:

90:10 in the Soviet Union's favour in Romania.
90:10 in the West's favour in Greece.
50:50 in Yugoslavia.
50:50 in Hungary.
75:25 in the Soviet Union's favour in Bulgaria.[95]

According to Churchill's account, he wrote this proposal on a piece of paper which Stalin studied and then ticked.[96] These ideas were discussed by Eden and Molotov the next day.[97] Molotov wanted some of the ratios to be changed. In particular, he said that Moscow desired a greater say in Hungary. Molotov suggested a ratio of 75:25 in Moscow's favour for Bulgaria, Hungary and Romania. Eden refused, but offered an alternative which was:

80:20 in the Soviet Union's favour in Bulgaria.
75:25 in the Soviet Union's favour in Hungary.
50:50 in Yugoslavia.

Eden and Molotov were unable to reach agreement and the matter was left open.[98] A great deal of controversy surrounded these negotiations. First, although Churchill believed that he and Stalin understood each other, the American ambassador in Moscow, Harriman, writes that Stalin understood that the United States would never countenance any arrangement which divided Europe into spheres of influence,[99] and that it would continue to protest against such deals. Second, it is not really clear what form of influence Churchill and Stalin were trading in. It was never, for example, made explicit exactly what the figure 75:25 would entitle either side to do.

What was clear, however, was the Soviet interest. Moscow regarded Romania, Bulgaria and Hungary as of primary importance and was prepared to forgo potential interests in the West. A trade-off took place. In return for the West accepting the pre-eminence of Soviet influence in Romania, Stalin was prepared to forgo whatever interest he may have had, or claimed to have, in Greece.[100] Again, this reflected military realities. The Red Army was already in control of Romania, Bulgaria and Hungary. The disposition of military forces during 1944 was actually the key to political influence. Realist historians are right in this respect, but much was still dependent on the outcome of the war. This was most obvious with regard to the negotiations over Germany.

At the January meeting of the European Advisory Commission on Germany, Moscow had ignored British proposals and seemed determined to obstruct progress on a German settlement.[101] In February, however, Moscow submitted a proposal to the EAC accepting the British proposals for tripartite zonal occupation of Germany as a whole and for Berlin. In addition, the Soviet paper envisaged that the Great Powers should impose tripartite control on Austria.[102] Throughout the paper, the principle of joint occupation was stressed. It has been suggested that this sudden reconciliation to Western views was founded on Soviet fears that the West would negotiate a separate agreement with Germany before the Red Army could reach German soil. It seems likely that Moscow, fearful that it would be excluded from the negotiations, sought 'legal' guarantees of its rights in any settlement of the German question. Joint occupation was also a way of tying the Western powers into the subjugation of Germany.

Anxieties over the future lines of demarcation in Germany inspired Soviet moves in the EAC during the spring and summer of 1944. In July, the Soviet delegate to the talks, Gusev, insisted that the British and American governments should formally agree upon which of the Western zones each would occupy.[103] Moscow was concerned to secure the agreements before Allied troops entered Germany. In September, with Eisenhower's troops within striking distance of Germany, Moscow signed the protocol for the surrender of Germany.[104]

The Yalta conference

By the time the Allies met at Yalta, in February 1945, the Allied armies were converging on Germany from both east and west. The initial discussions at Yalta were concerned with the timing and the character of the final blow against Hitler. The German counter-offensive in the Ardennes had been successful, and Roosevelt notified Stalin that, because of weather conditions, General Eisenhower did not intend to cross the Rhine until March.[105] Therefore, the decisive assault on Germany from the west would have to be postponed until the spring. There seemed, however, to be no impediment to the progress of the Red Army. It had made spectacular gains throughout late 1944 and early 1945, covering 300 miles through central Poland, across the German frontier and to within forty miles of Berlin.[106]

Despite the apparent strength of the Soviet onslaught upon Germany in early 1945, Moscow remained concerned by the tenacity of resistance. General Antonov predicted that the Germans would defend Berlin strongly and said that further fierce fighting was anticipated before the Red Army could move further west.[107] Stalin concurred with this forecast saying that, although the Red Army had established five or six bridgeheads on the west bank of the Oder, he anticipated stubborn resistance before Germany fell.[108] He was particularly concerned because the Germans were moving troops from the western battlefields to the eastern front.[109] Stalin suspected that this was in preparation for a separate peace with the West – a peace that would deprive Moscow of its share in the victory.[110] Reassurances were sought that Anglo-American forces would maintain pressure upon the Germans so that the removal of troops from the west would be impossible.[111] Contrary to the Soviet anxieties, it was widely believed in the West that the Red Army would soon take Berlin.[112]

It was not only the military advance of the Red Army that caused concern in the West over the future of Soviet power in Europe. The behaviour of Soviet forces in the liberated countries of East Europe caused anxiety. The United States was perturbed by the attitude of the USSR to the Western representatives on the Control Councils which governed the liberated territories.[113] It was believed that Soviet actions in countries such as Romania and Bulgaria were curtailing the option of establishing 'democratic' representative governments. Western officials in those countries had complained that their views were being ignored. The Soviet chairman of the Control Council in Romania, for example, had been issuing orders without consulting the Anglo-American representatives.[114] The Soviet Union counter charged that the Western officials were doing exactly the same in Italy.[115]

One of the primary aims of the American delegation at Yalta was to obtain agreement to a set of principles encompassed within the so-called 'Declaration on Liberated Europe' which aimed to create democratic institutions throughout Eastern Europe.[116] To achieve this, the Allies would agree that

> The three governments will jointly assist the peoples in any European liberated state or former Axis satellite in Europe where in their judgement conditions require (a) to establish conditions of internal peace; (b) to carry out emergency measures for the relief of distressed peoples; (c) to form interim governmental authorities broadly representative of all democratic elements in the population and pledged to the earliest possible establishment through free elections of governments responsive to the will of the people; and (d) to facilitate where necessary the holding of such elections.[117]

This was an attempt to claw back influence in those countries in which Moscow had established its interests. Despite the fact that Molotov viewed it as 'interference in the liberated territories',[118] Stalin accepted the proposal but wanted support to be given to the political leaders who had taken an active part in the struggle against fascism.[119] This suggestion was rejected by the Americans on the grounds that it would give Moscow the chance to promote its own followers at the expense of others.[120]

The fact that Stalin agreed to the proposal has been dismissed as a mere negotiating ruse to ensure continuing Allied unity. It has been alleged that no attempt was made to abide by the principles of the declaration. Stalin, according to this line of reasoning, planned simply to install communist governments throughout East Europe.[121] However, Soviet agreement to the declaration was not simply a matter of deception, and the apparent disingenuousness may be better construed in several ways.

The first explanation relates to the language of the declaration. It was recognised by American diplomats at Yalta that the declaration was open to varying interpretations.[122] The use of words such as 'democratic' illustrates this. It is possible that although the West assumed, or found it easier to assume,[123] that the Soviet Union understood 'democratic' in the Western sense, the Soviet Union did not. Immediately after the conference, a Soviet commentator, David Zaslavskii, wrote:

> England represents democracy in one of its historic types. The United States is another type and the USSR yet another. After the last traces of fascism and Nazism the people of liberated Europe will have the possibility of creating democratic institutions according to their own choice. They can take as an example any form of democracy that has been shaped by history.[124]

The second explanation for the supposed Soviet volte-face revolves around the question of expectations. It is possible that Stalin saw no reason at Yalta to oppose principles such as free elections in the liberated countries because he expected them to vote communist. It was widely believed that the Red Army would be welcomed by the peoples it had liberated and that this would be expressed in a vote for the indigenous Communist Party. In this spirit of confidence, elections took place in Hungary in November 1945.[125] The communists, however, gained only seventeen per cent of the vote,[126] undermining expectations of widespread popular support. Nevertheless, in February Stalin could not have been expected to foresee such a defeat.

A third explanation is that Moscow did not regard the Declaration on Liberated Europe as a matter of great importance. The agreements of the war years had proved that Stalin and the Soviet representatives believed in explicit agreements and achievements (e.g. a legally defined arrangement or a military presence) as the determining factors. Throughout the Great Power conferences the Soviet delegations had always tried to reach explicit agreements on matters they regarded as important – for example, the concern to reach agreement on Germany. Equally, it was Stalin who, in the hope of enlisting a US military presence in Austria, tried to persuade the Western Allies to arrive in Austria at the same time as the Red Army.

The declaration was neither an explicit agreement nor a troop presence. It was not inconsistent with Moscow's view of what was and was not binding for the Soviet government to ignore it. The problem was that respect for the proposals was crucial to the American view of a satisfactory post-war settlement. Many American diplomats believed that it was this declaration that would moderate Soviet behaviour in Europe. This, in many ways, was a reflection of the manner in which the United States liked to approach diplomacy – through the imposition of broad institutional structures. Charles Bohlen remarked that 'had it been implemented by the Soviet Union, it would have radically changed the face of Eastern Europe'.[127]

The effort made at Yalta to moderate Soviet behaviour was disputed within American diplomatic circles, most notably by George Kennan. He believed that it would be much wiser if, instead of trying to interfere in countries dominated by the Red Army, the United States made a Churchillian deal with the Soviet Union:

> Why could we not make a decent and definitive compromise with it – divide Europe frankly into spheres of influence – keep ourselves out of the Russian sphere and keep the Russians out of ours?[128]

In line with this proposal, Kennan suggested that the United Nations be disbanded and that Washington, unless it was prepared to go the whole way and militarily oppose Soviet domination of the area, 'write off' Eastern and South Eastern Europe.[129]

Kennan's suggestions, however, ran counter to the prevailing American view. As Bohlen wrote:

> As far as the partition of Germany, the domination of East Europe by the Soviet Union, and the general idea of dividing the continent into spheres of influence, I could not go along with Kennan. To me the acceptance of a Soviet sphere instead of relieving us of responsibility would compound the felony. Any formal or even informal attempt to give the Soviet Union a sphere of influence in East Europe would as soon as the agreement became known have brought a loud and effective outcry from our own Poles and Czechs.[130]

The clearest example of the Great Power debate over post-war planning arose with regard to Poland. The British and the Americans had accepted, unofficially, at Teheran, the Soviet view on the boundaries of the 'new' Poland. The Western concern was now to secure some influence in that country. This was the crux of the problem – how far would outside influence be permitted in an area regarded as a crucial security interest by the Soviet Union? The West, in particularly Britain, was determined to wrest some concessions from Moscow on the composition of any future government. The British objected to the Lublin government as 'undemocratic' and sought the installation of a more representative regime.[131] Stalin and Molotov were insistent, however, that the Allies should accept the Lublin government.

Churchill opened the discussions on Poland by pointing out that Britain had made concessions concerning the borders of Poland and now required concessions in return. He pointed out that, for Britain, the Polish question was a matter of honour. London had gone to war over the violation of Poland. Churchill said that Britain had conceded the Soviet view concerning borders but must insist on guarantees that a new 'national' government would be set up and that free elections would take place.[132] Stalin responded that Poland might be a matter of honour for Britain but, to him, was a matter of security. Poland had twice been a corridor through which Russia's enemies had passed to attack. He too wanted a strong and independent Poland, but one that was 'friendly' to Moscow. The London Poles would be unacceptable, since not only had their agents, operating in Poland, attacked Red Army supplies, but they had also killed Russians. Stalin, furthermore, defended the Lublin government: it was as democratic as De Gaulle's regime.[133]

An uneasy compromise was eventually achieved on the question of Poland. The Soviet Union agreed to a modification of the Lublin government. Additional representatives would be added in the form of emigres. Unfettered elections were guaranteed, and the Soviet Union agreed to the idea of a strong, free, independent and democratic state.[134] It was this agreement, or rather the various interpretations of it, that became the primary cause of Western allegations of 'betrayal' after Yalta.

Both the British and the Americans knew that they were in a weak position during the negotiations on the Polish issue. Bohlen wrote: 'The Red Army gave Stalin the power he needed to carry out his wishes regardless of his promises at Yalta.'[135] Not only did the Red Army occupy the country, but there was very little (short of military force — a strategy that was never seriously contemplated) that the West could do if the Soviet Union refused to concede any of the issues.[136] Indeed, it was the movements of the Red Army that overshadowed the Yalta conference. In February 1945, the Red Army was within forty miles of Berlin. The Americans and the British were concerned to secure written assurances that the Red Army would respect 'Western' zones in Germany.[137] On 1 February Stettinius and Eden agreed that it was imperative to secure an agreement before the Red Army entered Berlin.[138] The concern was that the Red Army would move into Western zones, and then refuse to negotiate the terms of occupation.[139]

Soviet plans did indeed exist to take Berlin in February. On 4 February general operational instructions were issued to Marshal Zhukov to consolidate, regroup and resupply up to 10 February before taking Berlin, with a rapid thrust, on 15 and 16 February.[140] However, on 6 February the orders were abruptly cancelled.[141] Earlier on the same day, at Yalta, the three Allies had reached agreement on the zonal divisions and the machinery to be implemented for the future control of Germany.[142] Following this agreement, the Red Army was redirected on a course of consolidation in Eastern Europe.[143] Stalin had been willing to take Berlin in order to assert Soviet interests in Germany, but once he had obtained assurances that the Allies had agreed to the Soviet zone in Germany such action was no longer an immediate necessity.

There had been some controversy over the question of zones. In particular, Churchill desired the re-establishment of French power and advocated that a zone in post-war Germany should be allocated to French control.[144] This suggestion was predictably and strenuously opposed by the Soviet leader. Stalin had never envisaged or desired that France should play a major role in the post-war order. Stalin had suggested rather that France should be treated as a holiday resort.[145]

Churchill argued that French power would be needed as a counterweight to German power. He pointed out that, just as he had accepted that Poland's 'friendship' was necessary to the Soviet Union, so Moscow should concede a similar role for France in relation to Britain. Churchill indicated that, without help in the West, the British would not be able to control the continent and any revival of German militarism.[146] Roosevelt reinforced the need for a French military contribution by stating that US troops would be withdrawn from Europe two years after the end of the war.[147]

This was not the first time that the President had voiced the opinion that American troops should not be regarded as a long-term solution to the problems of European security. It was, however, the first time that a two-year time limit had been put on a US military presence. The Soviet leader, it has been said, with the end of the conflict in sight, could now optimistically contemplate a Europe with only a self-confessedly weak Britain left to constrain Soviet ambitions.[148] However, this information appears to have had the opposite impact. Immediately after Roosevelt's confirmation that American troops would be stationed in Europe only for the immediate future, the Soviet leader agreed to France aiding the military effort in the West.[149] (Roosevelt later explained that he did actually foresee a long-term American military commitment to Europe. However, it would not be as part of Churchill's schemes for a new balance of power under the auspices of the United Nations.)[150] France, it was agreed, would be given a zone carved out of the Anglo-American sector of Germany.[151]

Stalin was reluctant, however, to agree to Churchill's second proposal, to allow the French to participate in the Control Council on Germany.[152] He was concerned that it would set a precedent for other small nations to claim a role in the decision-making.[153] Stalin feared that more Western powers on the Control Council would jeopardise Soviet interests. Once reassurances had been given that countries such as Belgium and Holland would not be permitted on to the Control Council, he agreed to French participation.[154]

Stalin became more reconciled to French participation in the control of Germany when the British and Americans agreed that a French zone would be carved out of the Anglo-American zones.[155] Moscow had clearly demonstrated that the Western powers could pursue their own policies within their sectors provided that those policies did not impinge upon Soviet interests in Germany. In July 1944, at an EAC meeting, the British, in an attempt to resolve their shortage of manpower, had proposed that military contingents from other countries should operate within the German zones of the three Allied powers.[156] The Soviet representative, Gusev, had objected to this suggestion on two grounds: first, that it would complicate matters in each zone; and, second, that these powers might then demand a share in the decision-making.[157] Later, however, he said that Moscow understood that the British should make use of Dominion forces in their zone.[158] Further, the Soviet Union did not object to the use of the troops of smaller countries during the occupation period, so long as they did not expect to participate in the control machinery by virtue of their military contribution.[159] In other words, they would not be allowed any control over Soviet activities.

In 1948, Stalin remarked that 'the West will make Western Germany their own, and we shall turn Eastern Germany into our own state'.[160] The roots of that philosophy are discernible in the Soviet attitude towards Germany in 1945. However, whilst Stalin wanted to maintain control of East Germany, he also wanted guarantees that a military stranglehold would operate upon the Western parts of Germany. This explains why Stalin had sought American management of West Germany at an early stage, and also why he had agreed to French help in maintaining an effective stranglehold on Germany.

It looked, at this point, as if the Soviet government was settling for the division and destruction of German power. This was apparent on the issue of reparations. Soviet proposals had a dual purpose. First, to ensure that Germany would never again be able to dominate Europe. Moscow wanted the destruction of German industries. Accordingly, it proposed that eighty per cent of all German industries should be dismantled, and Allied control established over the remaining industry.[161] Second, it sought to rebuild its own devastated country with German industrial plant. In pursuit of this aim, Stalin and Maisky proposed that a system should be implemented whereby reparations would be allocated according to a country's contribution to the war effort and be based upon its direct material losses.[162] They also suggested that reparations should be based upon a figure of $20 billion, with a Soviet share of $10 billion.[163]

Before the Yalta conference, both Britain and the United States had considered at great length the question of a German settlement. On the one hand, it was accepted that Germany should not be capable of posing a renewed threat to European security. On the other hand, it was understood that it should not be allowed to become an economic liability, literally dependent upon its Western conquerors.[164] London and Washington wanted to find a formula whereby Germany would be restrained militarily but economically self-sustaining yet not capable of a standard of living higher than that of the Allies.[165] However, they had not come up with any concrete plans. Whilst they were unwilling to implement Soviet suggestions, they lacked alternative proposals. The figure of $20 billion was agreed upon as the figure for the basis of reparations, which later gave rise to much ill feeling between the Allies, but the matter was referred to a reparations committee.

The Soviet aim, displayed at Yalta, was a patent desire to destroy German power. The Soviets sought affirmation of the Allied decision agreed at Teheran to the principle of dismemberment. The British and the Americans had reconsidered the matter; Churchill said that, although the British government was still inclined to favour partition, particularly any scheme that would isolate Prussia, it still had doubts over any really drastic measures.[166] Similarly, although Roosevelt still favoured the idea of Germany being divided into five or seven states, he preferred to delay the decision.[167]

The fact that Stalin sought Allied agreement to dismemberment has been explained as a ruse which would enable him later, in an attempt to communise the whole of Germany, to depict the West as the force that opposed German unity.[168] However, this idea lacks credibility. It is more convincing, given Stalin's fear that the West might form a separate peace, that he simply sought assurances that Germany would be treated as harshly as it deserved, and that the future Soviet role in Germany would be secured.

Soviet policy had consistently advocated joint occupation and control as the post-war settlement of Austria. In October 1944, Stalin had suggested that the Western Allies should transfer five or six divisions from the Italian front to Dalmatia for an advance on Zagreb, where they could join forces with the Red Army in south-eastern Austria. The German troops in Italy would then be forced to retreat and Soviet troops would be able to march on Vienna. Stalin proposed that eight to ten divisions should join them in the Austrian capital.[169]

The United States had initially been reluctant to join in the future 'policing' of Austria. In January 1944, the British proposed that the United States should be allocated a zone composed of southern Germany and all of Austria.[170] Washington rejected this suggestion for two reasons. First, it wanted to control a zone in northern Germany. Second, it did not wish to be involved in the physical occupation of Austria,[171] although it did want to be on the commission that would supervise the post-war occupation.

Soviet proposals on Austria envisaged tripartite control. In February 1944, Moscow suggested that the three Allies should join in the occupation of Austria. However, Roosevelt urged that Britain should take responsibility for southern Germany and the whole of Austria.[172] It was not until May 1944 that the United States agreed to allow American troops, a token force, to take part in the future occupation of Austria.[173] In January 1945, the United States finally agreed to the Soviet proposal that American troops should occupy a zone in Austria.[174]

Throughout the war, the British had sought to bind the Austrian settlement to the post-war treatment of Germany. Churchill had favoured the idea that southern Germany should be separated from the rest of Germany to form, with Austria, the basis of a Danubian confederation.[175]

At Yalta he expanded this scheme. He proposed the establishment of a second German state, aligned with Austria, with a capital in Vienna.[176] This was opposed by Moscow. It was felt that Churchill was attempting to construct a *cordon sanitaire*, which would result in a predominantly German[177] and Catholic state becoming the centre of an anti-communist bloc. The Soviet Union preferred Austria to be dealt with in the same manner as it agreed to treat a defeated Germany: with tripartite, or quadripartite occupation and a definite US military presence. However, unlike the German case, Soviet proposals envisaged the restoration of Austria as an independent state, with Allied occupation only a short-term measure. In Germany, occupation was, for Moscow, a long-term imperative.

From a Soviet perspective the Yalta conference produced mixed results. On the one hand, the USSR had failed to secure definite Allied agreement on the question of reparations from Germany. On the other hand, the Allies had agreed that it was appropriate to divide the responsibility for Germany between them. It was an arrangement that made the United States a long-term military fixture in Germany. Attempts to undermine Soviet influence in Eastern Europe had so far failed; the Declaration on Liberated Europe had not registered as a threat.

Soviet actions in February and March 1945 seemed to London and Washington deliberately to violate the Yalta agreements. In particular, Soviet intervention in Romania, which had resulted in the usurpation of the Radescu government and its replacement by the communist Groza government, was regarded with dismay.[178] Soviet representatives in Hungary, Bulgaria and Romania also continued to act without consulting with their Western colleagues.[179] But the allegation that the Yalta agreements had been 'betrayed' was based in particular on the Soviet attitude towards Poland. The commission which had been appointed at Yalta to 'compose' a new Polish government had failed to reach agreement.[180] Stalin insisted that the Yalta agreements had intended the existing provisional government to form the basis of any new government and that it, and only it, had the power to 'approve' new members.[181] A sence of grievance in London and Washington was fuelled in March, when Stalin refused to accede to demands for American servicemen in Poland to be returned and for observers to be allowed to supervise the process.[182] On 13 March, Churchill wrote to Roosevelt that the failure to resolve these problems meant that they were confronted by a total breakdown of the Yalta settlement.[183]

The question for Western historians has been whether Stalin did, in fact, cynically breach the Yalta agreements. There are two ways of looking at it. Soviet behaviour was actually consistent with its character before Yalta. The primary Soviet aim remained unchanged – the establishment and maintenance of so-called 'friendly' governments in Eastern Europe. Action such as dominating the Control Councils in Romania and Hungary was, from a Soviet perspective, legitimate. Throughout the wartime alliance, the Western powers had sanctioned the pre-eminence of Soviet interests in Eastern Europe. Consequently, Soviet moves after Yalta did not necessarily contravene the Yalta agreements or indeed any other political agreements concluded with the West on the future political composition of Europe. This was in fact acknowledged by Churchill:

> We were hampered in our protests because Eden and I during our October visit to Moscow had recognised that Russia should have a largely predominant voice in Romania and Bulgaria, while we took the lead in Greece. Stalin had kept very strictly to this understanding.[184]

The Western powers had, therefore, accepted, at least tacitly, Soviet domination in Eastern Europe; but there is little doubt that there was a problem of interpretation on the Western side. Churchill, for example, had hoped to influence the composition of the Polish government. The Soviet interpretation was that the existing government would continue to act. Stalin recognised that his views of Poland were in total opposition to those of Churchill. He remarked to Marshal Zhukov, with reference to the Yalta agreements, that 'Churchill wants the Soviet Union to share a border with bourgeois Poland alien to us, but we cannot allow this to happen.'[185]

The division of Europe

Many in the American administration realised that altering Soviet behaviour would not be easy. Harriman wrote that:

> It may be difficult for us to believe but it may still be true that Stalin and Molotov considered at Yalta that by our willingness to accept a general

wording of the declarations on Poland and liberated Europe, by our own recognition of the need for the Red Army for security behind its lines and of the predominant interest of Russia and Poland as a friendly neighbour and as a corridor to Germany, we understood and were ready to accept Soviet policies already known to us.[186]

At Yalta both sides had preferred to preserve Allied cooperation rather than risk a breakdown over the actual detail of agreement. Harriman's remarks are enlightening since they reveal American suspicions that Moscow, in all probability, would not accept Western definitions. Washington recognised that strategy would have to be altered accordingly. Harriman wrote on 6 April that 'Up to recently the issues we have had with the Soviets have been relatively small compared to their contribution to the war but now we should begin to establish a new relationship'.[187]

Churchill wrote that the destruction of German military power had brought with it a fundamental change in the relations between communist Russia and the Western democracies.[188] It would be wrong to state that there was strict Anglo-American agreement on this issue. There was no coherent approach to be implemented. This became apparent during the final assault on Nazi power in March and April. Churchill proposed that the West should use its military strength to compel Moscow to behave more reasonably. This could be done, he argued, by occupying as much territory in Eastern Europe as possible and by threatening not to relinquish it. However, Washington was reluctant to use its military strength for such a purpose. Its strategy was to exert economic influence.

From the standpoint of Moscow, the immediate cause of the deterioration in Allied relations took place in March 1945 when Stalin was informed that negotiations had been under way at Berne concerning a German surrender between General Wolffe, the commanding officer of the SS in Italy, and an American agent, Alan Dulles.[189] This constituted, for him, proof that the Western powers intended to betray their Soviet ally by signing a separate peace in the West.

This provoked quite a noticeable change in Soviet troop movements. Immediately after Yalta, Soviet military strategy seemed designed to synchronise the moves of the Red Army with the anticipated Anglo-American advance into Central Europe.[190] The Red Army would begin moving towards Bratislava on 10 March, with the aim of reaching Prague in forty to forty-five days.[191] This was not a rapid pace, and there was no major campaign scheduled for the northern sectors. Like Stalin's decision to halt at the Oder,[192] it appeared to be scheduled to wait for the Western advance.

The negotiations over the surrender of Germany conducted in March formed a watershed for Soviet views of the Western alliance. Suspicions of Western duplicity were fuelled by the fact that, since Yalta, the military position had become more complicated. The Red Army was bogged down in Hungary while Anglo-American forces triumphantly crossed the Rhine at Remegen on 7 March and were advancing rapidly through Germany. It appeared that the Germans were deliberately opening a route to Berlin and transferring forces to the east to deprive the Red Army of victory. On 3 April, Stalin wrote to Roosevelt 'that the Germans have already taken advantage of the talks with the Allied Command to move three divisions from Northern Italy to the Soviet front'.[193] Marshal Zhukov believed that there must have been some Nazi collaboration with the Western powers, since only 8,351 men out of an army of 3 million were lost in combat during the Anglo-American crossing at Remegen while the number of German prisoners of war ran into hundred of thousands of officers and men.[194] Stalin voiced his suspicions again in his correspondence to Roosevelt of 7 April:

> It is hard to agree that the absence of German resistance on the Western front is due solely to the fact that they have been beaten. The Germans have 147 divisions on the eastern front. They could safely withdraw some 15–20 divisions from the eastern front to aid their forces on the western front yet they have not done so, nor are they doing so. They are fighting desperately against the Russians for Zemlenice, an obscure station in Czechoslovakia, which they need as much as a dead man needs a poultice, but they surrender without any resistance such important towns in the heart of Germany as Osnabruck, Mannheim and Kassel. You will admit that this behaviour on the part of the Germans is more than strange and unaccountable.[195]

Such insecurity over future moves resulted in a change in Soviet strategy and a review of the US military role in Europe. Until March 1945, Anglo-American forces had been perceived as a necessary and integral part of the Soviet war effort against Nazi Germany. However, even before Hitler had surrendered, these Anglo-American troops became a threat to Soviet ambitions. Stalin realised that they could be used to frustrate the agreements reached on Europe such as the zonal protocol which enshrined Soviet rights in Germany. Given the 'freeze' that had now settled on Allied relations, he could not be certain where these troops would stop. Stalin's solution was to revise his strategy from one of cooperation to one of unilateral movement. His underlying intention was to locate the Red Army where it could safeguard Soviet interests and, perhaps, in addition hold 'Western' territory as a future bargaining chip.

Again, however, the British and the Americans were divided over what attitude to adopt towards the advance of the Red Army. Churchill advocated that Western troops should push as far east as possible and endeavour to take both Berlin, which was an agreed Soviet zone, and Prague.[196] He believed that, whenever possible, Anglo-American forces should occupy parts of the Soviet zone in Germany and also stake a claim to as much Austrian territory as possible.[197] This strategy had two main objectives. First, by maintaining a grip on agreed Soviet areas, the West would be able to force Moscow to modify its behaviour. Second, if Anglo-American troops could reach Prague before the Red Army, Czechoslovakia would be spared Soviet domination.[198]

The British now wished to repudiate the agreements on occupation zones. Churchill sought complete freedom of action. Military successes should dictate the 'stop' lines for both troops and post-war influence.[199] Churchill regarded it as a matter of urgency that Washington should agree to implement such a strategy. There were, however, several impediments to the adoption of such a course. Churchill recognised that the United States would oppose any attempt to maintain substantial numbers of troops in Europe in peacetime. He was aware even more urgently that the United States was already planning to transfer some of its forces to the Pacific theatre of war. He wrote to Truman that

> All these matters can only be settled before the United States armies in Europe are weakened. If they are not settled before the US armies withdraw from Europe and the Western world folds up its war machine there are no prospects of a satisfactory solution and very little of preventing a third world war.[200]

Washington, however, had a different conception of how the Anglo-American armies should behave as they advanced through Europe. Eisenhower and Truman both believed that their strategy should be to abide by the agreed zonal protocol rather than simply to aim to occupy as much territory as possible. This reluctance to acquiesce in Churchill's plans has been attributed to a lack of political–military foresight, but it actually resulted primarily from the fact that American actions were governed by the overriding need to transfer troops to the Pacific. Churchill's plans for a 'standfast' in the middle of Europe would have greatly impeded this transfer. In addition, the US administration was unwilling to incur additional casualties to capture targets in Europe that it felt would eventually have to be surrendered.[201] On 21 April, at a State Department conference, the question of how much leverage the United States had over Moscow was examined. The potential use of economic sanctions was discussed and considered viable. Military options were also discussed but no conclusions on this matter were reached.[202]

Washington was not unaware of the threat posed to Europe by the advance of the Red Army. However, unlike Churchill, the Americans believed that they possessed other forms of 'leverage' over Stalin, economic levers in the form of Lend–Lease and loans,[203] for example, and, correspondingly, they resisted Churchill's pleas to race for Berlin and Prague.

Eisenhower's memoirs stress the political restraints of the zonal protocol on his actions in Europe. He also underlines the fact that time and distance rendered it highly improbable that Western troops could have taken Berlin.[204] Eisenhower decided instead to concentrate on other strategic priorities, most notably the destruction of German forces within Germany that were not yet allocated to either East or West. With this aim in mind, Anglo-American forces were directed towards Austria and Denmark.[205] Eisenhower's decision to proceed in this manner meant that Anglo-American strategy was basically one of consolidation in the West and opportunism in Central Europe.

Throughout March, despite Churchill's protestations, Eisenhower continued to discount the possibility of taking Berlin. However, on 1 April he conceded to Churchill that if German resistance should crumble, and if it could be done cheaply, Berlin would be included in the list of important targets.[206] Throughout April, Churchill continued to press for the capture of Berlin by Western forces. Eisenhower resisted despite the fact that an American division had reached the Elbe on 11 April. According to

American calculations, the capture of Berlin would cost 100,000 American casualties.[207] Eisenhower regarded this as too heavy a price to pay. On 14 April Eisenhower outlined his strategy, which was to stop at the Elbe and destroy enemy resistance on his flanks. He judged that the Red Army was in the better position to capture Berlin,[208] even though the West had received messages from the Soviet high command which stated that Dresden, not Berlin, was the target of the offensive.[209]

On 24 April, Stalin agreed to Eisenhower's suggestion that a common border should be established along the Elbe–Mulde line.[210] Stalin informed Eisenhower that, when this border was formed, the Red Army intended not only to occupy Berlin, but, if possible, to clear out German forces east of the river Elbe.[211] This meant that the Red Army would be moving into Schleswig-Holstein, which was within the agreed British zone.

This signalled to the British and the Americans that the race was now on for Denmark. Eisenhower informed Stalin that Anglo-American forces were launching an operation across the lower Elbe to the Wismar–Donitz line.[212] The military rationale behind the Western race for the Wismar–Donitz line remains unclear. If the priority was to exclude the Red Army from Denmark it was only necessary to hold the line south of Lübeck.[213] However, taking the Wismar–Donitz line may be explained by the fact that it meant that the British would occupy part of the Soviet zone in Germany. They would have acquired an area of Soviet territory with which to bargain. Following the collapse of Hitler's Germany, Western forces held nearly half the Soviet zone to the west of the Oder–Neisse line.

In the spring of 1945, British and American conceptions of European strategy still differed considerably. The British wanted forces to penetrate further east than previous agreements had foreseen, in an attempt to forestall the extension of Soviet influence. The Americans preferred a process of consolidation in the west which involved the occupation of territory not already explicitly assigned to Soviet occupation. Washington was still unwilling to use military power to confront or moderate Soviet behaviour, not least because it still believed that Soviet forces were needed for the war in the Pacific. American views predominated, and Anglo-American forces failed to capture Berlin.

At the end of the war, with Anglo-American forces occupying parts of the Soviet zone in Germany, Churchill again advocated a strategy of holding on to the territory, and refusing to withdraw until 'an early and speedy show-down and settlement with Russia had been achieved'.[214] London did not wish the Americans to regard the war in Europe as over. It wanted to retain SHAEF, and it wanted troops to remain in considerable numbers. Truman rejected Churchill's pleas, arguing that the zonal protocol had to be abided by. However, he did accept that it was impossible 'from the present position to make a conjecture as to what the Soviet Union may do when Germany is under the small forces of occupation'.[215] In an attempt to reassure Churchill, he guaranteed that only 30,000 of the 3 million men in Europe would be withdrawn within the following twelve weeks.[216] Washington could not simply pack up and go home as it had done after World War I.

Stalin's belief that the British and Americans would conclude a separate peace with Germany had inspired a change in Soviet strategy. The most serious manifestation of this was the Soviet determination to take Berlin first. On 29 March, Stalin showed Zhukov a letter from a so-called informant describing a clandestine meeting between Nazi agents and official representatives of the Western Allies at Berne. The letter alleged that the Nazi agents had offered to cease all resistance and conclude a separate peace. A free passage to Berlin was also offered to the Western Allies, according to Zhukov. Stalin replied that 'Roosevelt won't violate the Yalta accords, but Churchill, he wouldn't flinch at anything'.[217]

Zhukov and Shtemenko claim that Stalin took the letter seriously. As Shtemenko writes: 'There remained no doubt that the Allies intended to capture Berlin before us.'[218] The Soviet high command persisted in this belief even when Stalin received General Eisenhower's message on 31 March that Berlin had lost its 'former strategic importance'. Stalin did not believe that Eisenhower was making an honest statement of opinion. On 1 April 1945 the plan for the Berlin operation was reviewed at Soviet Supreme Headquarters. Stalin concluded that it was necessary to take Berlin in the shortest possible time and that the operation must begin within twelve to fifteen days.[219] The priority Stalin attached to seizing Berlin before the Western Allies was illustrated by the encouragement he gave to two of his commanders, Zhukov and Konev, to compete for the prize of capturing it.[220] In taking Berlin, Stalin was asserting his interests in Germany.

Stalin's strategy in April and May involved deception. On 15 April he informed Harriman that a major offensive would begin and that Dresden would be the main objective. This was a ruse: Berlin was the true objective.[221] As the Red Army pursued its campaign in Germany, the Soviet leader grew more distrustful of his Western allies. Zhukov reports that, in March, Stalin was anxious and fatigued[222] and believed that the West might yet deceive him. Shtemenko recounts that, on 16 April, Stalin drew his attention to a claim by a captured German soldier that the remnants of the German forces had been instructed 'to open the gates in the West to stem the tide in the East'.[223]

Stalin's fears were reinforced when he learnt that Churchill had issued instructions to Eisenhower not to destroy captured Nazi weapons. The British leader asserted that they would be needed to rearm Germany.[224] From a Soviet perspective, this was an alarming prospect. It has been claimed that, in the spring of 1945, Stalin actually believed that the Western allies would unite with Germany against the USSR. In April, Soviet troops began building defensive installations in Austria. These included anti-aircraft facilities at a time when an operative German air force no longer existed.[225]

Stalin was not content simply to capture Berlin. He wanted Soviet troops to penetrate as far west as possible. On 24 April, Stalin informed Eisenhower that his immediate plans called for the occupation of Berlin and the destruction of the remaining forces east of the Elbe in the British zone.[226] Stalin, however, wanted Soviet troops to occupy part of the British zone in Germany. If, as Stalin suspected they would, Anglo-American forces refused to withdraw from designated Soviet areas, he would have a piece of territory with which to bargain. It does not appear that Stalin had any intention of permanent occupation of the British zone. Ulbricht discloses that, on 1 April, he and Dimitrov drew up their *Richtlinien* (guidelines) concerning future communist tasks in Germany. These applied only to the Soviet sectors in Germany.[227]

The Soviet strategy of taking territory in order to acquire a bargaining position is well illustrated by the 'foray' into Danish domains. On 8 May, Eisenhower had notified General Antonov that, in response to a Danish plea, Western forces intended to capture Bornholm, an island 135 km off the mainland.[228] Before the West could act, Soviet troops had been dispatched and on 11 May the Red Army captured the island. This incident has, on the whole, been ignored by historians, who have largely taken Stalin's remark to

Djilas – that whoever occupies a territory imposes his own social system upon it – as accurately reflecting Stalin's plans. In the main the evidence does support that view, but there were exceptions. In the case of Bornholm, for example, Stalin had no intention of imposing social systems but rather had in mind a pragmatic trading of interests.

After the Red Army had captured Berlin on 2 May, the main area of rivalry between the Allies was transferred to Czechoslovakia. Stalin's aim was to ensure that the Red Army liberated Prague. Churchill again advocated opposition. On 30 April, he wrote to Truman that: 'The liberation of Prague and much of the territory of Western Czechoslovakia by the US forces might make the whole difference in that country and influence events in nearby ones.'[229] However, an agreement existed between Moscow and Washington that American units would not move beyond the city of Plzen, fifty miles south of Prague.[230] When, on 5 May, General Bradley suggested to Marshal Konev that American troops join the Soviet assault on Prague, this agreement was cited by Konev. He explained that if Americans troops moved beyond the agreed boundary it could lead to confusion and the mixing of troops.[231] The truth is that Moscow wanted to be responsible for the liberation of Czechoslovakia. Events in Czechoslovakia were dramatically complicated when, on 5 May, an uprising broke out in Prague.[232] Churchill begged Eisenhower to exploit the situation and advance on Prague.[233] American troops did advance but then stopped at the agreed place. The same influences that had governed behaviour in Germany motivated Eisenhower in Czechoslovakia. He refused to risk casualties for 'purely political reasons'.[234] Stalin, in the belief that Eisenhower would try to take Prague, advanced the Soviet timetable by one day, from 7 May to 6 May.[235] On 8 May, the Red Army captured the Czech capital and secured Soviet interests.

In April and May 1945, Soviet strategy had two major aims. The first was to consolidate Soviet influence throughout East Europe and to exclude Anglo-American interference. The campaigns for Berlin and Prague were not just about defeating the enemy but were also about future interests. The second aim was to 'take' territory which if necessary could be used for 'bargaining' with the West. Hence the Soviet decision to capture Bornholm.

Conclusion

During the spring of 1945, American troops were viewed by the Soviet high command as potential competitors for influence in Eastern Europe. This was a misperception: American troops were not permitted to become contestants in a competition for either Berlin or Prague. American military ambition was limited strictly to western areas. During June and July, alterations to the lines that divided these areas of military influence in Europe were made. During this period, it became apparent to both sides that, although they had defeated Hitler's Germany, they now faced another form of competition – against each other. The future of American military power in Europe remained uncertain. Washington had yet to decide whether it would involve itself on a permanent basis in European security. Stalin had few doubts. In May he remarked that 'whether the United States wished it or not, it was a world power and would have to accept worldwide interests'.[236]

The question is, what did Stalin envisage the future relationship would be with the United States? He clearly differentiated between American and British aims in Europe. He understood that the British, in particular Churchill, sought to undermine Soviet interests. He was clear that Washington should not be allowed to interfere in Eastern Europe but also that the US presence had some utility in Germany. He wanted a US presence in Europe, but at the same time he wanted to deny it influence in what he considered to be his part of Europe. Stalin presented Western analysts with a paradox as the war with Germany drew to a close. They could not see why he was attempting both to include American troops in, and to exclude them from, Europe.

Notes

1 C. E. Bohlen, *Witness to History 1929–1969* (New York: W. W. Norton, 1973), p. 127.

2 'Personal and Secret Message from Premier J. V. Stalin to the Prime Minister, Mr W. Churchill, and the President, Mr F. D. Roosevelt', *Stalin's Correspondence with Churchill, Attlee, Roosevelt and Truman 1941–1945* (London: Lawrence and Wishart, 1958). Originally published as *Correspondence between the Chairman of the Council of Minsters of the USSR and the Presidents of the USA and the Prime Ministers of Great Britain during the Great Patriotic War of 1941–1945*, Vol. 2, (Moscow: Foreign

Language Publishing House, 1957), pp. 149–50. Hereafter *Stalin's Correspondence*.

3   See C. E. Bohlen, *Witness to History*, p. 127. Immediately before the conference he states that 'There was no question about the eventual outcome of the war'.

4   Lord Avon, *Memoirs*, Vol II, *The Reckoning* (London: Cassell, 1965), p. 301. Moscow was concerned at this point in the war by the fierce opposition that the Red Army was facing in the Ukraine. See G. Zhukov, *Reminiscences and Reflections* (Moscow: Progress Publishers, 1985), p. 244. See also S. M. Shtemenko, *The Soviet General Staff at War* (Moscow: Progress Publishers, 1986), p. 266.

5   Conference Document no. 1. Adopted Agenda 740.0011 Moscow/ 10–1943. US Department of State, *Foreign Relations of the United States Diplomatic Papers*, General 1943. Vol. 1, p. 703. Hereafter *FRUS*.

6   Summary of the Proceedings of the Third Session of the Tripartite Conference, 21 October 1943, 740.0011 Moscow/345 *FRUS* General 1943, Vol. 1, pp. 590–9.

7   Text of Telegram from Mr Eden to His Majesty's Ambassador at Moscow, 18 September 1943. *FRUS* General 1943, Vol. 1, p. 525.

8   *Moskovskaya konferentsiya ministrov inostrannykh del SSSR, SShA velikobritanii, 19–30 oktabrya 1943* (Moscow: Politizdat, 1984), p. 388.

9   R. Beitzall, *The Uneasy Alliance: America, Britain and Russia 1941–1943* (New York: A. A. Knopf, 1972), p. 168.

10   *Moskovskaya konferentsiya*, p. 338. See also S. M. Shtemenko, *The Soviet General Staff*, p. 266. General Shtemenko, who was the Soviet military representative at Teheran, wrote: 'The Soviet delegation literally compelled the British delegation to acknowledge that Operation Overlord should be the Allies' main effort and that it should begin not later than May of the following year.'

11   Text of Telegram from Mr Eden to his Majesty's Ambassador at Moscow. 18 September 1943. *FRUS* General 1943, Vol. 1, pp. 525–8.

12   Ibid.

13   See V. Mastny, *Russia's Road to the Cold War; Diplomacy, Warfare and the Politics of Communism* (New York: Columbia University Press, 1979), p. 114.

14   Text of Telegram from Mr Eden to his Majesty's Government.

15   *Moskovskaya konferentsiya*, pp. 159.

16   Memorandum by Eden, 28 September 1943, W. P. (43) 423. CAB 66/41. PRO: 135 conclusions minutes 4, 5 October 1943. W. M. (43) CAB 65/40/ PRO. Quoted in V. Mastny, *Russia's Road to the Cold War*, p. 114. See also Count Raczynski's report on his conversation with Mr Eden and Sir Orme Sargent dealing with the policy of the Soviet Union in General Sikorski Historical Institute. *Documents on Polish Soviet Relations* (London: Heinemann, 1961).

17 'The Beneš–Molotov–Stalin Conversations' in V. Mastny, 'Stalin and the Prospects of a Separate Peace', *American Historical Review* 72, 1972, pp 1365–88.

18 Summary of the Proceedings of the Seventh Session of the Tripartite Conference, October 25, 1943. 740.0011 Moscow/10–1845, *FRUS General 1943*, Vol. 1, p. 634.

19 Summary of the Proceedings of the Eighth Session of the Tripartite Conference, October 26, 1943. 740.0011 Moscow/10–1843, *FRUS General 1943*, Vol. 1, p. 640–2.

20 Summary of the Proceedings of the Third Session of the Tripartite Conference, October 21, 1943, 740. 0011 Moscow/345, *FRUS General 1943*, Vol. 1, pp. 596–7.

21 Ibid.

22 Ibid.

23 W. A. Harriman and E. Abel, *Special Envoy to Churchill and Stalin* (London: Hutchinson, 1976), p. 237.

24 W. S. Churchill, *The Second World War*, Vol. 5, *Closing the Ring* (London: Cassell, 1952), pp. 168–9. There is evidence that Moscow had tried to influence the Italian settlement at the time of the conference. Vyshinsky had in October 1943 negotiated with Marshal Badoglio in Naples to establish a special relationship between Moscow and liberated Italy. Moscow had even extended diplomatic recognition to Badoglio. See N. Kogan, *Italy and the Allies* (Cambridge, Mass.: Harvard University Press, 1956), chapter 5.

25 *Stalin's Correspondence*, Vol. 2, p. 84.

26 Ibid.

27 H. Feis, *Churchill, Roosevelt and Stalin. The War They Waged and the Peace They Sought* (London: Oxford University Press, 1957), p. 184.

28 Summary of the Proceedings of the Fourth Session of the Tripartite Conference, October 22, 1943, 740.0011 Moscow 10–1843. *FRUS General 1943*, Vol. 1, pp. 604–13.

29 *Moskovskaya Konferentiya*, p. 263.

30 H. Feis, *Churchill, Roosevelt and Stalin*, p. 187.

31 *Moskovskaya Konferentiya*, p. 263.

32 V. M. Molotov, 'The Question of Allied Troops abroad', Speech at the meeting of the First Committee of the General assembly, 22 November 1946 in V. M. Molotov, *Problems of Foreign Policy, Speeches and Statements. April 1945–November 1948* (Moscow: Foreign Languages Publishing House, 1949), pp. 283–300.

33 V. Mastny, 'The Beneš–Stalin–Molotov Conversations in December 1943', pp. 367–401.

34 C. Hull, *Memoirs* (London: Hodder and Stoughton, 1948), p. 1264.

35 J. Stalin, 'Order of the day of the Supreme Commander-in Chief, May 1, 1943', quoted in V. Mastny 'Stalin and the Prospects of a Separate

Peace in World War II'. *American Historical Review* 77 (1972), pp. 43–66.

36   H. Feis, *Churchill, Roosevelt and Stalin*, p. 219.

37   Both Hull and Eden were extremely uncertain over the approach their countries would adopt towards partition or dismemberment. Summary of the Proceedings of the Seventh Session of the Tripartite Conference, October 25, 1943, 740. 0011 Moscow/10–1843. *FRUS* 1943 General, Vol. 1, p. 631.

38   Conference Document no. 18. Memorandum from Mr Hull with Respect to Point 5 on the Agreed Agenda. 740. 0011 Moscow/10–1943. *FRUS* 1943 General, Vol. 1, pp. 720–3, pp. 710–11.

39   C. Hull, *Memoirs*, p. 1285.

40   Summary of the Proceedings of the Seventh Session of the Tripartite Conference, October 25, 1943, 740.0011 Moscow/10–1843, p. 631. *FRUS* General 1943, Vol. 1, pp. 629–34.

41   M. Djilas, *Conversations with Stalin* (New York: Harcourt Brace, 1962), p. 115.

42   Conference Document no. 2. Amended Draft on Austria. 740. 0011. Moscow/10–1943. *FRUS* General 1943, Vol. 1, p. 724.

43   Annex 6. Declaration on Austria. *FRUS* General 1943, Vol. 1, p. 761.

44   C. Hull, *Memoirs*, p. 1273.

45   For Stalin's view of the Polish government in exile, see *Stalin's Correspondence*, pp. 193–4.

46   See General Sikorski Historical Institute, *Documents on Polish–Soviet Relations, 1939–1945*, Vol. 1, Document. no. 303, pp. 523–4.

47   For Soviet demands on Poland, see General Sikorski Historical Institute, *Documents*, Vol. II, p. 5.

48   S. Mikolajczky, *The Rape of Poland* (London: McGraw-Hill, 1948), p. 45. Eden makes no mention of this encounter in his memoirs and his version of meetings with Mikolajzky differs in tone and context from that of Mikolajzky. See Earl of Avon, *Memoirs* II, p. 422.

49   S. Mikolajczky, *The Rape of Poland*, p. 45.

50   W. A. Harriman and E. Abel, *Special Envoy to Churchill and Stalin*, p. 242.

51   JCS Files, Combined Chiefs of Staff Minutes, *FRUS*, The Conferences at Cairo and Teheran, 1943, pp. 501–5.

52   W. D. Leahy, *I was There* (London: Victor Gollancz, 1950), p. 244.

53   This point is discussed by V. Mastny, 'Soviet War Aims at the Moscow and Teheran Conferences', *Journal of Modern History* no. 3, September 1975, pp. 481–505.

54   H. Feis, *Churchill, Roosevelt and Stalin*, p. 128.

55   JCS Combined Chiefs of Staff Minutes, *FRUS*, The Conferences at Cairo and Teheran, 1943, p. 542.

56   JCS Combined Chiefs of Staff Minutes, *FRUS*, The Conferences at

Cairo and Teheran, 1943, p. 528.

57 Ibid.

58 W. Leahy, *I was There*, p. 244.

59 W. A. Harriman and E. Abel, *Special Envoy to Churchill and Stalin*, p. 265. See also C. Bohlen, *Witness to History*, p. 146.

60 W. A. Harriman and E. Abel, *Special Envoy*, p. 266. See also Robert Conquest, *Stalin: Breaker of Nations* (London: Weidenfeld and Nicolson, 1991), pp. 262–3.

61 W. A. Harriman and E. Abel, *Special Envoy*, p. 277.

62 Bohlen Minutes. Roosevelt–Stalin Meeting, November 29, 1943, *FRUS*, The Conferences at Cairo and Teheran, 1943, pp. 530–1.

63 Ibid.

64 For American objections to spheres of influence agreements, see W. A. Harriman and E. Abel, *Special Envoy*, pp. 356–8.

65 Bohlen Minutes, Roosevelt–Stalin Meeting, November 29, 1943, *FRUS*, The Conferences at Cairo and Teheran, 1943, p. 531.

66 Ibid.

67 See, for example, T. Wolfe, *Soviet Power and Europe 1945–1970* (Baltimore: Johns Hopkins University Press, 1970), pp. 14–15.

68 W. A. Harriman and E. Abel, *Special Envoy*, p. 280.

69 W. A. Harriman and E. Abel, *Special Envoy*, p. 281.

70 Bohlen Minutes, November 28, 1943, *FRUS*, The Conferences at Cairo and Teheran, 1943, p. 511.

71 Ibid.

72 Bohlen Minutes, Roosevelt–Stalin Meeting, *FRUS*, The Conferences at Cairo and Teheran, 1943. p. 532.

73 W. A. Harriman and E. Abel, *Special Envoy*, p. 277. See also R. Sherwood, *The White House Papers of Harry L. Hopkins*, Vol. II, January 1942–July 1945 (London: Eyre and Spottiswoode, 1949), pp. 786–7.

74 R. Sherwood, *Hopkins*, pp. 786–7.

75 Ibid.

76 See W. A. Harriman and E. Abel, *Special Envoy*, p. 275.

77 R. Sherwood, *Hopkins*, p. 786.

78 W. S. Churchill, *Closing the Ring*, pp. 450–1.

79 See the discussion between Molotov and Beneš in V. Mastny, 'The Beneš–Stalin–Molotov Conversations', p. 398.

80 V. Mastny, 'The Beneš–Stalin–Molotov Conversations', p. 387.

81 C. E. Bohlen, *Witness to History*, p. 151.

82 C. E. Bohlen, *Witness to History*, p. 153.

83 J. R. Deane, *The Strange Alliance* (New York: Viking, 1947), pp. 147–50.

84 V. Mastny, *Russia's Road to the Cold War*, pp. 133–44.

85 S. Mikolajczyk, *The Pattern of Soviet Domination* (London: Sampson Low, 1948), pp. 104–7.

86   Squires (Istanbul) to Secretary of State, May 19, 1944. Communism US Embassy, Moscow, RG-84, NA, quoted in V. Mastny, 'The Beneš–Stalin–Molotov Conversations', p. 196.

87   S. Fischer-Galati, *The New Rumania* (Cambridge, Mass.: MIT Press, 1967), pp. 18–22.

88   A. Werth, *Russia at War* (London: Barrie and Rockcliffe, 1964), p. 903.

89   L. Woodward, *British Foreign Policy in the Second World War*, (London: HMSO, 1971), Vol. 3, p. 119.

90   Memorandum by William Strang, 27 August 1944, W. P. (44) 475 CAB 66/54, PRO. Quoted in V. Mastny, *Russia's Road to the Cold War*, p. 200.

91   L. Woodward, *British Foreign Policy*, p. 139.

92   Lord Avon, *Memoirs* II, p. 482.

93   A. Werth, *Russia at War*, p. 909.

94   W. S. Churchill, *The Second World War. Triumph and Tragedy* (London: Cassell, 1954), pp. 227–8.

95   Ibid.

96   Ibid.

97   Ibid.

98   Lord Avon, *Memoirs II*, p. 483.

99   W. Harriman and E. Abel, *Special Envoy*, p. 358.

100   W. S. Churchill, *Triumph and Tragedy*, pp. 227–8.

101   T. Sharpe, *The Wartime Alliance and the Zonal Division of Germany* (London: OUP, 1975), pp. 14–16.

102   Memorandum by the UK Representative to the European Advisory Commission (Strang), 15 January 1944, 740.00119 EAC/53. *FRUS* 1944, Vol. 1, pp. 139–54.

103   T. Sharpe, *The Wartime Alliance*, pp. 14–16.

104   Ibid.

105   Roosevelt–Stalin Meeting. February 4, 1945. Bohlen Minutes. *FRUS*, Malta and Yalta, 1945, p. 572.

106   W. Leahy, *I was There*, p. 351.

107   Combined Chiefs of Staff Minutes, February 4, 1945. *FRUS*, Malta and Yalta, 1945, p. 581.

108   Ibid, p. 581.

109   Combined Chiefs of Staff Minutes, February 5, 1945. *FRUS*, Malta and Yalta, 1945, p. 583.

110   W. D. Leahy, *I was There*, p. 353.

111   *FRUS*, Malta and Yalta, 1945, p. 599.

112   Lord Avon, *Memoirs* II, p. 510.

113   Joint Chiefs of Staff Minutes, February 4, 1945. *FRUS*, Malta and Yalta, 1945, p. 566.

114   Ibid.

115 Ibid.

116 Bohlen Minutes. February 9, 1945. *FRUS*, Malta and Yalta, p. 848.

117 W. A. Harriman and E. Abel, *Special Envoy*, p. 413.

118 CAB 99/31, PRO. Quoted in V. Mastny, *Russia's Road to the Cold War*, p. 251.

119 Memorandum of Conversation, February 9, 1945. 740. 5/9–1554. *FRUS*. Malta and Yalta, 1945, p. 863.

120 C. Bohlen, *Witness to History*, p. 193.

121 Ibid.

122 W. A. Harriman and E. Abel, *Special Envoy*, p. 413.

123 Ibid.

124 D. Zaslavaskii, 'The Rout of Germany'. BBC, Daily Digest of World Broadcasts 17 February 1945, no. 2042. Quoted in V. Mastny, *Russia's Road to the Cold War*, p. 255.

125 George Schopflin, 'Hungary', p. 99. Quoted in M. McCauley ed. *Communist Power in Europe 1944–1949* (London: Macmillan, 1977), pp. 95–110.

126 Ibid.

127 C. Bohlen, *Witness to History*, p. 193.

128 C. Bohlen, *Witness to History*, p. 176.

129 Ibid.

130 C. Bohlen, *Witness to History*, p. 177.

131 W. S. Churchill, *Triumph and Tragedy*, p. 321.

132 W. S. Churchill, *Triumph and Tragedy*, p. 322.

133 Ibid.

134 W. S. Churchill, *Triumph and Tragedy*, p. 334.

135 For Bohlen's realist approach to a deal with Moscow see Bohlen, *Witness to History*, pp. 173–93.

136 See W. A. Harriman and E. Abel, *Special Envoy*, p. 405.

137 Lord Avon, *Memoirs*, p. 511.

138 Lord Avon, *Memoirs*, p. 510.

139 E. R. Stettinius, Roosevelt and the Russians (London: Cape, 1950) p. 60.

140 I. V. Chuikov, *The End of the Third Reich* (London: MacGibbon and Kee, 1967), pp. 56–7. This is in fact denied by Marshal Zhukov. He states that it would not have been attempted because the Soviet supply lines were overstretched and incapable of sustaining the troops to Berlin. See G. K. Zhukov, 'On the Berlin Axis', in S. Bialer, *Stalin and his Generals* (New York: Pegasus, 1969), pp. 508–9.

141 I. V Chuikov, *The Fall of Berlin*, p. 120.

142 Bohlen Minutes, 5 February, 1945. *FRUS*, Malta and Yalta, 1945, p. 648.

143 I. V. Chuikov, *The Fall of Berlin*, p. 120.

144 Bohlen Minuutes, 5 February, 1945. *FRUS*, Malta and Yalta, 1945,

pp. 616–7.

145   Roosevelt, at Yalta, seemed to agree with the Soviet view of France: on one occasion he confided to Stalin that he agreed that De Gaulle had 'grandiose ambitions'. He remarked that the British were peculiar, they wanted to have their cake and eat it by trying to artificially build France up. W. A. Harriman and E. Abel, *Special Envoy*, p. 394.

146   Bohlen Minutes, 5 February, 1945. *FRUS*, Malta and Yalta, 1945. p. 617.

147   Ibid.

148   T. Wolfe, *Soviet Power and Europe*, pp. 14–15.

149   W. A. Harriman and E. Abel, *Special Envoy*, p. 402.

150   Bohlen Minutes, 6 February, 1945. *FRUS*, Malta and Yalta, 1945, p. 661.

151   W. A. Harriman and E. Abel, *Special Envoy*, p. 402.

152   Bohlen Minutes, 5 February, 1945. *FRUS*, Malta and Yalta, 1945, p. 619.

153   Matthews Minutes, 5 February, 1945. *FRUS*, Malta and Yalta, 1945, p. 629.

154   W. A. Harriman and E. Abel, *Special Envoy*, p. 402.

155   W. S. Churchill, *Triumph and Tragedy*, p. 307.

156   EAC Files File 144, Memorandum by the Military Adviser to the US Delegation to the European Advisory Commission, June 1 1944. *FRUS*, General 1944, Vol. 1, pp. 230–1.

157   Ibid.

158   740.00119 EAC/7–2844 Telegram to the Ambassador in the United Kingdom (Winant) to the Secretary of State, 28 July, 1944. *FRUS*, 1944, Vol. 1, p. 262.

159   Ibid.

160   M. Djilas, *Conversations with Stalin*, p. 153.

161   Bohlen Minutes, 5 February 1945. *FRUS*, Malta and Yalta, 1945, pp. 620–1.

162   Ibid.

163   Ibid.

164   W. S. Churchill, *Triumph and Tragedy*, p. 306.

165   On 4 January 1945 Churchill had written a memo to Eden in which he addressed the problem of the treatment of a post-war Germany. He expressed concern over what the public would allow to happen. He wrote that 'I have been struck at every point where I have sounded opinion at the depth of the feeling aroused by a policy of "putting Germany on her legs again".' Ibid.

166   W. S. Churchill, *Triumph and Tragedy*, p. 307.

167   W. A. Harriman and E. Abel, *Special Envoy*, p. 307.

168   Lord Avon, *Memoirs* II, p. 516.

169   W. S. Churchill, *Triumph and Tragedy*, p. 304.

170 British War Office 106/4228. Quoted in T. Sharpe, *The Wartime Alliance*, p. 36.

171 C. Hull, *Memoirs*, p. 1612. He quotes Roosevelt as saying, 'I do not want the US to have the post-war task of reconstructing the Balkans. This is not our natural task at a distance of 3, 500 miles or more. It is definitely a British task. '

172 C. Hull, *Memoirs*, p. 1612.

173 C. T. Grayson, *Austria's International Position 1938–1953*, (Geneva: Librairie E. Droz, 1953), p. 58.

174 Ibid.

175 W. S. Churchill, *Triumph and Tragedy*, p. 210.

176 E. Stettinius, *Roosevelt and the Russians*, p. 118.

177 *Pravda*, 7 April 1945.

178 W. A. Harriman and E. Abel, *Special Envoy*, p. 425

179 See H. B. Ryan, *The Vision of Anglo-America, The US–UK Alliance and the Emerging Cold War 1943–1946.* (Cambridge: Cambridge University Press, 1987), p. 137.

180 W. S. Churchill, *Triumph and Tragedy*, p. 371.

181 'Message, J. V. Stalin to W. Churchill', 7 April 1945, in *Stalin's Correspondence*, pp. 314–16.

182 'Message, J. V. Stalin to W. Churchill', 23 March 1945, in *Stalin's Correspondence*, p. 308.

183 W. S. Churchill, *Triumph and Tragedy*, p. 374.

184 W. S. Churchill, *Triumph and Tragedy*, p. 369.

185 G. K. Zhukov, *Reminisences and Reflections*, Vol. II, pp. 340–1.

186 711. 61/4–645 Moscow. Ambassador in the USSR, Harriman, to the Secretary of State, April 6, 1945. *FRUS*, 1945, Vol. V, Europe, pp. 822–3

187 Ibid.

188 W. S. Churchill, *Triumph and Tragedy*, p. 400.

189 W. A. Harriman and E. Abel, *Special Envoy*, p. 432.

190 S. M. Shtemenko, *Soviet General Staff*, p. 348–53.

191 Ibid.

192 This decision was disputed by Marshal Chuikov, who believed that the Red Army could have captured Berlin in March. See Marshal I. V. Chuikov, 'The Costly Delay', in S. Bialer, ed., *Stalin and his Generals* (New York: Pegasus, 1969), pp. 500–5.

193 Marshal J. V. Stalin to the President, Mr Roosevelt, April 3, 1945, in *Stalin's Correspondence*, Vol. II, pp. 205–6.

194 This was, however, a retrospective view. Zhukov can only have learnt of the Western casualties later. G. Zhukov, *Reminiscences*, Vol. II, p. 412.

195 Premier J. V. Stalin to the President, Mr F. Roosevelt, April 7, 1945, *Stalin's Correspondence*, p. 209.

196 W. S. Churchill, *Triumph and Tragedy*, p. 400.

197   Ibid.

198   W. S. Churchill, *Triumph and Tragedy*, p. 442.

199   W. S. Churchill, *Triumph and Tragedy*, p. 407.

200   Leahy Papers, Prime Minister Churchill to President Truman. *FRUS*, Potsdam, 1945, Vol. 1, p. 7.

201   D. D. Eisenhower, *Crusade in Europe* (New York: Doubleday, 1948).

202   W. A. Harriman and E. Abel, *Special Envoy*, p. 450.

203   Ibid.

204   D. D. Eisenhower, 'My views on Berlin', *Saturday Evening Post*, 9 December 1961. Quoted in T. Sharpe, *The Wartime Alliance*, p. 124.

205   The British in particular feared a permanent Soviet occupation of Denmark. W. S. Churchill, *Triumph and Tragedy*, p. 449.

206   W. S. Churchill, *Triumph and Tragedy*, p. 400.

207   O. N. Bradley, *A Soldier's Story* (London: Eyre and Spottiswoode, 1951), p, 535.

208   See G. K. Zhukov, *Reminiscences*, pp. 362–4.

209   This was not the case. The memoirs of Zhukov, Shtemenko and Konev all reveal that in spring 1945 the energies of the Red Army were concentrated upon Berlin.

210   T. Sharpe, *The Wartime Alliance*, p. 135.

211   J. Ehrman, *Grand Strategy*, Vol. VI (London: HMSO).

212   T. Sharpe, *The Wartime Alliance*, p. 137.

213   A possible explanation is that the British suspected that it might be an area of German atomic research and wanted to get there before the Red Army. W. S. Churchill, *Triumph and Tragedy*, p. 449.

214   W. S. Churchill, *Triumph and Tragedy*, p. 439.

215   Leahy Papers, President Truman to Prime Minister Churchill. *FRUS*, Potsdam, 1945, Vol. 1, p. 11.

216   W. S. Churchill, *Triumph and Tragedy*, p. 500.

217   G. K. Zhukov, *Reminiscences*, Vol. II, p. 347.

218   S. M. Shtemenko, 'The Battle for Berlin', in S. Bialer, *Stalin and his Generals*, p. 499.

219   G. K. Zhukov, *Reminiscences*, p. 349.

220   S. M. Shtemenko, 'Battle for Berlin', p. 493.

221   G. K. Zhukov, *Reminiscences*, Vol. II, p. 342–70.

222   G. K. Zhukov, *Reminiscences*, p. 341.

223   G. K. Zhukov, *Reminiscences*, Vol. II, p. 347.

224   G. K. Zhukov, *Reminiscences*, Vol. II, p. 456.

225   V. Mastny, *Russia's Road to the Cold War*, p. 270.

226   J. Ehrman, *Grand Strategy*, pp. 156–7.

227   C. Stern, *Ulbricht*, (New York: Praeger, 1956), p. 92.

228   V. Mastny, *Russia's Road to the Cold War*, p. 279.

229   W. S. Churchill, *Triumph and Tragedy*, p. 442.

230 M. Shtemenko, 'The Battle for Berlin', p. 624.

231 I. S. Konev 'Meeting with Bradley', in S. Bialer, *Stalin and his Generals*, pp. 551–7.

232 See V. Mastny, *Russia's Road to the Cold War*, pp. 277–9.

233 W. S. Churchill, *Triumph and Tragedy*, p. 442.

234 W. S. Churchill, *Triumph and Tragedy*, p. 442.

235 S. M. Shtemenko, 'The Battle for Berlin', pp. 423–42.

236 R. E. Sherwood, *The White House Papers*, Vol. 2, p. 889.

Chapter 3

Strategies of occupation

Some revisionist historians have claimed that, following the death of Roosevelt on 12 April 1945, Truman dramatically changed US strategy towards the Soviet Union, and that he pursued a more antagonistic line.[1] They allege that Truman was responsible for the Cold War through his determination to confront Stalin and through his use of atomic blackmail. In this version of history, Stalin was forced on to the defensive and Soviet foreign policy was merely reactive to an overtly aggressive American external agenda. In general the revisionist school of history is primarily concerned with the making of US foreign policy and in particular with the period of transition between the Roosevelt and Truman administrations. These historians have pointed to the problems that Roosevelt bequeathed to his successor through what had been his 'tacit' acceptance of Soviet foreign policy goals in Europe. The revisionists do not directly address the issue of US troops in Europe; but the underlying assumption is that Moscow was understandably and entirely hostile to their presence.

That assessment is not strictly accurate. US attitudes towards Moscow were far from fixed in the spring of 1945. Truman's stance was not wholly negative. His policies included some instances of a more aggressive line, but they were primarily a continuation of the approach established by Roosevelt, viz. to seek cooperation with Moscow. There were some instances of a tougher stance: Truman's riposte to Molotov on 23 April, for example, when the President reprimanded the Soviet Foreign Minister for the failure to implement the Yalta agreements in Eastern Europe;[2] and the suspension of Lend–Lease in May 1945.[3] Nevertheless, the Truman administration, on the whole, actually resisted the anti-Soviet line advocated by the British.

Churchill was continuing to urge that Soviet expansionism should be actively confronted. In May the Prime Minister once again suggested that British and American troops in Europe should be used to exact political concessions from Moscow. He proposed that Western troops already present in the future Soviet zone of Germany should remain there. Churchill wrote:

> We have several powerful bargaining counters on our side the use of which might make for a peaceful agreement. First, the Allies ought not to retreat from their present positions to the occupational line until we are satisfied about Poland and also about the temporary character of the Russia occupation of Germany and the conditions to be established in the Russianised or Russian-controlled countries in the Danube valley, particularly Hungary, Austria and Czechoslovakia and the Balkans . . . All these matters can only be settled before the United States armies in Europe are weakened.[4]

The Truman administration resisted the British overtures for a number of military and political reasons. First, as Secretary of War Stimson said 'the Russians would regard any attempt to reverse the decisions on zones as evidence that London and Washington had formed an alliance against them'.[5] The maintenance of good relations with Moscow was regarded as critical, primarily because the United States regarded Soviet military aid in the war against Japan as essential.[6] While the Truman administration recognised that there were political disagreements with Stalin over the post-war settlement it wished to postpone any confrontation in Europe until after victory in the East. Second, from a purely military point of view, logistical conditions in the Pacific war necessitated the transfer of US troops to that theatre.

Continued cooperation was not, however, universally supported within the administration. The Acting Secretary of State, Grew, supported Churchill's view and advocated keeping US troops in Europe to exert pressure on Moscow. On 14 May he asked Truman to instruct the military to cease the withdrawal of troops from Czechoslovakia so that US troops would only be withdrawn in tandem with their Soviet counterparts.[7]

Truman resisted pressure, both from the British authorities and from within his own administration, to confront Stalin and continued to operate a triangular policy between the three Great Powers.

On 26 May, Harry Hopkins, a close adviser to Roosevelt, was sent to Moscow to confer on the post-war settlement. The purposes of the meeting appear to have been to reassure Stalin that Truman was not hostile and to maintain harmonious relations whilst at the same time to secure an approximate date for the Soviet entry into the war in the Pacific.[8]

During these talks, Stalin made it clear to Hopkins that he understood that there were differences in Anglo-American thinking on the post-war world. He told Hopkins that responsibility for ill feeling between East and West lay with the British because of their intransigence on the Polish issue. He accused the British of trying to restore a *cordon sanitaire*. When Hopkins answered that neither the government nor the people of the United States had this intention, Stalin repeated that he was speaking only of the British.[9] Indeed, this line has been maintained until recently by Russian historians who have analysed the role of the British in the post-war world unfavourably. In the words of one study:

> The striving of England to occupy a leading position in Europe and to direct European policy against the USSR is marked by many international plans and measures undertaken ... in post-war years by England itself or by its supporters.[10]

During the meeting Hopkins attempted to reassure Stalin that Washington did not object to the pre-eminence of Soviet interests in Eastern Europe. He said that the United States wanted a Poland friendly to the Soviet Union. Stalin proposed a compromise agreement to resolve the issue of Poland. He advocated a scheme whereby the present Warsaw government would form the basis of any future government but that representatives from other Polish groups, friendly both to the West and to the USSR, should occupy a proportion of the ministerial posts.[11] Hopkins accepted this idea although he must have known that, in reality, it did not alter the balance of power in Poland. It did, however, allow President Truman to reassure the influential Polish-American lobby that Moscow was adhering to the Yalta principles.[12]

Truman's attempts to maintain some form of cooperation with Moscow were apparent during the Potsdam conference in July. In particular the US administration sought to alleviate Soviet suspicions over the formation of an Anglo-American bloc. The briefing book for the American delegation at the conference recommended that 'US policy should be to discourage the development of rival spheres of influence both Russian and British and also "dispel" the Soviet impression that the Western powers were "ganging up" against them'.[13]

It would appear, then, that, from the time of Roosevelt's death until the Potsdam conference, the revisionist account does not withstand scrutiny. More important, it fails to take account of Soviet aims and motivations and ignores the fact that Moscow possessed its own agenda. Stalin, irrespective of Roosevelt's death, perceived a territorial competition taking place in Central and Eastern Europe. Moscow's aim of trying to secure its sphere of influence remained unchanged. This was particularly obvious with regard to both Austria and Germany.

In the closing stages of the war in Europe, Stalin had attempted to exert influence in Austria through the establishment of the pro-Moscow Renner government in Vienna.[14] The Soviet leader had refused to allow British and American forces into the Austrian capital until they recognised the regime. The agreement on zones in Austria had been signed on 9 July, but Anglo-American forces were unable to move into the areas. It was only at Potsdam that Stalin agreed to Western forces entering Vienna after the British and the Americans had agreed that the Renner government's influence should be extended to the whole of Austria.[15] On 20 July he announced that Soviet forces would be withdrawn 100 km from the British zone in Austria.[16] He bargained not only for clear lines of demarcation, but also for the type of government he wanted in place in Austria.

Stalin hoped to secure the removal of Anglo-American forces from the Soviet zone in Germany. After VE day, British and American troops still held substantial areas that they had captured during the final days of the war. During the talks with Hopkins in May, Stalin had agreed to the inauguration of the Allied Control Commission as the supreme executive in Berlin, to take control on 5 June.[17] Zhukov subsequently made it a condition that, before the commission could meet, Anglo-American forces should be withdrawn from the Soviet zone.[18]

Despite Churchill's continued attempts to persuade Truman to maintain troops in the Soviet zone,[19] the American President once again rejected the idea and ordered the troops to prepare to start withdrawal on 21 June.[20] Paradoxically, Stalin then insisted that the withdrawal must be postponed until 1 July.[21] The paradox is easily explained, as the Soviets had a strategy of 'stripping' whatever industrial goods they could find in the Western zones and needed more time to transport them back to the USSR.[22]

The issue of German reparations was a key area of disagreement at the Potsdam conference in July. Despite the Soviet insistence on Allied troops moving into their designated zones, Molotov pressed for the creation of central German 'agencies' and demanded that for the purposes of economic planning Germany should be treated as one single unit. The Soviet delegation also suggested that the Ruhr area should be internationalised under the control of the Great Powers.[23] The emphasis upon Allied control of the whole of Germany was in part a ploy to extract as much reparations as possible. Byrnes, who was present at the conference, wrote that his overwhelming impression was that Moscow's primary concern was economic compensation.[24] The Soviet delegation demanded at least $18 million worth of reparations.[25] This policy failed, largely because the British and the Americans had begun to believe that Germany should not be completely stripped of its industrial and economic assets and allowed to sink into economic dependence on the rest of Europe. Indeed, many in the Truman administration believed that Europe as a whole should be rehabilitated.[26] A primary concern was that Moscow should be prevented from exacting such reparations from Germany that the latter would be unable to sustain itself. The Americans, therefore, constructed a plan that had at its core the principle that 'each country exacts reparations form its own zone of occupation'.[27] Agreement was eventually reached, at Potsdam, that each occupying authority could take whatever reparations it pleased, but only from its own zone. In return, Moscow was promised some additional deliveries from the Western zones.[28]

At Potsdam, Soviet hopes of making major gains from reparations were disappointed. Some scholars treat this as critical to the breakdown of US–Soviet relations.[29] This was important because it reinforced the sense of Soviet economic insecurity. However, the major part of the revisionist argument is that it was the emergence and advantage of US nuclear power that drastically changed both US and Soviet foreign policy. At the Potsdam conference Truman told Stalin that the United States possessed an atomic capability.[30] Contemporary accounts record that Stalin displayed little emotion at the news and did not seem, to Western observers, to understand the full importance of the weapons.[31] This view is reinforced by the recent work of Volkogonov, who makes little mention of the impact of the news on the Soviet leader.[32] It was only after the devastation of Hiroshima and Nagasaki that the Soviet leadership fully comprehended the new weapon's significance.[33]

A major concern appears to have been the effect that US possession of the bomb would have on the war in the Far East. By the time of the Potsdam conference and the news of the atomic bomb, Stalin had already begun to fear that the Americans would attempt to cut the USSR out of the post-war Japanese settlement. Just after the Yalta conference, the Soviet leadership had begun to make preparations for war with Japan, while in May 1945 a special Far Eastern Command was established.[34] However, Stalin had his doubts about whether the war with Japan would continue long enough for the USSR to make the necessary preparations. In particular, the Soviet leader was worried that Japan would surrender before the Soviet Union entered the war[35] and had had time to secure its territorial ambitions in the Far East. These included the recovery of Russian losses suffered during the defeat by Japan in 1904–05; the recovery of southern Sakhalin, the restoration of Port Arthur, annexation of the Kurile islands and the establishment of control along with the Chinese over the Chinese Eastern Railway. After the Potsdam conference, Soviet leaders were determined to enter the war as soon as possible. Shtemenko reports that after his return to Moscow from the Berlin conference, Stalin received reports that preparations for war were complete and issued orders for Soviet forces to move into action on 9 August. After that date, Soviet forces moved quickly to take territory in the Far East, without apparently allowing the examples of Hiroshima and Nagasaki to affect Soviet plans.

Despite this apparent lack of concern over the US possession of atomic power, Stalin fully understood the impact of the news and the importance of the United States' technological superiority and, hence, Soviet vulnerability. In the middle of August People's Commissar of Munitions Boris L'Vovich Vannikov and his deputies were summoned to the Kremlin. Stalin commanded that the Soviet nuclear programme be intensified to provide Moscow with atomic weapons in 'the shortest possible time'. Hiroshima, he said, had shaken the whole world. The equilibrium had been destroyed (*ravnovesie navrushilos*).[36]

The Soviet leadership knew that the economic and strategic con-
figuration of the world had been drastically altered. Soviet commentators asserted that a significant shift of forces had occurred
within the capitalist world in favour of the United States. The Soviet
estimate of whether Washington would use its new power in the
post-war world and whether it would be permanently involved in
Europe remained uncertain. There was a belief that Washington had
moved away from its former isolationism, The Soviet journal
Mirovoe khozyaistvo i mirovaya politika commented that

> Nowadays the foreign policy of the USA is based on active participation
> in the world and particularly in European military, political and
> economic problems. The lessons of history have convinced the
> American public that isolationism, the self-exclusion from world
> affairs, the refusal to take part in the struggle for peace throughout the
> world is fatal.[37]

The belief that a transformation had taken place in the attitude of the
United States towards its role in international affairs was reinforced
by other analyses. There was a view that, despite its current
economic strength, the United States would inevitably face a
recession. During the war, it was argued, the American economy had
been producing at full capacity, but with the end of the war demand
would decrease and, as a consequence, Washington would be compelled to find new overseas markets in order to continue to produce
at full capacity. The search for new markets, it was presumed, would
lead the Truman administration away from isolationism.[38]

There was a further consequence of this Soviet expectation,
namely that the American search for new markets would necessitate
trade with the Soviet Union. As early as April 1945, Averell
Harriman detected this view. He reported that some quarters in
Moscow believed that American business needed, as a matter of life
and death, the development of exports to Russia.[39]

In early 1945 Molotov handed Harriman an *aide-memoire* stating
that the USSR was ready to place $6 million worth of orders with
American industries after the war. The note explained that the Soviet
offer would aid the American economy to make the necessary transition from wartime to peacetime production, would prevent mass
unemployment and would provide new markets.[40] This attitude
struck Western officials at the time as rather peculiar.[41] It may be
explained as a bargaining technique which had been used by the

Soviet leadership in the past to induce Washington to trade with Moscow. It also indicates Moscow's continuing belief that economic benefits could be obtained through cooperation with Washington.

This was a tactical arrangement; it does not mean that Moscow trusted Washington, or that antagonisms had been forgotten. Moscow, nevertheless, believed that, in the shorter term, cooperation was possible. There was obviously unease at the capitalist threat to the Soviet system. Spokesmen were adamant that the continued existence of capitalism made war inevitable, but not yet. In April, the main journal of the party argued that 'the possibility of war will exist as long as antagonistic class contradictions exist'.[42] A little later in the year, the party's Agitprop chief, G. Alexandrov, quoted Stalin to the effect that the capitalist tendencies towards war had not abated and that the risk of war was 'an objective historical fact'.[43]

Yet for all the warnings of the inevitability of conflict between capitalism and socialism, theorists did not consider war to be imminent. In August 1945, an article in *Bolshevik* made it clear that 'war was nor irreversible under present conditions'.[44] In September, Stalin himself endorsed this view when he commented that he discounted a war between the three Allies in the foreseeable future.[45]

The Soviet leadership was, in any case, in no state to fight a war at this stage. The Joint Intelligence Staff (JIS) finalised a report in July 1946 that examined the state of the Soviet Union's infrastructure after the war. It concluded that Moscow was not capable of launching an attack on Western Europe. Approximately 91,000 km of roads and 90,000 bridges had been rendered unusable. The armaments industry was only producing at the production levels of 1938 and damage to regions such as Ukraine was so great that coal production was less efficient than in 1938.[46] The priority of the Soviet leadership after World War II, as it had been after World War I, was to ensure a period of peace in which to reconstruct its economy and armed forces.

The Soviet army was demobilised after the war. By the end of 1945, the army had been reduced by 3 million from 11,365,000 men in May.[47] By 1948 numbers were reduced to 2,874,000.[48] This was accompanied by a large-scale reorganisation. The decision to cut the manpower available for defence was not motivated by a feeling of security. There is at least one indicator of the fear of imminent attack. One of the first actions that the Soviet leadership took was to establish modern air defences.[49] In 1946, the Air Force was elevated to the same level as the Navy and Army Ground Forces.[50]

Although Moscow was aware of the inferiority of its strategic power, and despite its perception of an external threat, the Soviet government did not allow these factors to overtly affect its diplomatic policy. There was no outward show of concern about US nuclear power.

The London meeting of the Council of Foreign Ministers opened on 11 September. It had been set up at Potsdam to prepare peace treaties with Germany and its allies. Molotov pursued the linkage between Western and Eastern power in Europe. When the Americans refused to accept the peace treaties with Romania and Bulgaria, the Soviet delegation refused to sign the peace treaty with Italy.[51] Molotov also linked any post-war settlement in Europe with that for the Pacific. On 27 September he told Byrnes that if Washington would only agree to Moscow taking a prominent role in the Allied Control Council for Japan it would be easier for him to accept the Italian treaty.[52] Implicitly, Molotov was stating that if the United States wanted to influence the settlement in Eastern Europe then he would demand similar rights in Japan.

Byrnes had hoped that the US atomic capability would make the Russians more tractable.[53] He took a forceful stance towards Moscow. He refused to allow Soviet influence in the future control of Japan. On the whole Byrnes's belief in the power of the atomic weapon seemed to make little difference to Moscow, which remained intransigent in asserting its interests in Eastern Europe. Molotov even seemed to joke about the US nuclear capability at the conference. He remarked that 'we must pay attention to the US, they are the only ones who have the atomic bomb'.[54] Moscow appeared determined to demonstrate it would not be cowed by the American technological advantage. Soviet analysts have subsequently remarked that the London meeting of Foreign Ministers marked the first attempt by the Americans to practise 'atomic diplomacy'.[55]

Despite this outward show of confidence, in the autumn of 1945 there were indications that Moscow was uncertain of its future course in foreign policy. In October, Stalin indicated an alternative course to cooperation with the West. In an interview with Averell Harriman, he intimated that the option of isolationism remained viable for the Soviet Union. He added that, although he had personally opposed the adoption of this course (which implied that others had supported it), he must now consider it carefully.[56] This threat appears as a ploy to bargain with Washington for continued Soviet cooperation. During the same conversation, Stalin stated that he might be forced along this road because of American intransigence over issues such as the Japanese settlement.

Yet, during the autumn of 1945, the Soviet leader also seemed intent on not antagonising Washington. He remarked to George Kennan that 'our troops are going to get out' of Eastern Europe.[57] Although it obviously would not be correct to deduce policy from one remark, Soviet troops were withdrawn from Czechoslovakia at that time.

The withdrawal from Czechoslovakia

During the war, the Roosevelt administration had concluded an informal agreement with the Czech government that US troops would remain on Czech soil for as long as Russian forces remained. On 9 July, after Truman had told Churchill that American forces could not remain in their advanced positions in Germany, the State Department reassured the American chargé d'affaires in Czechoslovakia that

> SHAEF has instructed Twelfth Army Group to maintain the existing line of demarcation with Soviet forces. The United States has no intention of making complete unilateral withdrawal at this time.[58]

Throughout July, according to Czech sources, the Soviet Union steadily reduced its forces in Czechoslovakia from about 150,000 to 40,000.[59] By August, the United States had withdrawn four of the eight divisions originally stationed in the country.[60] In August, a debate was under way within the Truman administration over both the desirability and the feasibility of maintaining US troops in Czechoslovakia.[61] Domestic pressures were mounting to withdraw forces from Europe. The War Department too began pressing for withdrawal in accordance with the demobilisation programme. In September, the Acting Secretary of State wrote to the US ambassador in Czechoslovakia describing his attempts to persuade the Secretary for War to allow two divisions to remain.[62] By late autumn 1945, the administration believed that there was no alternative to complete withdrawal from Czechoslovakia. Although the Americans had decided to withdraw their forces unilaterally, Secretary of State

Byrnes proposed to the Soviet Union that American and Soviet troops be withdrawn simultaneously. While he believed that there was little hope of Soviet agreement, he argued that: 'If Stalin does not agree to our proposal we would be in no worse position and could then make our independent decision whether to withdraw or not.'[63] Much to Byrnes's surprise, Stalin accepted the American proposal, replying that it fully accorded with Soviet plans for the demobilisation and withdrawal of armies.[64] On 6 December, the US ambassador in Czechoslovakia reported that the Soviet government had kept to its agreement to evacuate Czechoslovakia by 1 December.[65]

The Czech case illustrates Soviet motives and aspirations in the autumn of 1945. Stalin's remark to Djilas that 'he who occupies a territory imposes his own system on it' is often presented as the key to Soviet strategy in Europe. Yet Czechoslovakia shows that Stalin was prepared to withdraw Soviet troops from occupied territory. This might be explained as an attempt to maintain good relations with Washington. More pragmatically, it might also be explained as an exercise that cost Moscow little to perform. There seemed to be every reason for Moscow to expect that the Communist Party would dominate Czech politics in the post-war period,[66] and, indeed, Moscow would not have found it difficult to replace troops in Czechoslovakia. Nevertheless, the multilateral withdrawals demonstrate that all forms of cooperation between Moscow and Washington had not disappeared. In fact in this period, despite American protests over Soviet behaviour in Eastern Europe, Washington and Moscow managed to come to some form of settlement on those countries which had caused disagreement at the London conference.

At the Foreign Ministers' conference in Moscow in December 1945, Byrnes held a meeting with Stalin and agreement was reached on the Romanian and Bulgarian settlements. In return for Soviet assurances concerning free elections and press freedoms, to be monitored by a tripartite Allied Commission, Romania would be recognised by the West. Moscow agreed that the Bulgarian government should include two democratically elected Ministers.[67] In return for these Soviet concessions, it was agreed that an Allied Control Commission would be established in Japan in which Moscow could play a consultative role. These agreements were clearly linked: token Western involvement in Eastern Europe in return for token Soviet involvement in Japan.

A significant feature of the Moscow conference was that Anglo-American differences were clear. Byrnes held a meeting with Stalin independently of the British delegation and told Stalin that 'even though we were supposed to have a bloc with Britain I had not informed Bevin about my proposal to Mr Molotov as I should have done'.[68] The British delegation was upset, not only by its exclusion from the meeting but also by Byrnes's attitude towards the emerging crisis in Iran. This was a critical episode in the Cold War for two reasons. First, it demonstrated Moscow's belief that there was room to manipulate for advantage the differences between the British and the Americans, and, second, it pushed Washington into a harder line *vis-à-vis* Moscow.

Moscow and Iran

Bevin attempted to negotiate a fixed date for the removal of both Western and Soviet troops from Iran. Byrnes, rather than supporting Bevin's position, accepted the Soviet proposal and agreed with Molotov that the question of troop withdrawals should be postponed. The British regarded this as a failure by the Americans to protect Western solidarity in the face of Soviet intransigence.[69]

The Iranian problem of early 1946 constituted one of the first crises of the Cold War. In 1941, British and Soviet troops had entered Iran under joint agreement to prevent the oilfields from falling into the hands of the Germans and to ensure the security of the southern supply route to the Soviet Union. The Red Army occupied the northern provinces whilst Britain controlled the southern parts of the country. In 1942, the so-called Anglo-Iranian-Soviet Tripartite Agreement was signed providing for British and Soviet troops to remain in Iran until six months after the end of the war. This understanding was reaffirmed at both the Teheran conference and at the London Foreign Ministers' conference in the autumn of 1945.

Moscow was concerned to exact long-term oil concessions from the Iranian government and to protect its economic interests generally. Stalin told Byrnes at the Foreign Ministers' conference in Moscow in December 1945 that if Soviet forces were pulled out, saboteurs might attempt to blow up the Baku oilfields. Nevertheless, Stalin reassured Byrnes that he would accept the Western proposal that all troops would be withdrawn by the March deadline.[70]

Britain feared, however, that Moscow would attempt to prolong its stay in the northern provinces. This fear had been fuelled by the creation, in December 1945, of the independent Republic of Azerbaijan and of the Kurdish Mahabad Republic by the communist-led Tudeh party. There is little doubt that Moscow wanted to exercise influence in northern Iran. Even before the Allied invasion of Iran in 1941, during the period of alliance with Germany, Molotov had sought to advance its interests in Iran. His condition for joining the Four Power Pact had been that 'the area south of Batum and Baku and in the general direction of the Persian Gulf would be recognised as the centre of the aspirations of the Soviet Union'.[71]

During the war years, Soviet troops had exercised considerable influence in the northern provinces. They had been aided in this by the state of near anarchy which existed in Azerbaijan and also by popular hostility towards the government in Teheran. There is some evidence that Soviet forces actively encouraged this anti-government sentiment.[72] Soviet influence was strengthened by control over food supplies to the region, most notably grain. With control over the harvests in the north, Soviet troops could hamper the efforts of Iranian authorities to distribute food and relieve local discontent. While Soviet forces remained in occupation in the northern provinces they could maintain pressure upon Teheran to negotiate on the critical issue of oil concessions. When the oil negotiations failed at the end of 1944, Moscow began to show greater reluctance to discuss the issue of troop withdrawals in any detail. The Soviets continued to maintain that they would pull out of Iran, but it was noticeable that they began to express concern over the security of oil supplies.

In January 1946, Molotov told Bevin of Moscow's worries about the oil supplies in Baku.[73] At the same time, reports from the American vice-consul at Tabriz, Robert Rossow, noted fresh Soviet troop movements into northern Iran.[74] Rossow described Soviet activities as 'no ordinary reshuffling of troops but a full scale combat deployment'.[75]

The American response to the developing crisis evolved rapidly. In early January 1946, despite British and Iranian appeals, the United States refused firmly to support the Iranian protest to the United Nations over Soviet behaviour. On 2 January, Byrnes wrote to the US ambassador in Iran:

While the American Government has in no way changed its policy as regards Iran, which is based firmly on the declaration regarding Iran and on the UN charter, the American Government could not undertake to give advance assurances of the position it would take in any case of this kind to be brought before the UNO. The United States has friendly relations with both the Soviet Union and with Iran and for us to give advance commitment to either side would not be in harmony either with those friendly relations.[76]

The March deadline for the withdrawal of foreign troops from Iranian soil was reached and Soviet forces remained in place. American officials began to harden their attitude. Reports of heavy Soviet troops movements in Azerbaijan confirmed the view of some within the administration of the need to act. On 5 March, Dean Acheson stated that the United States should 'let the USSR know that we are aware of its move but leave a graceful way out if it desired a showdown'.[77] However, the next day Byrnes took a more forceful line; when informed of alleged Soviet troop movements towards Teheran he stated that a Soviet 'military invasion' meant that the United States could 'give it to them with both barrels'.[78] Byrnes sent a telegram to Stalin asking for an explanation of the Soviet manoeuvres but Moscow simply ignored the message.[79]

Moscow continued to put pressure on the Iranian Prime Minister, Qavam, to grant oil concessions, and, throughout March, remained adamant that Soviet troops would remain in northern Iran. A combination of US diplomatic pressure and an Iranian appeal to the UN Security Council appears to have persuaded Moscow to change its strategy. In early April, Moscow reached an agreement with Teheran that Soviet forces should be withdrawn by early May.[80] President Truman recorded that

The Soviet Union persisted in its occupation until I personally saw to it that Stalin was informed that I had given orders to our military chiefs to prepare for the movement of our ground, sea and air forces. Stalin then did what I knew he would do. He moved his troops out.[81]

No documentary evidence has been found to substantiate Truman's claim that he threatened the USSR with such drastic action;[82] nevertheless, it was the American interest in Iran which appeared to compel the Soviet withdrawal and end any hope of Soviet influence in Iran.

Throughout January and February, Moscow had made it a *sine qua non* for the withdrawal of its troops that a joint Iranian–Soviet company should be established,[83] but the agreement signed between Prime Minister Gavam and the Soviet ambassador to Iran, Sadchikov, on 4 April gave Moscow little of any value.

So long as the Soviet Union was opposed primarily by the British in Iran, Stalin pushed to the limit his ability to extend Soviet influence. Once it had become clear in early 1946 that the United States was concerned, Stalin was unwilling to persist. What is interesting is that Moscow did not expect a forceful American response: it believed that America would leave the area to the British. This misperception was understandable. As late as December 1945, Byrnes had signalled a lack of interest over the future of British imperial possessions and reassured the Soviet negotiators that Washington would not always side with the British. Further, the Americans had, up to that point, not been over-concerned with the future of Iran.

The withdrawal of Soviet forces from Iran appears to have been undertaken with the intention of limiting US hostility. In early 1946 there was considerable uncertainty in Soviet foreign strategies. Not only had Moscow been forced from Iran, but there was a noticeable hardening in US attitudes towards it. The Soviet failure to withdraw troops from Iran by the agreed deadline indicated that Moscow had territorial ambitions which overrode agreed boundaries. American analysts deduced from this that Soviet conduct was untrustworthy in other areas.[84] The shift in American perceptions was inspired not only by Soviet behaviour in Iran. The Truman administration was compelled by a variety of internal factors to adopt a harder line towards the USSR. If it did not it risked losing its domestic bipartisan support.[85]

This pressure coincided with the promotion of views advocating the implementation of a tougher strategy within the administration itself. The views of these 'hard-liners' prevailed in the spring of 1946. Noteworthy among them was the work of George Kennan, the American chargé in Moscow, which provided the rationale for the new approach. For many months prior to the Iranian crisis, Kennan had been sending dispatches from Moscow analysing Soviet behaviour in the gloomiest terms and stressing the futility of policies which sought conciliation and cooperation with Moscow.[86] These reports had largely been ignored until February, when they struck a responsive chord within the administration. Kennan's analysis of Soviet foreign policy, as an outgrowth of an ideologically pre-

determined set of expectations and ambitions, provided the intel-
lectual basis of a new American strategy towards the Soviet Union.[87]
Secretary Byrnes gave an indication of the new American attitude on
28 February when, in a speech to the Overseas Press Club, he
proclaimed: 'If we are to be a great power we must act as a great
power, not only in order to ensure our own security but in order to
preserve the peace of the world.'[88]

The tougher American stance was reinforced a week later by what
appeared to be a considerable tightening of the Anglo-American
bloc. Ex-Prime Minister Churchill gave a speech at Fulton in the
United States which called for an Anglo-American alliance.[89] President Truman sat next to him, endorsing the view that an iron curtain
had come down over Europe.[90] Washington had publicly abandoned the posture of trying to operate a triangular policy between
Britain and Moscow.

Moscow responded with some public anger at Churchill's Fulton
speech. *Pravda* published an indignant editorial.[91] On 13 March,
Stalin branded Churchill's speech a dangerous act. He accused
Churchill of acting as an incendiary for war.[92] Moscow was, however, reluctant to accept the complete breakdown of cooperation
with Washington. Even after American intervention in the Iranian
dispute, and even as American attitudes hardened into anti-Soviet
ones, Stalin refused to accept the reality of an Anglo-American bloc.
There seems to have been genuine uncertainty over the future course
of Soviet foreign relations.

Moscow and Germany

There were indications among the Soviet leadership of two strands of
thinking over the the path that foreign relations should take. These
were expressed by two leading figures in early 1946, A. Zhdanov and
G. Malenkov. The struggle between the two was a major theme of
the immediate post-war period.[93] The origins of this intra-elite
conflict can be traced back to the Eighteenth Party Congress of
March 1939.[94] During discussion, Malenkov stressed the role of the
Secretariat in providing industry with guidance, and advocated a
technocratic and economic approach to the running of Soviet
industry. Zhdanov, on the other hand, proposed that the Primary
Party Organisation, the PPO, which was more concerned with
ideological orthodoxy, should monitor local factory managers and

workers. He emphasised the importance of the 'ideologically' correct line in factories.[95] The conference endorsed Zhdanov's idea,[96] but disagreements between the two continued throughout the war years.

Zhdanov had been responsible for Marxist–Leninist education since 1938. During 1939, he was appointed Director of Agitprop with responsibility for the supervision of the press and education of party members. In 1939, Malenkov became Director of the new Cadre Directorate of the Secretariat with responsibility for the supervision of industry and personnel management. Malenkov occupied a more prominent position in the Soviet heirarchy in this period. Zhdnaov's position was noticeably downgraded after 1941, mainly because of his former association with advocacy of the Nazi–Soviet pact.[97] Upon the Nazi invasion of 1941, Zhdanov was given charge of the Leningrad military district whilst Malenkov assumed control, alongside Beria, of the State Defence Committee. Malenkov ended the war as the more powerful figure, having spent the period in Moscow in charge of the home front.

In 1946, Zhdanov and Malenkov assumed divergent positions on international issues. Malenkov was associated with an isolationist, anti-Western line while Zhandov pursued a line that called for the active encouragement of socialism beyond socialist borders. These differing approaches to international affairs were revealed in the election speeches of February 1946. Malenkov called for a reinvigoration of the Soviet homeland.

> We must continue, first of all, to strengthen the Soviet state created by Lenin and Stalin . . . We already represent a very great power. Let us not forget that we are strong enough to maintain the interest of our people . . . we have achieved victory for ourselves and wish to safeguard our motherland against any eventualities. We do not wish to pull chestnuts out of the fire for others.[98]

The major theme of Malenkov's speech was 'self-sufficiency'. He stated that the tasks of the USSR were 'to strengthen our might, strengthen our air force, strengthen our socialist state, strengthen our glorious Red Army and Navy'. Beria, a close associate of Malenkov, reinforced this view, stating that sooner or later 'the Soviet states will have to withstand the onslaught of hostile imperialist states'.[99] Another associate of Malenkov, Kagonovich, stressed the dangers of capitalist encirclement.[100]

Within this group there was a high level of mistrust of the West. It is of some significance that not one of them mentioned the wartime alliance with the Western states. This does not mean that they sought confrontation, but rather that they regarded the wartime alliance as over, and preferred a strategy of what might be termed isolationism or self-sufficiency.

Zhdanov, on the other hand, in his speeches of 1946, emphasised the primacy not of the USSR, but of socialism. He appeared more optimistic about the international environment and less hostile towards the West. In his election speech of February, he made no mention of armed conflict with the West and declared that 'we have entered a period of peaceful development'.[101] He stressed that the position of socialism had been strengthened by victory in World War II.[102] On 8 February, speeches by both Malenkov and Zhdanov appeared on the same page in the newspaper *Krasnaya Zvezda* and illustrated their divergent emphases on the future policies of the USSR. Malenkov stressed the need for self-sufficiency and spoke of the need to strengthen the USSR. Zhdanov said that there was no need to remain in isolation, as socialism was spreading.[103] These differences proved to be of practical significance in dealing with Germany.

During the winter of 1944–45, the Council of People's Commissars had set up a committee, chaired by Malenkov, to supervise the extraction of reparations from the occupied zones of Germany.[104] The removal of reparations, in particular the transfer of the industrial and economic materials of Germany, was seen as serving two purposes. It was viewed as a means of strengthening the Soviet economic and industrial base; it was also a means of depriving Germany of any future economic or industrial potential. An article in *Bolshevik* in August 1945 made this point explicitly. It stated that the 'military potential of the country was determined by heavy industry' and that it was imperative for the decisions of the Berlin conference which included the 'full disarmament and demilitarization' of the country to be carried out. If Germany was deprived of a heavy industrial capacity it would be less of a threat. The August timing of this article ties in with the Stalinist directive to provide the Soviet Union with an atomic capability as quickly as possible. While justification of the regime's behaviour in its zone in Germany was couched in the language of reparations,[105] it was determined by the need for resources. Malenkov seems to have been mainly in charge of the process of dismantling the eastern zone, but he received support in this endeavour from Kagonovich and Beria. Beria was in charge of the Soviet atomic programme while Kagonovich was head of the Ministry of Construction; both had a vested interest in stripping the zone.[106]

Malenkov had been in the Soviet zone, in charge of the dismantling process, during the winter of 1944. Soviet dismantling teams had arrived in the zone with the second echelon of the occupying armies. Soviet officers from the period testify to the importance attributed to this process. It has been claimed that, in order to collect all the wealth possible from Germany, special units were formed within the Red Army at division and army level, whilst other units were organised to guard and transport back to the USSR the property which was collected.[107] By the autumn of 1945, according to witnesses, vast quantities of dismantled machines, materials and instruments were piled up at the transhipment points of the Special Committee at Brest-Litvosk, Poznan and Stettin, and unloaded on the ground along the railway tracks for a distance of 100 km.[108]

The process of dismantling and stripping the zone appears to have been carried out in a hasty and disorganised fashion. Colonel Koval'chikov, the commander of the Trophy Administration of the First Ukrainian Front, described the dismantling of German industry as 'characterised mainly by the almost complete absence of any overall direction'.[109] Highly valuable machines and goods were ruined in the process through exposure and breakage. The whole operation appears to have been dictated by Malenkov's belief that the Soviet priority should be to transport as rapidly as possible whatever was of any technical or industrial value. Malenkov's haste, interestingly enough, seems to have been premised on the belief that USSR would eventually have to withdraw from the eastern zones.[110]

Malenkov's strategy in Germany was not one which was supported among the Soviet leadership. Zhdanov, in particular, seems to have advocated what might be termed a strategy of Sovietisation. Zhdanov, however, was not the first actively to oppose the Malenkov line in the eastern zone of Germany. During 1945, for example, the Group of Occupation Forces in Germany had already come into conflict with the Special Committee's policy of economic disarmament. In May 1945, GSOVG, in conjunction with the Political Administration of the Soviet Army headed by General Mekhlis, complained to the Special Committee specifically about the dismantling of printing plant and paper factories.[111] The Political Administration of the Soviet Army believed that, after the war, the need would again arise for large-scale Soviet agitation in both Germany and the East European countries. A prerequisite for this task would be a number of printworks and paper factories.[112] In May 1945, the Special Committee had ordered the dismantling of all the factories making tarred roofing paper in Berlin. Colonel General N. Berzarin, the Commandant of Berlin, used his authority to countermand the execution of the order in the case of one factory in Spandau.[113] From this it can be deduced that some Soviet military officials were already thinking in terms of the Sovietisation of the eastern zone or, at the very least, did not share Malenkov's view that the zone existed merely to be stripped.

The Malenkov programme for the eastern zone was not regarded as a success. The chaos and wastage of the dismantling process aroused opposition in Moscow, as did the failure of the programme to provide all the reparations needed.[114] In early 1946, alternative ideas were beginning to surface in Moscow. In January 1946, the Soviet Council of People's Commissars issued a degree calling for extraordinary measures to increase the output of materials.[115] Mikoyan, the Minister of Trade, suggested that, in order to achieve higher levels of production, it might make more sense to maintain a certain level of production in the zone.[116] A commission was appointed in the summer of 1946 to look into the causes of the failure in the eastern zone;[117] dismantling was blamed.

In the spring of 1946, Malenkov's influence appeared to be relatively downgraded within the Soviet hierarchy. In May, he was removed from the Party Secretariat.[118] Meanwhile, in Germany, men associated with Zhdanov were placed in prominent positions in the eastern zone. Marshal Zhukov was replaced by Marshal Sokolovsky.[119] Zhukov's removal coincided with the demise of Malenkov's influence and a change in Soviet strategy for the eastern zone. There is some evidence that Zhdanov exerted pressure to remove Zhukov. In January, Colonel S. I. Tiul'panov had confided to SPD leaders in Germany that Zhukov would not be commander in Germany for much longer.[120] Sokolovsky and Tiul'panov, who assumed command of the eastern zone, especially Tiul'panov, had very close links with Zhdanov. Sokolovsky, in his first major speech, had made it clear that he fully supported the Zhdanov strategy in Germany. He denounced outright the stripping or dismantling of

German industry and supported the idea of a divided Germany. In 1946, Tiul'panov became chief of the Information and Propaganda Department of the Soviet Military Administration, and Head of the Party Organisation and representative of the CPSU in the occupation zone. Tiul'panov had close links with Zhdanov. He had, initially, been trained as an engineer in Leningrad. Zhdanov had been party boss in Leningrad from 1934 and had worked within the Political Administration of the city until he was transferred to the main Ukrainian front in 1943.[121] Tiul'panov told Gniffke that he had been exiled to Siberia for 'deviationism' but that Zhdanov had intervened on his behalf and saved him from such a fate. As Tiul'panov owed his position to Zhdanov, it is hardly surprising that he was one of the most ardent proponents of the Zhdanov strategy.

The change in personnel altered the political composition of the eastern zone quite dramatically. Under the Sokolovsky–Tiul'panov command, Walter Ulbricht, the head of the Kommunistische Partei Deutschlands (KPD), exerted far greater influence. Ulbricht had spent some of the war years in Moscow.[123] During this period he had been involved with the foundation of the National Committee for a 'free Germany' in July 1943. This group had determined that all Germans had contributed to the rise of Hitler to power. They concluded that all efforts should be devoted towards the long-term goal of a socialist Germany.[124] The philosophy suited the Zhdanovite plans for the creation of a future East German socialist state. The pre-eminence of the KPD line in Germany was assured in the spring of 1946 when the Sozialistische Einheitspartei Deutschlands (SED) was created through the forcible merger of the KPD and the SPD. This development was associated with Tiul'panov.

In the spring of 1946, the United States made a series of offers to test Soviet designs in Germany. In April, Byrnes proposed to Molotov that the United States, the USSR, Britain and France should agree to a treaty which would guarantee the disarmament and demilitarisation of Germany for the next twenty-five years.[125] Four days later, on 4 May, General Clay announced the suspension of further reparations from the American zone until all four powers had agreed to treat Germany as an economic entity.[126] Both of these proposals were designed to discover Moscow's aspirations in Germany.

During the spring and summer, Washington and London moved inexorably towards the fusion of the Western zones. In July 1946, they commenced the process of integrating their zones, beginning the consolidation, under one authority, of almost sixty per cent of German and Austrian territory, and, indeed, the great bulk of the industrial capacity of both countries.[127] In the same period, the Americans not only cut off reparations from their zone to the east, but quashed any hopes that Moscow might have had of a future reconstruction loan.[128] Washington also withdrew its support from the UNRRA.[129]

The issue of reparations remained a major stumbling block between the powers. At the Council of Foreign Ministers' meeting in July, Molotov insisted that what Moscow wanted was what it had demanded at the Yalta conference – $10 billion in reparations and quadripartite control of the Ruhr region.[130] The Americans refused to countenance such demands. The Soviet insistence upon huge payments and control of the Ruhr would, Western analysts believed, have led to a centralised government, adapted to the seizure of absolute control of the country by communists. Germany was thought particularly vulnerable because of its relative poverty and large population.[131]

The second major issue at the Council of Foreign Ministers was control of Germany. Molotov made it clear that Byrnes's proposal for a twenty-five year quadripartite regime was not satisfactory to Moscow. He reiterated that what Moscow wanted was a completely disarmed Germany and internationalisation of the Ruhr.[132]

> The Soviet Government reaffirms that disarmament and the demilitarization of Germany are absolutely essential. The Soviet Government feels that Germany should be kept disarmed and demilitarized not for 25 years as suggested in the draft but for at least 40 years. Experience has shown that the short period of time during which restrictions on Germany's armaments were enforced after the First World War proved to be absolutely insufficient to prevent Germany's renascence as an aggressive force endangering the peoples of Europe and the world. Only 20 years had passed since the end of the First World War when Germany unleashed a Second World War.[133]

Molotov outlined what he saw as crucial objectives with regard to Germany: first, to bring to a conclusion the military and economic disarmament of Germany; second, to secure the democratisation of the regime in Germany; third, to assure reparation deliveries. Molotov also made it clear that Moscow actively sought a US military presence in Europe: 'We hold that the presence of occupation forces in Germany and the maintenance of zones of occupation are absolutely essential as long as these objectives have not been achieved.'[134]

Some American officials, Kennan in particular, assumed that Soviet leaders had a clear and cogent strategy in Germany. He believed that Moscow planned to consolidate its power in the eastern zone and then to attempt to overcome the three weak and divided Western zones, drawing Germany into the eastern camp. Western indecision, Kennan argued, would make this increasingly likely.[135]

On 7 September, Byrnes made a speech in Stuttgart and stated that Washington was committed to the unification of the Western zones and to the economic, social and political recovery of Germany with or without Soviet cooperation.[136] Byrnes also stated that: 'I want no misunderstanding. We will not shirk our duty. We are not withdrawing. We are staying here. As long as there is an occupation army in Germany, American forces will be part of that occupation army.'[137]

Some Western analysts have concluded that this commitment to maintain US forces in Germany must have been deeply disturbing to the Soviet leadership. They have argued that Moscow was still relying on Roosevelt's policy of limiting a military presence in Germany to two years.[138] This is doubtful. The issue of US troops did not appear to be Moscow's central concern. It did not press for their removal. There are several explanations. A first possibility is that US troops in Western Germany actually provided a certain justification for Soviet activity in the eastern zone. Washington could hardly object to a Soviet presence whilst its own troops were still in the adjacent Western zones. A second explanation is that Soviet leaders actually and understandably believed that US forces still performed a useful function in maintaining a stranglehold on German militarism. Soviet criticisms were, in this period, mainly directed against the creation of a German army.[139]

The Soviet acceptance of US troops in Germany was evidenced by the fact that Moscow appeared eager to establish some form of quadripartite demilitarisation regime in at least some parts of Germany. It is true that Molotov rejected Byrnes's suggestion that the four Allies should run a demilitarised Germany for the next quarter of a century; but he countered with a plan that would have meant a demilitarised regime in Germany for forty years,[140] a time scale thought necessary for the rehabilitation of the Soviet Union itself.

From Moscow's perspective, US troops could act as a stranglehold upon the resurgence of German militarism in the short term, and provide the vital security from German aggression essential for Soviet recovery.

The alarming feature of Byrnes's speech for Soviet leaders was that it signalled that the United States intended to rebuild and rehabilitate the western parts of Germany. This provided the Soviet leaders with a problem: US troops could act as a guard against German militarism, but might also form the basis of an anti-Soviet military-political alliance in Europe.

Moscow and Italy

While the Soviet leadership remained ambivalent about a long-term strategy towards US troops in Germany, it had little doubt that it wanted to deny the Americans the use of bases in Italy.

The Allied Control Commission established in Italy was dominated by American and British representatives.[141] This, of course, conformed to the general pattern of occupation throughout Europe: countries occupied tended to absorb the political colouring of their occupation forces. However, despite the preponderant Western influence, from the spring of 1946 Moscow made determined efforts to influence the Italian settlement and to modify Anglo-American influence in the region.

The internal political situation in Italy affected Soviet perceptions. The Italian Communist Party (PCI), led by Togliatti, suffered a major setback in the Constituent Assembly elections of February 1946.[142] The communists polled less than 19 per cent of the vote, gaining only 104 of 556 seats. Their representation lagged far behind that of the Christian Democrats, led by De Gasperi, who had gained 35 per cent of the vote.[143] De Gasperi saw his primary task in the late 1940s as to secure the state against communism, and to solicit American support to withstand communist pressure.[144] Although the link between Moscow and domestic communist strategy in Italy remains ambiguous,[145] the failure of the PCI to acquire decisive support in the elections meant that Moscow could not really rely upon the domestic communists to dilute Western influence in Italy. Any countervailing Soviet influence would have to be exerted from outside the country. Attempts of this kind began two months after the failure of the communists in the 1946 elections.

Soviet efforts to influence the Italian settlement took several forms: endeavours to persuade the West to remove occupation forces; attempts to moderate the degree of economic involvement; and efforts to deny the West the use of military bases in any part of Italian territory.

East–West negotiations over the future of Italy began at the Potsdam conference in 1945 and were continued subsequently at the Foreign Ministers' conference in September 1945.[146] Soviet efforts to negotiate the withdrawal from Italian soil began in earnest only in May 1946 at the Council of Foreign Ministers. Molotov sought a guarantee that, after the conclusion of the peace treaty, troops would be withdrawn. The Western representatives, Byrnes and Bevin, agreed, but stipulated that some troops were necessary to maintain lines of communication with Austria. Molotov offered a deal. He said that the Soviet delegation was ready to consider the question of terms of reciprocity. If Allied troops were withdrawn from Italy, the Soviet delegation would be ready to discuss the Bulgarian question.[147]

In 1946, the Americans and the British were anxious to reduce the number of Soviet occupation forces in Eastern Europe. In May 1946, an American estimate put Soviet troop figures at 700,000 in Romania, 65,000 in Hungary and 280,000 in Bulgaria.[148] Shortly afterwards, the British War Office estimated that there was an approximate total of 905,000 troops in south-east Europe.[149] Eager as the West was to persuade the USSR to withdraw troops from Eastern Europe, the British delegation did not believe that the Italian situation could be equated with that which prevailed in Bulgaria. Instead, it suggested that Soviet troops in Romania and Hungary should be measured against Western forces in Italy.[150]

This idea was vehemently rejected by Molotov: Soviet troops in Romania were necessary to protect Red Army lines of communication with Austria. Eventually, Molotov appears to have won the point, and Byrnes and Bevin not only accepted the Bulgaria–Italy idea but also conceded that Soviet troops should remain in Hungary and Romania.[151] This 'troop trading' is significant in that Molotov might otherwise have conceded the withdrawal of troops from other parts of Eastern Europe in a *quid pro quo* to modify Western influence in Italy. The Soviet outlook remained subject to the need to avoid any substantial weakening of the Soviet grip on Eastern Europe.

In addition to 'troop trading', the Soviet Union pressed for an early conclusion of a peace settlement for Italy.[152] Once peace was officially concluded, Molotov reasoned, the West would be denied any pretext for leaving troops in place. Hence Molotov vehemently objected to the Western idea in mid-1946 of a provisional peace. In May, Bevin proposed that 'provision' should be made for the establishment of Allied machinery to enforce the naval, military and air clauses of the peace treaty until such time as Italy could be accepted as a reliable member of the United Nations.[153] The idea met with general agreement from the British and French representatives but was opposed by the Soviet delegation. It was perceived as a Western attempt to maintain forces in Italy. Molotov stated that 'this policy has nothing in common with Italy's national interests'. On the contrary, protraction of the occupation for a long term would place Italy in ever-growing dependence on foreign states. He said that he feared that such an arrangement 'might be used as a pretext for keeping troops in Italy after the conclusion of the peace treaty'.[154]

These objections should not, however, be taken at face value. In fact it was unusual for the USSR, during the negotiations for the post-war settlements, to defend the interests of a former enemy state. On the whole, Moscow differentiated very clearly between the treatment of former enemy states and others. In general, no objections were raised against the maintenance of foreign troops on the soil of Axis states. Molotov made this distinction explicit in November 1946. He objected to troops on foreign soil except in the case of ex-enemies.[155] This points to deeper Soviet motives for the championing of Italian independence from occupation throughout 1946. Moscow feared that the United States would seek to maintain heavy troop contingents in Italy which might be used to the detriment of Soviet security.[156]

Moscow was seeking to reduce Western influence by engineering troop withdrawals; attempts were also made to dilute the potential Western political and economic preponderance. In May 1946, Molotov called for agreements to ensure that no one power should exert undue influence on the Italian settlement, and made a proposal 'to restrict excessive claims of foreign powers and foreigners generally in Italy'.[157] Molotov also called attention to the 'danger that strong foreign states possessing large capital and wielding powerful means of pressure may use these practically unrestricted rights to the detriment of the national interests of the Italian republic'.[158] These proposals were intended to establish the economic neutrality of Italy.

Despite the calls for Western economic influence to be prohibited, the question of troops in Italy continued to be the dominant issue in the Italian settlement. This reflected a broader Soviet concern over the establishment of American military influence in Europe generally. Throughout 1946, Soviet protests on the issue of US troops grew stronger, particularly in connection with the establishment of American bases throughout the continent.[159] In November 1946, Molotov stated that

> We know that there are armed forces belonging to the USA and to Great Britain on the territory of a number of states of the United Nations . . . suffice it to say that armed forces including air and naval bases belonging to the United States of America and to Great Britain are disposed . . . in every part of the globe, including various territories of the Pacific, Atlantic and Indian oceans.[160]

The perception of the United States and Britain as states bent on the establishment of bases around the globe became a predominant concern of the USSR in 1946–47. This was particularly pertinent to the Italian situation. Throughout mid-1946 and 1947, the USSR perceived the West as intent on turning Italy into a territory for Western air and naval bases, forming part of a wider attempt to establish a network throughout Europe, from Iceland round to Italy, to encircle the Soviet Union. From May to June 1946, the Soviet military press began to comment unfavourably on the influence of Washington in both Iceland and Italy.[161] Even in the early 1980s, the Soviet press commented on Italy as a critical link in the Western scheme of things, and characterised it as a military springboard for Western aggression.[162] The post-war settlement for Italy provided that all troops should be withdrawn within ninety days of the treaty coming into force, except those necessary to maintain lines of communication.[163] However, it was agreed that a maximum of 5,000 troops from the United States, Britain and Yugoslavia would be made available to the governor of Trieste for a period of ninety days.

Stalin had shown little interest, during 1945, in exercising power in Italy. It was only as mistrust began to characterise the Soviet-American relationship that Moscow began to perceive US power in Italy as a threat. In particular, once plans began to be made to consolidate US air power in Europe, Moscow began to advocate plans for demilitarisation and neutrality.

In 1946 several interesting suggestions were raised for demilitarised zones in Italy. There appears to have been a coincidence of interest between Soviet and French views in favour of security zones on the territorial borders of Italy. The French sought some form of demilitarised frontier between French and Italian soil.[164] This idea was endorsed by Moscow, provided that a similar arrangement was made for the Italian–Yugoslav frontier.[165] These schemes were opposed by Washington. Byrnes believed that, as Italy was being disarmed anyway, through a limitation on its forces and a prohibition on long-range guns, 'it was unnecessary to provide for a thirty kilometre demilitarisation zone'.[166] The endorsement of the demilitarisation notion by both France and the Soviet Union indicates a similar concern on the part of both European land powers to contain the possibility of any future Italian offensive.

Soviet efforts to deny the West influence or bases in Italy are illustrated by the East–West struggle over Trieste and Venezia Giulia in the period 1945–47. During the war, both East and West had jostled for position in Venezia Giulia. As Hitler's armies in Italy had retreated, Tito's forces had advanced rapidly into the north-east territories. Tito seemed determined to seize the Trieste area before the Western allies could lay claim to it.[167] The Western allies were equally determined in April-May 1945 to capture the area themselves.[168] Trieste was regarded by both sides as a point of significant strategic value. The Western Allies were intent on securing Trieste: it was a major port and was viewed as an essential supply point for future occupation zones in Austria.[169]

In the spring of 1945, the Americans appeared to have both short-term and long-term plans for Trieste. Washington wished to control the area for the duration of the war. In the longer term, it appears to have favoured the idea of turning Trieste into an international port which would act as an outlet into the Adriatic.[170]

In April, Anglo-American task forces were ordered to seize those parts of Venezia Giulia essential to military operations, including Trieste and the communications leading to it and into Austria.[171] Allied military government was to be set up as in the other parts of Italy. It was recognised that the Yugoslavs would object to Anglo-American dominance. Western leaders sought to avoid the possibility of US and Yugoslav forces fighting for control of the area, but the Western powers were determined to deny Tito any claim to the area.[172] Truman went so far as to state that although he was unwilling to involve his country in a war with the Yugoslavs unless they attacked the Allies, in that eventually 'we should be justified in using Allied troops to throw them back far enough to stop any further aggression'. Truman believed that if Tito was to assume control of Trieste, Yugoslav ambitions in Hungary, Austria and Greece would be encouraged.[173]

Truman was determined to hold on to the area. Washington decided to solicit Soviet support to exert pressure on the Yugoslavs to remove their forces. If cooperation could not be obtained, the Western forces were instructed to take control anyway. During April, Allied forces (New Zealand troops) raced the Yugoslavs to take over Venezia Giulia, and during May portions of Trieste were occupied by both Western and Yugoslav troops.[174]

The policy of attempting to enforce Allied military government over the whole of Venezia Giulia, which the State Department had strongly emphasised, was abandoned in the face of Yugoslav opposition. Washington settled for control over a more limited area: Trieste and Pola, lines of communication through Gorizia and Monfalcone, and a large enough area to the east to ensure what the British and the Americans termed 'proper administration'.[175] A telegram was sent to Stalin which asked him to 'request' Tito to comply with this arrangement, since the Yugoslavs had proved unwilling to accede to Western demands.[176] It is significant that Moscow's influence appears to have been decisive. The Western notes presented lines of demarcation for Venezia Giulia on 15 May, but, on 19 May, Tito declined the Western offers. On 21 May, however, he agreed to those ideas with a few modifications.[177] The territory was divided into two. The area of Venezia Giulia west of the Morgan line and Pola came under the command of the Supreme Allied Commander. Yugoslavia was allowed to maintain 2,000 troops in this area.[178] Italy, backed by the Western powers, claimed the Trieste area as an Italian possession, while the Yugoslavs, backed by the Soviet Union, made equally powerful claims upon it.[179]

The Soviet backing of the Yugoslav position in 1946 was understandable on several levels. First, in mid-1946, in the wake of the Iran crisis, Soviet–American relations had deteriorated to a level of mutual distrust. It was natural that Stalin should support another regime against the British and Americans. Second, Trieste was a major port, of great strategic and economic value, providing both

Yugoslavia and the Soviet Union with access to the Adriatic. Third, Yugoslav possession of Trieste would have denied the Italians, and more important the Americans and the British, the use of a vital base. The latter appears to have been a major source of concern to Moscow in 1946. Molotov expressed the hope that Trieste would not be converted into a new base in the Balkans for someone else's armed forces.[180]

Negotiations over Trieste reached deadlock and a compromise agreement was suggested, by the French, that Trieste should be a free port. The Western powers wanted Trieste to be demilitarised, but the Soviet proposals insisted that the free territory must also be neutral.[181] Recognition of neutrality, from the Soviet perspective, meant that 'there will be no armed forces either domestic or foreign on this territory'.[182] The Soviet proposal for Trieste had two essential components. The first was that Trieste should be demilitarised and neutral. The second was that all foreign troops stationed in the free territory should be withdrawn within thirty days of the date of the enactment of the peace treaty with Italy.[183]

This was one of the earliest Soviet proposals for the neutralisation of an area in the post-war era. During the rest of 1946, Moscow espoused neutrality as the solution to the problem of Trieste. This appears to reflect the unique circumstances of Trieste. The area did not fall obviously into either the Western or the Eastern camp. From the Soviet perspective, when it became obvious that the British and the Americans were not going to allow the Yugoslavs to take Trieste, neutrality offered perhaps the best solution. It meant the establishment of a free port which could be used by both the USSR and Yugoslavia. More significantly, it denied the United States a base in the Balkans. Neutrality also meant the removal of Western troops.

The Kremlin's strategies of occupation in Eastern Europe, its intransigence over Iran, and its negotiating posture over Italy, confirmed to many in the West their conceptions of the Soviet Union as an inherently aggressive and expansionist power. Although no extra pressure was exerted upon Iran in 1946 and 1947, Washington remained concerned by what it perceived as similarly aggressive acts elsewhere in Europe. It was particularly anxious about Soviet involvement in the Greek civil war which had broken out again in the winter of 1946. A report by the State Department concluded that the EAM, the Greek Communist Party, was being used, by Moscow, to undermine British influence in the region.[184] There was concern over

Yugoslav aid to the Greek communists. It was assumed, in Washington, that Moscow was both coordinating and directing TitoUs activities. Already, in February 1946, the State Department had been informed that the situation in Greece was serious and that the Greek government might at any moment collapse.

While Greece was not strategically critical to Washington, the Truman administration saw civil war in Greece as part of a Soviet plan to dominate Europe. George Kennan noted that a communist victory in Greece would be followed shortly afterwards by communist control of Italy.[185] It was believed that once Italy had fallen, nothing would prevent the communist take-over of France, Germany and Britain.

Communism was regarded as a particularly potent force during the winter of 1946–47 because of the economic crisis.[186] The winter was particularly severe and, in March 1947, the British Cabinet warned the American ambassador that Britain was heading for a financial crisis and that funds for British forces abroad would have to be reduced. During May 1947, the French coalition government fell, and Washington feared that the communists would seek power through illegal methods. During the spring of 1947, American officials considered that the situation in Europe was so serious that Moscow was being encouraged to take a harder line in negotiations on European issues. It was believed that Soviet intransigence over Germany was strengthened by the Soviet belief that Europe would succumb to communism.[187]

The US reaction to the threat to the stability of Western Europe took the form of the Truman Doctrine, announced on 20 June 1947, which made financial aid available to both Greece and Turkey, and Marshall Aid, announced on 5 June 1947, by the Secretary of State, George Marshall. The purpose of both the Truman Doctrine and Marshall Aid was to strengthen the structures, economies and institutions of West European states to withstand the threat from communism. The theoretical basis of these initiatives was wholly ideological: democratic structures based firmly on liberal ideals would not be subverted by communism.

Initially, the offer of Marshall Aid was open to the Eastern bloc, although the terms on which it was offered were unacceptable to Moscow. Indeed, it appears that both the Americans and the West Europeans intended that this should be the case. Both Bevin and Bidault assured the US ambassador in Paris, Jefferson Caffery, that an invitation to Moscow to join in Marshall Aid was 'little more than window dressing'.[188]

Nevertheless, there is evidence that at first the Soviet leadership was prepared to consider seriously taking up the offer of Marshall Aid. In early June, for example, Molotov asked Eugene Varga to assess American intentions with regard to the plan. Varga actually prepared a report and handed it to Molotov on 26 June. His analysis was that while economic self-interest motivated the American interest in the economic rehabilitation of Europe, not least its search for new markets, he also advised that Moscow might be able to obtain some benefits without succumbing to Western pressure.[189] Moscow agreed to send a delegation to attend the Paris conference to discuss Marshall Aid, but the Soviet leadership retained its suspicions that this was one more element in a scheme to form a Western bloc that excluded the Soviet Union. The Soviet ambassador to Washington, Nikolai V. Novikov, gave voice to those suspicions on 9 June when he warned Moscow that 'the outlines of a West European bloc directed against us are patently visible'.[190] The Soviet delegation in fact withdrew from the conference convened to discuss the issue of European economic recovery and refused to allow East European countries to accept American aid. The American commitment to fostering a West European recovery forced a reappraisal of Soviet strategies.

Conclusion

Moscow employed several strategies of occupation in the period after the end of the war in Europe. One was to secure control over Eastern Europe. Moscow did this by physically occupying territory and denying the Western allies access and political influence. In this manner, Moscow carved out an area of political and military control where it was, on the whole, unwilling to cede any influence to Washington, despite American atomic and economic superiority.

In the months after the war in Europe had ended, Moscow sought to benefit from continued cooperation with Washington for both economic and security reasons. Moscow's prime concern was the subjugation of Germany. It wanted US aid to restrain future German ambitions. To this end, Moscow actively sought US military occupation in part of Germany. Division, between East and West, offered, at least in the short term, the best option for occupation.

The crisis in US–Soviet relations came about because of the Soviet attempt to maintain forces outside agreed boundaries in northern Iran. This attempt to extend influence, mainly at the expense of the British, was resisted by Washington. Soviet withdrawal was undertaken in a bid to limit American hostility, but it was too late. Soviet aggression, together with growing concern over Moscow's activities in Eastern Europe, combined to promote a hardening of US attitudes. As some of the revisionist school have pointed out, in many respects this was a result of Roosevelt's pigeons coming home to roost for Truman. Roosevelt had been able to avoid confronting Stalin over Eastern Europe, whilst at the same time maintaining to a US audience that Eastern Europe (in particular Poland) would not be betrayed. Truman had no such option. The tougher line, which was adopted from the autumn of 1945, appeared, most obviously, in the promotion of the view that the Western zones of Germany should be rehabilitated against communist encroachment. This, in turn, engendered a much harder line within Moscow, and the relatively benign view of US troops in Europe did not extend to their presence beyond German soil. Moscow sought to limit American influence in areas such as Italy. It should not, however, be suggested that Moscow operated to a blueprint for occupation in this period. There seems to have been genuine ambivalence over what course in Germany offered the best solution to the security concerns. There also remained an attempt to cooperate with Washington.

Notes

1 G. Alperovitz, *Atomic Diplomacy. Hiroshima and Potsdam* (New York: Simon and Schuster, 1965), pp. 19–40.

2 H. S. Truman, *Memoirs*, Vol. I, *Year of Decisions 1945* (London: Hodder and Stoughton, 1955), p. 85.

3 The abrupt end to Lend–Lease to the USSR can, it is claimed, be attributed to bureaucratic zeal, and did not reflect Truman's real intentions. See G. C. Herring Jr, *Aid to Russia 1941–1946. Strategy, Diplomacy, the Origins of the Cold War* (New York: Columbia University Press, 1973), p. 207.

4 See W. S. Churchill, *The Second World War*, Vol. VI. *Triumph and Tragedy* (London: Cassell, 1954), pp. 498–9, 523–4.

5 *Foreign Relations of the United States*, 1945, Vol. III, pp. 235–6. Hereafter *FRUS*.

6 For Grew's view that SHAEF held the line in Czechoslovakia, see

Department of State 740.0011 EW/ 5–1445. May 14, 1945. *FRUS* 1945, Vol. V, p. 254.

7   Ibid.

8   Hopkins had been a personal adviser to Roosevelt and his visit appears to have been designed to emphasise the continuity in US policies towards the USSR. *FRUS*, Potsdam, Vol. 1, pp. 26–32.

9   Department of State 740.00119. *FRUS*, Potsdam, Vol. I, pp. 26–32.

10   See, for example, V. G. Turkhanovsky and N. K. Kapitonova, *Sovetsko-angliyskie otnosheniya 1945–1978* (Moscow: Mezhdunarodnye otnosheniya, 1978), pp. 41–2.

11   Department of State, 740/00119. *FRUS*, 1945, Vol. V, pp. 299–388.

12   W. D. Leahy, *I was There* (New York: McGraw-Hill, 1950), Admiral Leahy describes the domestic pressures from the Polish American lobby, p. 467.

13   Briefing Book, US Delegation. *FRUS*, Potsdam, Vol. I, 1945, pp. 299–388.

14   See previous chapter.

15   Thompson Minutes. Fourth Plenary Meeting, 20 July, p. 176.

16   Cohen Notes. Truman Papers. *FRUS*, Potsdam, Vol. II, p. 181.

17   Ibid.

18   Eisenhower to Joint Chiefs of Staff, 6 June. *FRUS*, 1945, Vol. III, p. 328.

19   W. S. Churchill, *Triumph and Tragedy*, pp. 604–5.

20   Ibid.

21   Some analysts believe that Stalin had not expected such a rapid response. See V. Mastny, *Russia's Road to the Cold War. Diplomacy, Warfare and the Politics of Communism, 1941–1945* (New York: Columbia University Press, 1979), p. 291.

22   Ibid.

23   Meeting of the Economic Subcommittee July 20, 1945. US Delegation Memorandum. *FRUS*, Potsdam, Vol. I, pp. 143–55.

24   Bohlen Minutes. *FRUS*, Potsdam, Vol. I, p. 449–51.

25   Informal Meeting of the Foreign Ministers, 23 July 1945. Department of State Minutes. *FRUS*, Potsdam, p. 297.

26   Secretary of War (Stimson) to the President. Memorandum for the President. The Rehabilitation of Europe as a whole. *FRUS*, Potsdam, Vol. I, pp. 808–9.

27   US Delegation Memorandum. Department of State Minutes. *FRUS*, 1945, Potsdam, Vol. I, p. 514.

28   Ibid.

29   D. F. Fleming. *The Cold War and its Origins 1917–1960* (London: Allen and Unwin, 1968).

30   H. S. Truman, *Year of Decisions*, p. 416.

31   J. Byrnes, *Speaking Frankly* (New York: Harper and Brothers,

1947), p. 263.

32 D. Volkagonov, trans. Harold Shukman, *Stalin. Triumph and Tragedy* (London: Weidenfeld and Nicolson, 1991), pp. 501–2.

33 Quoted by A. Lavrent'yera in *Stroiteli novogomira' V mire knig* 70. Quoted in D. Holloway, *The Soviet Union and the Arms Race* (New Haven and London: Yale University Press, 1983).

34 See M. V. Zakharov, *Finale* (Moscow: Progress Publishers, 1972).

35 N. S. Khrushchev, *Khrushchev Remembers. The Glasnost Tapes* (Boston: Little Brown, 1990), p. 81.

36 Ibid.

37 'Znachenie vneshnei torgovli dlya 1945', *Mirovoe Khozyaistvo i mivovaya politika*, 10, 1945, p. 41.

38 Soviet economists actually disagreed about the future of US might. Most notably Varga put forward the idea that the experience of wartime planning might bring about a stabilisation of the capitalist economies. Eugen S. Varga, *Izmeniia v ekonomike kapitalizma v itoge vtoroi mirovoi voiny* (Moscow: Gospolitizdat, 1946). This will be discussed in chapter 5.

39 *FRUS*, 1945, Vol. V, p. 232.

40 *FRUS*, 1945, Vol. V, p. 942–5.

41 For a discussion of the American response see *FRUS*, 1945, Vol. V, p. 860.

42 Propaganda i Agitatsiya, no. 18, 1945. Quoted in W. O. McCagg Jr, *Stalin Embattled 1943–1948* (Detroit: Wayne State University Press, 1978), p. 204.

43 P. Fedoseev, 'Marksizm–Leninizm ob istochkakh i kharaktere voin', *Bolshevik*, no. 16, 1945, pp. 38–9. See also P. Chuikov, 'Uchenie Lenina–Stalina o voynakh spravedlivykh i nespravedlivykh', *Bolshevik*, no. 7–8, pp. 14–26.

44 Ibid.

44 See Stalin's comments to George Kennan, quoted in *FRUS*, 1945, Vol. V, pp. 882–3. This view was shared by Washington. The JCS did not at this stage believe that the immediate threat was war with Moscow. SWNCC 282. Basis for the Formulation of US Military Policy, 19 September, 1945. *FRUS*, 1945, Vol. I, pp. 1160–5.

46 JIS 80/26, 'Capabilities and Intentions of the USSR in the Post-war World', 9 July 1946.

47 *50 let Vooruzhennykh Sil SSSR* (Moscow: Voenizdat, 1968), pp. 474–9.

48 See J. Erickson, L. Hansen and W. Schneider, *Soviet Ground Forces* (Boulder: Westview, 1986), p. 21. See also the claims made concerning Soviet demobilisation after World War II in V. Zhurkin, S. Karaganov and A. Kortunov, 'Reasonable Sufficiency', *New Times* 12, 1987, p. 14.

49 R. A. Kilmarx, *A History of Soviet Air Power* (London: Faber and Faber, 1962), p. 222.

50   R. L. Garthoff, *Soviet Strategy in the Nuclear Age* (New York: Frederick Praeger, 1958), p. 178.

51   740.00119 Council 9–1945, Memorandum of Conversation by Mr Charles E. Bohlen, Special Assistant to the Secretary of State, September 19, 1945, *FRUS*, 1945. Vol. II, p. 243.

52   740.00119 Council/9–2745, Memorandum of Conversation by Mr Charles E. Bohlen to the Secretary of State. September 27, 1945. *FRUS*, 1945, Vol. II, p. 426.

53   For the revisionist claim that Washington did intend to blackmail Moscow through nuclear weapons, see G. Alperovitz, *Atomic Diplomacy*.

54   Quoted by D. Yergin, *Shattered Peace* (Boston: Houghton Mifflin, 1978), p. 132.

55   V. G. Trukhanovsky and N. K. Kapitonova, *Sovetsko-angliiskie otnosheniya 1945–1978* (Moscow: Mezhdunarodnye otnosheniya, 1978), p. 33. The authors allege that London and Washington wanted to end cooperation with Moscow. However, despite the fact that Trukhanovsky was in the Soviet Foreign Ministry at the time of the Foreign Ministers' meeting, this source seems to owe much to having been written at the onset of the Second Cold War. It is generally hostile towards the West.

56   A. Harriman and E. Abel, *Special Envoy to Churchill and Stalin 1941–1946* (New York: Random House, 1975), pp. 514–15.

57   See note 43.

58   740.00119 Control Germany/10–2645, The Secretary of War (Patterson) to the Secretary of State, October 26, 1945. By the autumn the United States had 30,000 troops spread over a 266 mile front in Czechoslovakia. *FRUS*, 1945, Vol. IV, p. 502.

59   860.F.01/7–545, The US Political Adviser for Germany (Murphy) to the Secretary of State, *FRUS*, 1945, Vol. IV, p. 469.

60   860F.01 8–2545, Telegram, The Ambassador in Czechoslovakia (Steinhardt) to Secretary of State, August 25, 1945, *FRUS*, 1945, Vol. IV, p. 485.

61   860.F.01 / 8–3145 Telegram, the Ambassador in Czechoslovakia (Steinhardt) to Secretary of State. *FRUS*, 1945, Vol. IV, p. 486.

62   860. F. 01/9–445, Telegram, The Acting Secretary of State to the Ambassador in Czechoslovakia (Steinhardt), September 11, 1945, *FRUS*, 1945, Vol. IV, p. 489.

63   740.00119 EW/10–1645 Record of a meeting of the Secretaries of State, War and Navy, October 16, 1945. *FRUS*, 1945, Vol. IV, pp. 496–7.

64   860. F 01/11–945, Telegram, the Secretary of State to the Ambassador in Czechoslovakia, November 9, 1945. *FRUS*, 1945, Vol. IV, p. 508.

65   F860.F.01/11–3045, Telegram, Ambassador in Czechoslovakia (Steinhardt) to Secretary of State, November 30, 1945. *FRUS*, 1945, Vol. IV, p. 509.

66   See A. Ulam, *Expansion and Coexistence, Soviet Foreign Policy*

1917–73, Second Edition (New York: Holt, Rinehart and Winston, 1974), p. 421.

67   Enclosure 2. Memorandum of the US Delegation at the Moscow Conference of Ministers, Moscow, December 18, 1945. *FRUS*, 1945, Vol. II, pp. 567–76.

68   J. F. Byrnes, *Speaking Frankly*, pp. 116–17.

69   CFM, Lot M-88-CFM, London Decisions. Record of Decisions of the Seventeenth Meeting of the Council of Foreign Ministers, London, September 22, 1945. *FRUS*, 1945, Vol. II, pp. 315–16.

70   740.00119 Council/12–2645, Memo of Conversation by US Delegation at the Moscow Conference of Foreign Ministers, December 19, 1945. *FRUS*, 1945, Vol. II, pp. 680–7.

71   See R. K. Ramazani, *Iran's Foreign Policy 1941–1973*, Charlottesville: University of Virginia Press, 1975), chapters 4–5, and W. Eagleton Jr, *The Kurdish Republic of 1946*, (London: Oxford University Press, 1963).

72   Department of State, 861.24591/3–446 CS/HS.

73   FO 371/52662, 19 January, 1946, quoted in L. Fawcett, *Iran and the Cold War* (Cambridge: Cambridge University Press, 1992), p. 96.

74   761.91/3–546, Telegram, Vice Consul at Tabriz (Rossow) to the Secretary of State. *FRUS*, 1946, Vol. II, p. 340.

75   Rossow to the Secretary of State, James Byrnes, 7 March 1946. *FRUS*, 1946, Vol. II, pp. 344–5.

76   F891.00/1–246, The Secretary of State to the Ambassador in Iran. *FRUS*, 1946, Vol. VII, pp. 292–3.

77   Editorial Note. *FRUS*, 1946, Vol. VII, p. 347.

78   Ibid.

79   Department of State Memorandum, *FRUS*, 1946, Vol. VII, p. 347.

80   The Ambassador in Iran (Murray) to the Secretary of State, Teheran. April 4, 1946. *FRUS*, 1946, Vol. VII, pp. 322–415.

81   Quoted in the *New York Times*, 26 August, 1957.

82   See the Editorial Note, *FRUS*, 1946, Vol. VII, pp. 348–9.

83   The Ambassador in Iran (Murray) to the Secretary of State, Teheran, March 22, 1946. *FRUS*, Vol. VII, 1946, p. 369. The Soviet Ambassador to Iran, Sadichikov, had stated that the 'Soviets might withdraw from Iran if the Shah and the Prime Minister would sign letters to him assuring Russia that arrangements would be made for joint Iranian-Soviet exploitation of North Iranian oil.'

84   The Chargé in the Soviet Union (Kennan) to the Secretary of State. Moscow, March 14, 1946. *FRUS*, 1946, Vol. VI, p. 716.

85   See A. H. Vandenburg, *The Private Papers of Senator Vandenberg* (Cambridge, Mass.: Riverside, 1952), pp. 247–51.

86   The Chargé in the Soviet Union (Kennan) to the Secretary of State, Moscow, February 22, 1946. *FRUS*, 1946, Vol. VI, pp. 696–709.

87   Ibid.

88   Department of State *Bulletin* XIV, 10 March 1946, pp. 355–8.

89   *New York Times*, 6 March 1946.

90   For a discussion of the emergence of the Anglo-American bloc, see Henry Butterfield Ryan, *The Vision of Anglo-America: The US–UK Alliance and the Emerging Cold War 1943–1946* (Cambridge: Cambridge University Press, 1987).

91   *Pravda*, 11 March 1946; *Izvestiya*, 12 March 1946.

92   *Pravda*, 14 March 1946.

93   There are obvious dangers in simply looking at the disputes between Soviet leaders and deducing policy differences. One analyst, W. O. McCagg, suggested (*Stalin Embattled 1943–1949*, Detroit: Wayne State University Press, 1978, pp. 231–3) that: 'the conflict between the two leaders was deliberately manipulated by Stalin in order to constrain his powerful "lieutenants" and more significantly, as an elaborate scheme to control the party, which Stalin regarded as having grown excessively powerful during the war years.' McCagg's theory is that Stalin deliberately placed Zhdanov and Malenkov in opposition. In the early months of 1946 the institutions associated with Malenkov's powerful wartime position were eliminated. On 19 January the Chief Administration for War Industry was abolished. The Politburo was restored to its pre-war supremacy and, while Malenkov's position was confirmed within it, Zhdanov's position was also strengthened to equal that of his rival. Zhdanov's place in the Party Secretariat was reaffirmed. A. A. Kuznetsov, who was regarded as within the Zhdanov faction, was also placed within that body. This resulted in an accrual of power to Zhdanov which was sufficient to challenge Malenkov directly. McCagg writes that 'under these circumstances, for whose emergence Stalin was patently responsible, Malenkov and Zhdanov could hardly help but clash'. Whilst there can be little doubt that prominent members of the Soviet elite assumed short-term policy positions to outmanoeuvre political opponents (see J. A. Armstrong 'W. G. Hahn and Post-War Soviet Politics. The Fall of Zhdanov and the Defeat of Moderation', Book Review, *Soviet Studies*, Vol. XXXV, no. 3, 1983, pp. 418–19), it is equally undeniable that there were genuine differences of opinion on both domestic and foreign affairs.

94   T. Harris, 'The Origins of the Conflict between Malenkov and Zhdanov 1939–1941', *Slavic Review*, Vol. 35, no. 2, June 1976, p. 291.

95   Ibid.

96   Ibid.

97   Zhdanov had been closely associated with advocacy of the Nazi–Soviet pact in the 1930s. See A. D'Agnostino, *Soviet Succession Struggles. Kremlinology and the Russian Question from Lenin to Gorbachev* (Boston: Allen and Unwin, 1988), p. 164.

98   *Pravda*, 8 February 1946.

99   Ibid.

100   Ibid.

101   Ibid.

102   Ibid.

103   *Krasnaya Zvezdya*, 8 February 1946.

104   R. Slusser, *Soviet Economic Policy in Post-War Germany* (New York: Research Programme on the USSR, 1953), p. 19.

105   Ibid.

106   See D. Holloway, *The Soviet Union and the Arms Race* (New Haven and London: Yale University Press, 1983), p. 22.

107   V. Yershov, 'The First Phase of the Occupation, Confiscation and Plunder by the Army of Occupation', in R. Slusser, *Soviet Economic Policy*, pp. 1–14. See also Y. Andreyevich, 'Kak proizodili demontazh v Germanii', *Novoye russkoye slovo*, 29 July, 1949. Quoted in R. Slusser, *Soviet Economic Policy*, p. 36.

108   Ibid.

109   R. Slusser, *Soviet Economic Policy*, p. 19.

110   For Beria's apparent willingness to give up the Eastern zone, see chapter 6.

111   V. Rudolph, 'The Administrative Organization of Soviet Control 1945–1948', in R. Slusser, *Soviet Economic Policy*, p. 19

112   Ibid.

113   R. Slusser, *Soviet Economic Policy*, p. 28.

114   The recently opened Party Archive in Moscow reveals that the activities in the Eastern zone caused an enormous amount of concern to the Kremlin. In September 1946, the Central Party Committee sent a special party commission to check out the activities. They were critical of the whole situation in the zone. See op. 128, p. 87, 92–95, 99, 104. Documents of the Central Committee. quoted in S. Kudryashov, 'The Central Committee of the All-Union Communist Party and Eastern Europe. New Documents', paper prepared for the British International History Group, Annual Conference, Leeds University. September, 1992.

115   R. Slusser, *Soviet Economic Policy*, pp. 42–7.

116   Ibid.

117   V. Rudolph in R. Slusser, *Soviet Economic Policy*, pp. 52–4.

118   See W. Hahn, *The Fall of Zhdanov and the Defeat of Moderation, 1946–1953* (New York: Cornell University Press, 1982), p. 45.

119   Zhukov's demotion should not simply be attributed to his association with a discredited strategy in the Eastern zones of Germany. Zhukov's removal from the German command and his subsequent demotion in July 1946 to the command of the Urals region to a large extent reflected considerations unrelated to the controversy over strategy towards Germany. His fall from grace may also be attributed to his very success as a wartime commander and his highly visible public profile. See S. Bialer, ed., *Stalin and*

his Generals (New York: Pegasus, 1969), p. 294.

120　E. W. Gniffke, *Jahre Mir Ulricht* (Cologne: Verlag Wissenschaft und Politik, 1966), pp. 250–1.

121　G. D. Ra'anon, *International Policy Formation in the USSR, Factional Debates during the Zhdanovshine* (Hamden, Conn.: Archon, 1983), p. 89.

122　W. E. Gniffke, *Jahre mir Ulricht*, p. 178.

123　H. Duhnke, *Die KPD zwischen 1933–1945* (Cologne, 1972), p. 395, quoted in M. McCauley, 'East Germany', in M. McCauley, ed., *Communist Power in Europe 1944–1949* (London: Macmillan, 1977), p. 60.

124　Ibid.

125　Memorandum of Conversation by Charles E. Bohlen, Assistant to the Secretary of State, Paris, April 28, 1946. *FRUS*, 1946, Vol. II, pp. 146–7.

126　Telegram 1160, May 2 1946, Berlin. *FRUS*, 1946, Vol. V, p. 545.

127　For an account of Washington's motivations over financial aid to Moscow see J. L. Gaddis, *The United States and the Origins of the Cold War 1941–1947* (New York: Columbia University Press, 1972).

128　Ibid.

129　Ibid.

130　For a discussion of the negotiations on reparations see *FRUS*, 1946, Vol. II, p. 882.

131　For a discussion of American views of the effect of large reparations payments on Germany see *FRUS*, 1946, Vol. V, pp. 516–20.

132　This was a consistent call by the Soviet delegation at every one of the meetings.

133　US Delegation Record. CFM Second Session. 38th Meeting, Palais du Luxembourg, Paris, July 9, 1946. *FRUS*, 1946, Vol. II, pp. 842–3.

134　Ibid.

135　George Kennan believed that Moscow intended to subvert the West through playing upon its economic weakness. See George Kennan, ('X'), 'The Sources and Conduct of Soviet Foreign Policy', *Foreign Affairs*, July 1947.

136　*Department of State Bulletin* XV, 15 September 1946.

137　Ibid.

138　See the analysis in W. Taubman, *Stalin's American Policy. From Entente to Detente to Cold War* (New York and London: W. W. Norton, 1982). The tenor of his argument is that Stalin's European policies were geared to the removal of a US military presence in Europe.

139　V. M. Molotov, *Problems of Foreign Policy. Speeches and Statements, April 1945–November 1948* (Moscow: Foreign Languages Publishing House, 1949), pp. 272–9.

140　*FRUS*, 1946, Vol. II, p. 147. In July they rejected the idea. *FRUS*, 1946, Vol. II, pp. 842–3.

141　See chapter 2.

142   G. Galli 'Italian Communism' in W. E. Griffiths, ed., *Communism in Europe* (Oxford: Pergamon, 1967).

143   P. A. Allum and D. Sassoon, 'Italy' in M. McCauley, ed., *Communist Power in Europe 1941–1949* (London, Macmillan, 1977), p. 178.

144   Ibid.

145   Ibid.

146   *Berlinskaya (Potsdamskaya) konferentsiya rukovoditelely trekh soyuznykh derzhav SSSR, SShA i Velikobritanii* (Moscow: Izdatel'stvo politicheskoy literatury, 1980), p. 364.

147   *FRUS*, 1946, Vol. II, pp. 376–7.

148   FO 371/58633, Hayter letter to Holman, Bucharest. Quoted in E. Barker, *The British between the Superpowers 1945–1950* (London: Macmillan), p. 61.

149   US Delegation Record. Second Session, Sixteenth Meeting, Paris, 14 May 1946. ibid.

150   *FRUS*, 1946, Vol. II, p. 376.

151   See E. Barker, *The British between the Superpowers*, p. 61.

152   US Delegation Record, CFM, Second Session, Sixth Meeting, Paris, 1 May 1946. *FRUS*, 1946, Vol. II, p. 196.

153   Ibid.

154   Ibid.

155   V. M. Molotov, *Problems of Foreign Policy*, p. 290.

156   Ibid. Molotov linked his objections to foreign troops 'abroad' with the issue of bases. For a commentary on the issue of foreign bases see 'Sozdanie amerikansky sistemy baz v gody vtoroy mivovoy voyny', *Voprosy Istorii*, no. 9, 1984.

157   For Molotov's comments see the discussions recorded in *FRUS*, Vol. 2, p. 375.

158   Ibid.

159   Memorandum of Conversation, Paris, May 5, 1946. *FRUS*, p. 247.

160   V. M. Molotov, *Problems of Foreign Policy*, p. 275.

161   See, for example, 'Prityazaniya SShA na Voennye bazy v islandii', *Krasnaya Zvezda*, 12 May 1946; 'Amerikanskie bazy v islandii', *Krasnaya Zvezda*, 11 June 1946, I acknowledge the help of Mary Dea in finding these articles.

162   A. Vinogradov, 'Velikie derzhavy i mirnoe uregulirovania s italiey v 1945–1947 godakh', *Voprosy Istorii*, 1984.

163   For the details of this agreeement see *FRUS*, 1946, Vol. II, p. 180.

164   One suggestion for demilitarization is recorded in *FRUS*, 1946, Vol. II, p. 338–9.

165   Ibid.

166   Ibid.

167   C. R. S. Harris, *Allied Military Administration of Italy 1943–1945* (London: HMSO, 1957), pp. 328–44.

168 C. R. S. Harris, *Allied Military Administration*, p. 340.

169 W. S. Churchill, *The Second World War*, Vol. VI, *Triumph and Tragedy* (London: Cassell, 1954), pp. 482–9.

170 C. R. S. Harris, *Allied Military Administration*, pp. 328–44.

171 Ibid.

172 W. D. Leahy, *I was There*, p. 430.

173 Ibid.

174 C. R. S. Harris, *Allied Military Administration*, pp. 328–44.

175 C. R. S. Harris, *Allied Military Administration*, p. 340–1.

176 W. D. Leahy, *I was There*, p. 430.

177 Ibid.

178 C. R. S. Harris, *Allied Military Administration*, p. 342.

179 For the Yugoslav claim see *FRUS*, 1946, Vol. II, p. 140.

180 V. M. Molotov, 'The Statute of Trieste and Major Questions of International Cooperation', in V. M. Molotov, *Problems of Foreign Policy*, pp. 173–91.

181 V. M. Molotov, *Problems of Foreign Policy*, pp. 190–1.

182 Ibid.

183 For the Soviet suggestion see *FRUS*, 1946, Vol. II, pp. 1215, 1225.

184 State Department, Lot 55 D 638, January 1947.

185 PPS/,8 US Policy in the Event of the Establishment of Communist Power in Greece, 18 September 1947. See also Department of State Papers 868.00/2–2047.

186 PPS/1, Policy with Respect to American Aid to Western Europe, 23 May 1947.

187 The Assistant Chief of the Division of Commercial Policy, Ben Moore, to the Director of the Office of International Trade, 28 July, *FRUS*, 1947, Vol. III, p. 240.

188 See Caffery to Secretary of State Marshall, 18 June 1947, *FRUS*, 1947, Vol. III, p. 260.

189 Report of Academician Varga to Foreign Minister Molotov, 24 June 1947. Archive of the Foreign Policy of the Russian Federation (abbreviated in Russian AVP RF), AVP RF, 06.op.9.d. 213, p. 18.1.2. Quoted in Scott D. Parrish and Mikhail M. Narinsky, 'New Evidence of the Soviet Rejection of the Marshall Plan, 1947. Two Reports.' Working Paper no. 9. Cold War International History Project. Woodrow Wilson International Center for Scholars, March 1994, p. 166.

190 9 June 1947, AVP. RF, f.059. op.18. p. 39. d.250.11. 207.209, printed in *Mezhunarodnaya Zhizn*, 5 May 1992, pp. 118–19. Quoted in Parrish and Navinsky, 'New Evidence', p. 18.

Chapter 4

Strategies of consolidation

Historians are generally agreed that, in 1948, Soviet strategies in Europe underwent a dramatic alteration. On the one hand, this shift has been characterised as a conscious decision, taken by Moscow, to embark upon a more expansionist policy, designed to roll back Western influence. Examples of militant behaviour on the part of Moscow have been catalogued in support of this view. Analysts have pointed to the coup in Czechoslovakia, communist militancy in Western Europe and the crisis over Berlin.[1] An alternative explanation of Soviet behaviour is that it was governed by a desire to maintain Soviet power in the East and should be viewed as primarily defensive.[2] This chapter examines these claims and puts forward the idea that Moscow's actions should be seen in terms of 'consolidation' and 'denial'. Moscow attempted to consolidate its hold over the East and Central European countries, and attempted to prevent what it viewed as the prospective military and economic encirclement of the USSR by denying Western influence in key areas.

Consolidation

The first Soviet priority in response to the Marshall Plan was to tighten Soviet control over the East European Communist Parties. In September 1947, representatives of the Communist Parties of the USSR, Bulgaria, Romania, Czechoslovakia, Hungary, Poland, France, Italy and Yugoslvia met in Poland to create an organisation to coordinate their activities. Moscow sought to centralise control over the parties. The Czech desire to break ranks and accept Marshall Aid had indicated a worrying independence, while the activities of Tito's Yugoslavia had been regarded with acute alarm.

The Soviet delegation tried to insist that Tito should concede certain privileges to Moscow.[3] This would have rendered Yugoslavia far less independent. Some analysts have claimed that the primary purpose of the meeting was to whip the Yugoslav parties back into line.[4] There is little doubt that this was part of the purpose. After the Yugoslavs had rejected his demands, Stalin attempted to force them into a Balkan federation, in what seems to have been an attempt to integrate Yugoslavia into the Eastern bloc more firmly.

Cohesion in the communist bloc was critical to Stalin in a period when Washington was beginning to exert what appeared to be much greater influence in Western Europe. That does not mean that the Cominform meeting was not a response to Western integration. Speeches at the Cominform marked a far more militant line towards the West and firmly divided the world into two camps. Part of the motivation for this was a Soviet desire to secure an Eastern bloc.

The series of bilateral treaties imposed upon East European states during early 1948 illustrates the attempts by the Soviet leadership to formalise its control of a bloc in the east. On 4 February 1948, the first such treaty was concluded with Romania. Two weeks later a similar treaty was agreed with Hungary. The following month, a Treaty of Friendship and Mutual Cooperation was signed with the Bulgarian government. All these documents contained clauses outlining the duties of both parties in the event of future military conflict. They all provided for the eventuality of German aggression. While this reflected the Soviet preoccupation with the experience of World War II and the possible formation of another German-led East European alliance, the primary Soviet concern was over the establishment of a military coalition based in the Western zones of Germany. Soviet historians have explicitly linked the two issues. They explain Moscow's actions thus:

> At the beginning of 1948 the USSR concluded treaties of friendship, cooperation and mutual assistance with Romania, Hungary, Bulgaria and Finland, fully corresponding to the goals and principles of the United Nations Organisation and having great significance for strengthening peace and security in Europe . . . Together with them the Soviet Union continued its efforts to prevent the shameful consequences of the policy of the Western powers in relation to Germany.[5]

During early 1948, the Soviet leadership used a range of instruments to try to maintain control in the east and to ensure the cohesion of a communist bloc. Whilst making treaties of friendship and co-operation was one method, a less subtle means was tried in February in Prague. A great deal of controversy surrounds the degree of influence exerted by Moscow on the events of February 1948, when the Czech coalition government was ousted by the communists. Various interpreters have offered the view that the coup was actually the result of indigenous causes. It has been argued, for example, that with the onset of the Cold War, the Czech right wing initiated a political offensive to which the communists responded with the coup.[6] Some historians have argued that the events of February represented the culmination of long-held ambitions of the Czech Communist Party. They claim that the events of 1948 were a natural outcome of internal factors working towards socialism.

This interpretation is favoured by M. R. Myant, whose work examines this issue.[7] Myant suggests that while the communists were in the Czech coalition government they were able to gain support for, and implement, socialist plans. These, he argues, found general acceptance and were the basis of the gradual evolution of the state towards a socialist model. Myant, therefore, has emphasised the domestic forces behind the coup. However, the role of Moscow in the coup is not satisfactorily explained. Myant points out that the Czech Communist Party underwent an 'unmistakable' change in the latter part of 1947 and became more radical. The question is: was this ordered by Moscow? Some claim that the link is indirect while others argue that, after the foundation of the Cominform, and Zhdanov's proclamation of two camps, the Czech communists assumed that Moscow was encouraging a more radical stance and reacted in a militant manner. The coup was, in fact, sparked by the zeal of the more radical elements within the Communist Party, who, independently, staged demonstrations and strikes to weaken the government and to ensure the success of socialism.

A more feasible explanation of the events of February 1948 in Czechoslovakia is that communist actions were triggered by the fear of losing power within the coalition. Elections were actually set to take place in the spring and there were indications that the communists faced substantial losses. By mid-January, the Communist Party was entering a period of crisis. It was at this point, on 7 February, that the communists began organising a series of demonstrations designed to bring workers into Prague on the 22nd of the month.[8]

While there is little evidence that Stalin directly ordered a communist seizure of power, it seems unlikely that Moscow could have viewed the loss of communist influence with any degree of detachment. Moscow had, in the summer of 1947, intervened to prevent the Czech government accepting Marshall Aid. A more convincing explanation is that Moscow had been prepared to allow socialism to develop at its own pace in Czechoslovakia. Indeed, until late 1947 this is what appears to have happened, but once the possibility began to disappear, Stalin could not afford to allow Prague to turn Westwards. Conclusive evidence for this theory is scarce, but the very speed with which Moscow acted after the coup seems to indicate some foreknowledge of events. The right of passage through Czechoslovakia for the Red Army was requested and Soviet officials, such as the Deputy Foreign Minister, V. Zorin, were dispatched to Prague to supervise economic matters. Zorin, apparently, conveyed a message from Stalin to Gottwald, the leader of the Czech communists, that 'The USSR would not allow the West to interfere in Czechoslovakia's internal affairs'.[9]

The process of consolidation of Soviet influence was also visible further to the north. The target was Helsinki and the Soviet–Finnish relationship. On 22 February 1948, Stalin sent the Finnish President, Paasikivi, a letter containing a suggestion for a Soviet–Finnish treaty.[10] In his proposal, the Soviet leader directly alluded to the bilateral treaty with Hungary as a possible model. It was suggested that the treaty should provide for mutual assistance 'against a possible attack by Germany'.[11] Molotov described the treaty as a joint defence pact.[12] At the time there was widespread concern in both Finland and in the West that Moscow intended to 'swallow' Finland. Paasikivi believed, at least initially, that the Soviet intention was to bring Finland under military control and into a Soviet bloc.[13] Western diplomats believed that Stalin was pursuing a policy of East European military integration.[14]

During February 1948, American diplomats in Helsinki reported fears of a coup similar to the one that had taken place in Prague. It was widely expected that the communists in the Finnish government would engineer a domestic crisis and that Soviet troops would be 'requested' to help restore order.[15]

Throughout January, sources in Helsinki reported rumours of a build-up of Soviet forces on the Finnish border,[16] and Stalin himself pressed Paasikivi to agree to a treaty confirming a 'special' relationship. There seems little doubt that Moscow sought influence in

Finland. It was, however, influence of a different kind from that gained in Czechoslovakia. Moscow wanted to prevent Helsinki looking West, but, in particular, it wanted to prevent the Finns from joining a prospective Nordic alliance which was under discussion. Specifically, Moscow wanted to keep Sweden, and possibly Norway, neutral. By not obviously 'browbeating' the Finns into the treaty Moscow could achieve its security aims in the north without frightening the other Nordic countries. In a conversation in mid-February, the new Soviet ambassador to Finland, General Savonenkov, revealed these intentions. He suggested to the Finnish Foreign Minister, Enckell, that the Finns should publicly take the initiative over the treaty because, he claimed, such action would make it less likely to create tensions in Scandinavia and affect the security choices of other Nordic powers.[17]

It is of some significance that Moscow was also approaching Oslo to negotiate a similar treaty.[18] Some Western analysts have claimed that the actual terms of the Friendship and Mutual Cooperation Treaty between Moscow and Helsinki was evidence of moderation on the Soviet side. Moscow did not, for example, demand bases in western Finland.[19] However, a more convincing explanation was provided by some Finnish political observers at the time. They were extremely critical of the treaty and put forward the notion that what Moscow sought was to exclude Western influence from the northern area. According to them, Moscow sought control,

> . . . but did not want bases in Western Finland or any military con-cession that would alarm the Scandinavian countries to the extent of abandoning their traditional policy of neutrality and eventually joining the Western bloc.[20]

During early 1948, Moscow consolidated its control over the Eastern and Central European states it had dominated since the end of World War II. Activity in both Czechoslovakia and Finland demonstrate that Moscow was concerned to establish its power firmly, and to prevent the extension of Western influence. The ambitions of consolidation and denial were also apparent in the Soviet conduct of the Berlin crisis.

Denial

The Soviet leadership hoped to achieve a range of objectives through the imposition of the Berlin blockade in 1948. These may be characterised as 'All-German' and 'East German' aims. 'All-German' aims were: first, an attempt to coerce the West into abandoning its strategy of building up a coalition encompassing a new West German state; second, an attempt to persuade the West to reopen negotiations with Moscow on the question of Germany as a whole; and third, an initiative to test the West's degree of commitment to its current policy in Europe, especially in West Germany. The 'East German' aims were: to build a separate state structure in the Eastern half of Germany; to consolidate control within eastern Europe; and to deny the West influence.

To achieve both sets of aims, the instrument of persuasion was the application of pressure upon the Western presence in Berlin. If this failed to achieve Soviet ambitions with respect to Germany as a whole, it could perhaps achieve another Soviet goal – the withdrawal of troops from Berlin and the abandonment of the sole Western outpost in Eastern Europe.

'All-German' objectives

By the spring of 1948, the Western powers had succeeded not only in merging their zones of occupation in Germany, but also in laying the foundations of military-political integration into a Western coalition. The Soviet government was implacably hostile towards this idea, claiming it to be an attempt, utilising German military and industrial strength, to create an anti-Soviet, Western bloc.

A variety of tactics was used by Moscow to persuade the Western Allies to negotiate on the issue of Germany as a whole. The Soviet leadership sought discussion of the demilitarisation and denazification of Germany. It demanded participation in the control of the Ruhr area,[21] and a uniform German currency to avert the introduction of a separate currency for the Western zones.[22] Currency reform was regarded as detrimental to Soviet economic rehabilitation in the east. It was perceived as part of a strategy, inherent in the Marshall Plan, to build up the West against the Soviet Union, and was a powerful symbol of the intention to unify the Western zones and reinvigorate the West German economy.

Soviet actions over Berlin in 1948 were closely linked to Western measures aimed at German military and political integration. On 13 February 1948, a note to the Western powers stated that the Soviet government had learnt, from press reports, of their intention to call a conference in London to consider questions such as three-power policy in the Western zones, control of the Ruhr and problems of security and reparations in Germany. The note asserted that, in the absence of the USSR, this conference constituted a violation of the Potsdam agreement.[23] Despite these protests, the London conference of the Western Allies was held from 23 February until June.[24]

In March, Marshal Sokolovsky, the Soviet commander of Berlin, walked out of the Allied Control Council.[25] On the 31st of that month, the United States military government in Berlin was informed that, as from 1 April, new restrictions were to be imposed on Allied personnel travelling into Berlin by rail and road.[26] On 18 June, the Western allies informed Marshal Sokolovsky of their intention to implement a new currency reform in the Western zones of Germany two days later.[27] On the same day the Soviet military authorities ordered 'obstructions' to Allied road traffic between Berlin and the Western zones.[28] Sokolovsky followed this with a decree, on 23 June, announcing a currency reform for the Soviet zones of Germany and the whole of Berlin.[29] Sokolovsky was officially informed of the Western intention to introduce currency reforms in the Western sectors of Berlin on 24 June. On the same day the remaining waterways, road and rail links were closed by order of the Soviet military authorities.[30]

Throughout the spring of 1948, Moscow attempted to persuade the French to oppose Anglo-American plans for the Western zones of Germany. Moscow counted upon traditional French fears of German militarism overriding US persuasion. The French certainly had serious doubts over the wisdom of creating a West German state. Before the first session of the London conference in February, French Ministers had informed Washington that they wanted both a federal government and the demilitarisation of the whole of Germany.[31] In April and May, there was intense discussion in Paris on the future of Germany. Anxiety over the military potential of a new German state competed with a desire to benefit from US economic aid. The French considered a range of options through which they hoped to gain both military security and economic assistance. Some French Ministers argued for a policy of Franco-German reconciliation through a Western federation. The paramount concern was the fear that, if Paris did not agree to the merging of all the Western zones in Germany, the British and Americans would simply proceed without France.

In May, Moscow attempted to influence French actions by leaking an exchange of letters between Walter Bedell Smith, the US ambassador in Moscow, and Molotov. Washington had not informed its Western allies of the contents of the letter, which contained an attempt to negotiate with Stalin over Germany. What is interesting is Moscow's calculation that enough room existed on the Western side for them to manipulate the debate.[32] The French eventually agreed with Washington that the negotiations for the Western zone should proceed, although they maintained reservations about the revival of German militarism. Moscow continued to try to exploit these French fears throughout the rest of the Berlin crisis.

Throughout the ensuing crisis, Stalin attempted to make the creation of a West German state the focal point of all East–West negotiations. In August, Moscow advanced a proposal that 'assurances that the implementation of the London decisions would be suspended until such time as the four powers met and tried to reach agreement on fundamental questions affecting Germany'.[33] On 3 August, US ambassador Bedell Smith held a meeting with Stalin and Molotov in Moscow. The Soviet leader agreed to lift the blockade, but called for a conference of the Council of Foreign Ministers on the future of Germany.[34] On 24 August, the USSR dispatched a note proposing a meeting of the Council of Foreign Ministers to discuss any unresolved matters regarding either Germany as a whole or Berlin in particular.[35] In January 1949, Stalin stated that the blockade could be resolved 'provided the Western allies agreed to postpone the establishment of a separate West German state, pending a meeting of the Council of Foreign Ministers to consider *the German problem as a whole*'.[36]

In January 1949 a Western interviewer asked Stalin:

> If the governments of the United States of America, the United Kingdom and France agree to postpone the establishment of a separate West German state until the convocation of a session of the Council of Foreign Ministers devoted to the examination of *the German question as a whole*, would the Government of the USSR be prepared to remove the restrictions introduced by the Soviet authorities on communications between Berlin and the Western zones of Germany?

Stalin replied that he would agree to a lifting of the blockade, provided that Germany was indeed discussed as a whole:

> If the United States of America, Great Britain and France observe the

conditions stipulated in the . . . question, the Soviet government sees no
obstacle to a removal of transport restrictions, provided however that
the transport and trade restrictions introduced by the three powers are
removed simultaneously.[37]

Soviet aims were not directed simply at retarding the creation of a
West German state. The Soviet leadership was also preoccupied with
the political and military composition of any future West German
state. Throughout the blockade, the USSR made allegations over
ostensible Western violations of the Potsdam Agreements: it alleged
a failure by the Western powers to denazify and to make any serious
attempt to demilitarise the Western zones.[38] Soviet claims that the
Western powers were fuelling Nazi revanchism had a potent propaganda function, not least to justify a regime of political and military
controls in Eastern Europe and within the USSR itself.

Nevertheless, Soviet accusations that the military potential of
West Germany was being regenerated were not groundless. By 1948,
the West had assessed the likely contribution of a West German state
in a European military political coalition. Soviet fears that West
German power would be harnessed to the coalition proved to be
justified. However, Soviet claims that the West would countenance a
resurgence of German revanchism were unfounded. The United
States had committed itself to the demilitarisation of Germany and
the destruction of Nazi power.

The USSR attempted to resurrect the spectre of German militarism
to break up the coalition. It sought to dissuade France from supporting strategies of integration. In 1948, the Soviet press commented on
the future nature of France's relationship with a reconstructed West
Germany, and the general effects of German power in Europe. The
article questioned whether the French understood the potential of
the future West German state.[39] Soviet leaders had a natural anxiety
over the creation of an anti-Soviet, American-sponsored bloc in
Europe. They were also worried by the prospect of the Western
powers building up a new German state which they would be unable
or unprepared to shackle. If the USSR could not prevent Western
integration then it at least sought guarantees over the character of the
new German state.

Throughout 1948 and into 1949, the Soviet Union vigorously
protested against the alleged reinstatement of former Nazis in key
positions in West Germany. In November, Molotov alleged that 'in

the American, British and French zones of occupation in Germany, people who were prominent under the fascist regime are being restored to key positions in industry and administration'.[40] In January 1949, an article in *Pravda* entitled 'Hitlerite Generals in the Service of the Americans' alleged details of ex-Nazis allowed to resume public office, and maintained that Germany was being reconstructed into an anti-Soviet state with former wartime military figures in the contemporary administrative and military apparatus:

> . . . the training and preparation of German soldiers and officers is already taking place on the territory of Western Germany . . . Preference is given to men who formerly served in the SS troops, parachute or tank units, and also former servicemen decorated in the Hitlerite army and possessing references that they were 'exemplary soldiers'.[41]

The Western powers were accused of transforming Western Germany into a new appendage of the American empire.[42] Underlying the propagandist message of such statements one may discern growing Soviet frustration over the issue of the economic resources of the Ruhr. The denial of Soviet access to any part of the Ruhr deprived the USSR of any guarantees against its industrial potential being used to regenerate German military capabilities.[43]

While Soviet publications described the resolution of the German question as the key to future peace in Europe,[44] Soviet leaders expressed concern that Germany was no longer regarded by the West as a defeated adversary. In January 1949, for example, Pravda commented that

> . . . in contrast with all the treaties of mutual aid concluded by the Soviet Union with the other European states, including France and Britain, which are aimed at preventing the possibility of new aggression on the part of Germany and thereby fostering a strengthening of peace in Europe, the military alliance of the five Western states . . . was formed against the USSR and the states of people's democracy.[45]

The policies of the Western states, Moscow asserted, in contrast to Soviet policies in its zone, had failed to eradicate German militarism. *Bolshevik* claimed that, basically, all the military factories, objects and installations on the territory of the Soviet occupation zone which should have been dismantled, according to the reparations plan, had been. The Soviet journal also noted that the German military forces

and quasi-paramilitary organisations had been disbanded. The journal asserted that this was evidence that 'the material basis of
militarism and fascism has been destroyed in the Soviet zone'.[46]

Moscow advanced numerous alternatives to the creation of a West
German state throughout the period of the blockade. The Warsaw
statement of June 1948 (made after a conference of Soviet and East
European representatives in Poland) concluded by proposing that
the four major powers should adopt a five-point programme for all
of Germany. This would include the implementation of measures
ensuring the final demilitarisation of Germany by agreement
between Great Britain, the USSR, France and the United States.
Another requirement would be the institution of a quadripartite
control regime for a definite period over the heavy industries of the
Ruhr to preclude the re-establishment of German capacity to wage
war. Moscow also asked for the conclusion of a peace treaty with
Germany to enable the withdrawal of occupation forces within a
year of the treaty.[47] The latter proposal was reiterated on 21
September 1948[48] and throughout 1949, when the USSR reaffirmed
its support for the withdrawal of all foreign troops from German
soil.[49]

The concept of demilitarisation was a constant theme in Soviet
proposals and publications. It appeared to be the option most
favoured by the USSR for the future of Germany. A Soviet commentator expressed the view that

> The basis of such a resolution of the German problem, and also the
> preparation for a peace treaty with Germany, is offered by the known
> resolutions of the Crimean [Yalta] and Berlin conferences of the Allied
> great powers, which planned a programme of demilitarisation and
> democratisation of Germany.[50]

Soviet suggestions for the demilitarisation of Germany and for the
joint withdrawal of occupation forces were intended to offer the
West alternatives to the division of Germany. There may also have
been a second motive. Western acceptance of such proposals, the
USSR may have reasoned, would ensure that the traditional forward
base area in Germany for assaults upon the Russian homeland could
not in any circumstances perform that function.

It is likely that Soviet suspicions of offensive intentions were raised
by the issue of US bases in Europe. By early 1948, the United States
had acquired the right to military bases in Greenland, Iceland,

Morocco, Libya, Turkey and Saudi Arabia, as well as in Britain and Japan.[51] The United States had also deployed 120 B-29 Super-Fortress bombers in Europe in July and August 1948.[52] In June 1948, B-29s had been dispatched to bases in Britain. B-29s stationed in Germany had flown into Berlin before the blockade.[53] The Soviet leadership could not have failed to realise that a demilitarised Germany would deprive the West of strategic bases in the centre of Europe. It must have been equally clear that the West would lose its forward line of defence against a Soviet offensive in Central Europe.

At this time, the USSR suggested that Japan should be demilitarised. The demilitarisation of both Germany and Japan would have neutralised the strategic potential offered by those territories to the Western powers in any future East–West conflict. In January 1949, *Pravda* explicitly linked Western strategies in the two countries: 'the USA is attempting to prepare both West Germany and Japan as its weapons for carrying out aggressive plans'.[54] The Soviet strategic appraisal of Germany is indicated by the Soviet incorporation of East Germany into the forward air defences of the Eastern bloc in 1948. From the Soviet perspective, a demilitarised Germany would have extended the territorial scope of the Soviet buffer in Europe and deprived the West of a strategic redoubt. It would also have gravely weakened the defence of Western Europe in protracted East–West hostilities.

All this apparent enthusiasm for demilitarisation represented a turnabout in the Soviet position. In 1946, Moscow had rejected the suggestions of Byrnes, the American Secretary of State, for a demilitarised Germany.[55] In the absence of occupation forces and quadripartite control, a demilitarised Germany would, from a Soviet perspective, have reinvoked a traditional Soviet preoccupation with military ambitions. The reversal of the Soviet stand on the demilitarisation of Germany may be attributable to the fact that, by 1948, faced with the imminent creation of a West German state, the Soviet initiatives were advanced less as concrete proposals than as a means to persuade the West to enter into negotiations on the overall future of Germany and to concede rights in the Western zones to the Soviet Union. This assessment is reinforced by a study of Soviet proposals for a demilitarised Germany. All such proposals involved Soviet participation in the Ruhr area and partial Soviet control over Western Germany. The Western powers were unprepared to accept these terms, since they were regarded as attempts by the USSR to create the conditions for a communist Germany.

It is uncertain whether the Soviet leadership had any confidence in the demilitarisation of Germany as an effective means of subjugating German power in the long term. The Kremlin may have believed that the enforcement of a demilitarisation regime of this kind would have required a residual quadripartite military presence in Germany, and, in this fashion, Soviet military and US, British and French military responsibilities for West Germany could perhaps be retained in a much reduced or looser form. This was a poor substitute for the clear-cut military control exercised by the USSR over East Germany in the absence of demilitarisation. Soviet declaratory support for German demilitarisation was largely directed at German indigenous military capabilities; this idea was intended to preclude the development of strong organised West German military forces.

The blockade

The Berlin blockade represented a Soviet attempt to apply pressure on the Western powers. The latter's position in the city was anomalous because Berlin was particularly vulnerable to direct Soviet political and military pressure. The vulnerability of the Western powers derived not only from their difficult logistical position, but also from the unclear character of the wartime agreements governing the Western right of access to Berlin.[56]

The blockade challenged not only the commitment of the United States to Berlin, but also, in a wider sense, its commitment to Western Europe itself. The notion that Stalin was 'testing' the United States is supported by a study of the Soviet conduct of the blockade. The actual imposition was preceded by numerous warnings over the 'technical' difficulties that might prevent Western access to Berlin. This incremental process of raising the level of East–West tension permitted the West opportunities to accede to Soviet demands and to discuss the German issue as a whole. However, Western resolve contributed to Stalin's decision to raise the stakes on Berlin and to impose a full blockade of that city which resulted in the sharpest confrontation to date between the former wartime allies.

The operational conduct of the blockade by the USSR is revealing. The Soviet authorities were careful only to interfere with Western access to Berlin by land. Following an incident which ended in loss of life, the USSR made little attempt to interfere with Western rights of access to Berlin by air. An aide to President Truman reported on

Soviet conduct as follows:

> Incidents have occurred sporadically, but none has interfered with the airlift. The Russians certainly do possess the capability of seriously interfering with the airlift operation, of even closing the air corridors should they desire to do so.[57]

The Soviet reluctance to employ military measures is underlined by a US estimate that, of the 162,275 flights that took place into Berlin between June 1948 and June 1949, less than one per cent were interfered with.[58] Two possible explanations may be advanced. The first is that Stalin underestimated the lengths to which the Western powers would go to ensure the success of the airlift, especially through the winter of 1948–49. This was understandable, since many in the West doubted the ability of the West to sustain the airlift.[59] Second, Stalin recognised that any interference with Western air access would push the conflict into an area where the margins of error and accident might be reduced, and infringements lead to war. Following the single incident in which Western and Soviet aircraft collided over Berlin, Western officials received the impression that the USSR was defensive and concerned over possible repercussions.[60]

As the success of the airlift became more apparent, Stalin moderated his demands in an attempt to salvage something from the twelve months of tension. By January 1949 he was no longer making the withdrawal of Western currency reforms a *sine qua non* of lifting the blockade.[61] However, it remains uncertain whether the USSR had either the intention or the ability to widen the confrontation into a military conflict. Soviet intentions were dependent upon Western reactions; given the success of the airlift and Western resolve in the face of the Soviet challenge, it is doubtful whether Stalin could have expected that any attempts to probe deeper into Germany would fail to meet resistance. It is also a matter of some debate whether the USSR had the military capacity necessary to take the conflict any further into Europe.

According to certain Western estimates, the Soviet Union was prepared to engage in military confrontation. In July 1948, a US military memorandum to Admiral Leahy reported that

> ... it is important to note the build-up of Russian fighters and para-troopers in the Berlin area: and also the rearrangement of divisions on the Russian western borders to bring their best combat troops near and

around the Berlin area. This is, in my opinion, not a show of force or a training manoeuvre, it is strictly a build-up and preparation for the shooting war which the Russians will at this time precipitate if they fail in other means to gain their end.[62]

By autumn 1948 the American view had changed. The primary danger was now regarded as accidental war rather than a deliberate Soviet offensive. The 286th State Department Policy Planning Staff meeting, in September 1948, illustrated this new perception: it concluded that the USSR 'would not undertake a deliberate military attack on say one of our concentrations of aircraft at Wiesbaden' but the possibility of accidental war was acknowledged. The situation had 'potentialities for incidents that could lead to war'.[63] What is also interesting is the debate on the Western side about Soviet troop levels.

Controversy surrounds the number of troops that the USSR deployed in Europe in the post-war period. In 1948, for example, the Joint Chiefs of Staff estimated the number of Soviet divisions in East Europe as 175[64] (excluding the Western areas of the USSR). However, this estimate did not specify whether these divisions were at full strength, combat-ready or at partial strength and not fully trained. By December 1948, the Joint Chiefs of Staff's estimates had changed considerably. They now placed the number of Soviet divisions occupying Eastern Europe and Germany at thirty-one out of a total of 175, with an armed strength of 2.5 million out of the 4 million men in total in the Soviet armed forces.[65] CIA estimates at the time suggested a Soviet attacking force of approximately twenty-five divisions. It has been pointed out that, if this figure is reliable, the twenty-five to thirty divisions (at full complement) and the twelve divisions of strategic reserve would mean a total of 700,000–800,000 Soviet troops available for an invasion of Western Europe.[66] On the Western side, this was matched by a total of approximately 800,000 Allied troops.[67] These figures dispel the idea of an overwhelming Soviet numerical superiority and the idea that the USSR could feel sure of military superiority in an armed conflict in Europe.

The diverse range of functions performed by Soviet forces in the immediate post-war period belies the notion that Soviet troops, at the time of the Berlin blockade, were wholly oriented towards involvement in an imminent offensive in Europe. Their tasks included occupation duties, such as the implementation of reparations policy, in particular the stripping and transfer of industrial plant from occupation zones to the USSR; and the exercise of political repression in East European countries and certain areas of the USSR itself.

Soviet troops were extensively used in East Germany to carry out Moscow's reparations strategies. The scale of this task was enormous and, for a period after the war, the USSR dedicated itself to the dismantling of German industry. It has been estimated that, by mid-1947, 500,000 wagonloads of reparations goods had been moved from Germany to the Soviet Union.[68] Other troops were stationed in those East European countries which Stalin considered least reliable and in areas of the USSR with traditions of opposition to Soviet rule. Some estimates have placed the number of Soviet troops involved in occupation duties in the Western Soviet Union at approximately fifty to sixty divisions.[69] One CIA report of 1948 speculated that the Soviet hold on these areas was so uncertain that, in the event of a war in Europe, Stalin would have to face not only mass desertions from the army but also guerilla warfare in the Ukraine.[70] The internal Soviet difficulties may, to some extent, explain Stalin's reluctance to broaden the Berlin confrontation. Another factor that may have discouraged any greater Soviet ambition was the Western possession of a nuclear capability.

Throughout the period from Potsdam, when Stalin was informed of US atomic power, until 1953, the USSR exerted considerable efforts to play down the significance of nuclear weapons. Not one article appeared in the Soviet military press discussing nuclear power and its role in warfare. Stalinist military doctrine dismissed nuclear power as a decisive factor in warfare. From an analysis of Western nuclear potential in the late 1940s some specialists have concluded that these Soviet views had some foundation.[71] The United States had a relatively small stockpile of nuclear weapons. General Spaatz recalled that, until April 1948, the United States possessed only about a dozen bombs,[72] whilst only thirty-two B-29 bombers had a nuclear capability in 1948.[73] It has, therefore, been asserted that Stalinist military doctrine was correct in assuming that the US nuclear capacity could not be decisive. However, whilst this analysis may be valid for the early part of 1948, by late 1948 the US nuclear capability had increased substantially. It was predicted in official US government circles in September 1948 that by December 'the United

States would possess 202 adapted B29s'.[74]

A non-nuclear Soviet Union obviously had an interest in playing down the significance and potential of nuclear weapons, but public pronouncements on nuclear weapons are belied by the fact that in the 1940s the USSR was striving to create its own nuclear force. Soviet concentration upon the production of nuclear weapons in the 1940s signals clearly the Soviet recognition of the strategic power of such weapons. This recognition must have been reinforced by the examples of Nagasaki and Hiroshima. The Soviet fear of a strategic air attack in the late 1940s is indicated by the emphasis upon the forward integration of East European countries into Soviet air defences. The fact was that Soviet conventional military power in Europe in the late 1940s was not what it was assumed to be at the time. Soviet appreciation of the US nuclear potential was acute. A military conflict arising from the Berlin blockade cannot, to say the least, have been viewed with equanimity in Moscow.

The Berlin crisis therefore should be seen as a localised confrontation (but one with much wider possibilities) in which Moscow eventually had to accept defeat. By the beginning of 1949, the Soviet Union had decided that it could no longer contest the effectiveness of the Western airlift and Western resolve in Europe. In February 1949 *Pravda* published an article entitled 'On the Question of the Concept of Diplomacy'. In this article the author points out that diplomacy has certain advantages over war. He cites Lenin's use of Clausewitz: 'that war is a continuation of politics by other means'. Lenin pointed out that 'Marxists have always, and justly, considered this proposition the theoretical foundation of views on the significance of each given war'. The author continued that: 'Diplomacy, however, is not merely one of the methods of foreign policy. Among all the methods of foreign policy, it is of primary importance in time of peace, and usually it dominates over other methods.'[75] This article, in February 1949, could be regarded as an *ex post facto* justification of Stalin's policy, which permitted the United States to 'win' the battle of the airlift and failed to take stronger military measures during the blockade. It could also be suggested that it signalled that the USSR was not prepared to resort to military means to achieve its aims in Europe.

It was ironic that in attempting to coerce the West, through the blockade, to negotiate on the question of Germany's future, and in attempting to persuade Western leaders to abandon plans for a new

West German state, the Soviet Union strengthened the justification for the West to rearm. There is evidence that the West deliberately exaggerated 'war' scares and Soviet capabilities to obtain support for a 'defence' build-up in the West.[76] The USSR had hoped to force the West to negotiate on larger issues through the application of pressure on a small isolated enclave of the Western occupation troops in Germany. Moscow succeeded only in providing the rationale for Western rearmament. The evident failure of the Soviet blockade and the success of the Western airlift and counter-blockade meant that towards the end of 1948 and in 1949 Stalin had to resort to the full implementation of his East German strategy.

The 'East German' strategy

The second aim of the blockade was a continuation of Moscow's broader European strategy of consolidating the territorial and political gains made during and after World War II. As previously discussed, this strategy took the form of ensuring complete Soviet control over East Europe. The USSR retained this as a fall-back approach to Berlin, to be used if the primary Soviet objective, Soviet–Western negotiations over Germany, failed to materialise. Indeed, throughout the blockade, the USSR had moved slowly towards the creation of an East German state in response to Anglo-American moves in the bizone. This process was accelerated once the blockade had failed to compel the West to abandon its plans for a West German state.

It is difficult to pinpoint the moment at which Stalin decided to accept the 'East German option'. The evidence that he appeared to accept the division of Germany is usually taken to begin in January 1948 when Stalin told Djilas that 'the West will make West Germany their own and we shall make East Germany ours'.[77] However, this did not preclude Stalin's attempt to force the West to negotiate over the wider issue of Germany as a whole. The contention here is that Stalin carried out the two policies concurrently.

In February 1948, the East German communists took some preliminary steps towards the construction of an administrative apparatus for the future East German state. These were very cautious steps and there was no public announcement of any change in Soviet attitudes towards Germany. In March, the German communists convened another *Volkskongress* as if they stood for an all-German state.[78] Reunification was an enduring theme of Soviet propaganda in 1948. Stalin used it to improve the Soviet position *vis-à-vis* the German population and also to stimulate German opposition to the creation of a West German state.

Conclusion

There were points during the Berlin crisis at which Stalin's strategies, 'all-German' and 'East German', appeared somewhat contradictory. Even at the time when the USSR was demanding quadripartite control for all of Germany, the Soviet Union also appeared to accept division, and proceeded to consolidate control in East Germany. In June 1948, for example, Colonel Vyrianov, the chief of SMA liaison in Berlin, suggested that 'possibly, an adjustment of present zonal lines in Germany should be made'. A US officer inquired whether he meant 'our departure from Berlin and return to Thuringia and Saxony, originally occupied by American forces', in other words a return to the immediate post-war arrangements. Vyrianov suggested that some such readjustment might be a solution.[79] Even if the blockade were to fail to convince the West of the necessity of negotiating upon the question of Germany as a whole, Moscow could have hoped at least to persuade the Western Allies to leave Berlin. This outcome would have ensured that Eastern Europe was totally under Soviet control without any Western outposts. The success of the airlift and the Western counter-blockade again thwarted this ambition and the USSR failed to deny the West a foothold in the east. The failure of the Soviet blockade of Berlin resulted not only in a divided Germany, but in the creation of an anti-Soviet, West German state and a fundamental reassessment by Moscow of the American role in Europe.

Notes

1   T. W. Wolfe, *Soviet Power and Europe 1945–1970* (Baltimore: Johns Hopkins University Press, 1970).

2   G. F. Kennan, *Memoirs 1925–1950* (Boston: Little Brown, 1957), p. 401.

3   W. O. McCagg Jr, 'Domestic Politics and Soviet Foreign Policy at the Cominform Conference in 1947', *Slavic and Soviet Series*, Vol. 2, no. 1, spring 1977, pp. 3–31.

4   Ibid.

5   V. G. Trukhanovsky, ed., *Istoriya Mezhdunarodnykh Otnosheniy i*

vneshnei politiki SSSR, Vol. III, *1945–1963* (Moscow: Izdatel'stvo mezhdunarodnykh otnosheniy), p. 219.

6 J. Opat, 'K metodě Studia a výkladu některých problému v obdobi 1945–8', *Přispěvky k dějinám KSĆ*, 1967. Quoted in M. V. Myant, *Socialism and Democracy in Czechoslovakia 1943–1948* (Cambridge: Cambridge University Press, 1981), p. 4.

7 M. V. Myant, *Socialism and Democracy*, p. 4.

8 M. V. Myant, *Socialism and Democracy*, p. 185.

9 J. Belda *et al.*, *Na rozhrani drou epoch* (Prague: Svoboda, 1968), pp. 264–5. Quoted in W. O. McCagg, *Stalin Embattled* (Detroit: Wayne State University Press, 1978), p. 402.

10 US Department of State, 27 February 1948. 760D. 6111/2–2748.

11 US Department of State, 28 February 1948. 760D. 6111. 2–2848.

12 US Department of State, 30 March 1948. 760D. 6111./3–3048.

13 US Department of State, 16 March 1948. 760D. 6111/3–1648.

14 US Department of State, 27 February 1948. 760D. 6111/2–2748.

15 US Department of State, 28 February 1948. 760D. 6111/2–2848.

16 US Department of State, 22 January 1948. 760D. 6111/2–2248.

17 US Department of State, 27 February 1948. 7460D. 6111/2–2748.

18 US Department of State, 29 March 1948. 760D. 6111/3–2448.

19 R. Allison, *Finland's Relations with the Soviet Union 1944–1984* (London: Macmillan, 1986), p. 20.

20 US Department of State, 14 July 1948. 760D. 6111/7. 1448.

21 All Soviet proposals for the resolution of the Berlin crisis contained clauses that would have required Western acceptance of Soviet involvement in the question of Germany as a whole.

22 The issue of currency reform was a clause in all Soviet proposals for the resolution of the crisis until January 1949, when Stalin suddenly removed it from the agenda. See Stalin's interview with Kingsbury-Smith, January 1949 in Committee on Foreign Affairs, *Soviet Diplomacy and Negotiating Behaviour, Emerging New Context for U.S. Diplomacy* (Washington: US Government Printing Office, 1979), p. 242.

23 Statements of Marshal Sokolovsky at the Meeting of the Control Council, 29 March 1948. Union of Soviet Socialist Republics, Ministry of Foreign Affairs, *The Soviet Union and the Berlin Question* (Documents) (Moscow, 1948), pp. 18–20.

24 For details of the conference see H. Adomeit, *Soviet Risk-Taking and Crisis Behaviour* (London: George Allen and Unwin, 1982), pp. 80–1.

25 L. Clay, *Decision in Germany* (New York: Doubleday, 1950), p. 335.

26 J. E. Smith. ed., *The Papers of Lucius D. Clay. Germany 1945–1949* (Bloomington: Indiana University Press, 1974), Vol. II, pp. 600–1.

27 O. M. van der Gablentz, Marshal Sokolovsky, 'Proclamation to the German People on the Western Currency Reform', 19 June 1948, *Docu-*

ments on the Status of Berlin 1944–1959 (Munich: Oldenburg Verlag, 1959); see also *FRUS*, 1948, Vol. II, p. 907.

28   L. Clay, *Decision in Germany*, p. 362.

29   M. Carlyle, ed., *Documents on International Affairs, 1947–1948* (London: Oxford University Press, 1952), pp. 580–1.

30   See A. Shlaim, *The United States and the Berlin Blockade, 1948–1949* (London: University of California Press, 1983), p. 162.

31   Bidault Papers, Box 21 (6 April). Quoted in J. Young, *France, the Cold War and the Western Alliance 1944–1949* (Leicester: Leicester University Press, 1990), p. 188.

32   M. Carlyle, *Documents on International Affairs*, pp. 153–9.

33   US Department of State, *The Berlin Crisis. A Report on the Moscow Discussions* (Washington, DC: Government Printing Office, 1948), pp. 22–3, p. 318.

34   Union of Socialist Soviet Republics, Ministry of Foreign Affairs, *The Soviet Union and the Berlin Question* (Moscow, 1949), Second Series, Documents, pp. 8–9. See also *FRUS*, 1948, Vol. II, pp. 999–1006.

35   Smith to Marshall, 25 August 1948, in *FRUS*, 1948, Vol. II, pp. 1065–9.

36   *FRUS*, 1948, Vol. V, p. 562.

37   For the change in Soviet demands, see *Soviet Diplomacy and Negotiating Behaviour*, pp. 242–3.

38   *Pravda*, 12 January 1949.

39   B. Leont'ev, 'Anglo-amerikanskaya politika raskola Evropy', *Bolshevik*, no. 13, 1948, p. 67.

40   Anniversary of the Great October Socialist Revolution. Speech Delivered at a Celebration Meeting of the Moscow Soviet, 6 November 1948. V. M. Molotov, *Problems of Foreign Policy. Speeches and Statements, April 1945–November 1948* (Moscow: Foreign Publishing House, 1949), p. 585.

41   *Pravda*, 12 January 1949.

42   *Pravda*, 3 January 1949.

43   *Izvestiya*, 1 January 1949.

44   D. Monin, 'O bor'be drakh napravleniy v mezhdanarodnoy politike', *Bolshevik*, no. 24, 1947, p. 53.

45   *Pravda*, 14 January 1949.

46   D Monin, 'O bor'be drakh napravleniy v mezhdanarodnoy politike', p. 51.

47   *Pravda*, 25 June 1949.

48   *Pravda*, 21 September 1948.

49   *Pravda*, 3 January 1949.

50   D Monin, 'O bor'be drakh . . .', p. 51.

51   See M. McGwire, 'The Genesis of Soviet Threat Perception', Washington, D.C.: The Brookings Institution, p. 18. For Soviet comments

on the American acquisition of bases, see V. M. Molotov, *Problems of Foreign Policy*, p. 592.

52 See M. McGwire, 'Genesis', p. 18.

53 See A. Shlaim, *The United States and the Berlin Blockade*, p. 238.

54 V. M. Molotov, *Problems of Foreign Policy*, p. 592.

55 *FRUS*, 1948, Vol. II, p. 61.

56 See discussion on the Berlin occupational agreement, Forrestal Papers, 25 June 1948. Princeton Library. I am grateful to Dr Avi Shlaim for this reference.

57 Memorandum for the President: from Colonel Robert B. Landry (an aide to the President), 28 September 1948. Truman Papers. National Archive, Washington.

58 Robert Rodrigo, *Berlin Airlift* (London: Cassell, 1960), p. 214.

59 Record of meeting on 'Berlin Situation', Forrestal Papers, 27 June 1948, Princeton Library. I am grateful to Dr Avi Shlaim for this reference.

60 740.00119 Control Germany 4-68, US Political Adviser for Germany (Murphy) to the Secretary of State, Berlin, April 6, 1948. *FRUS*, 1948, Vol. 2, pp. 890–91.

61 *Soviet Diplomacy and Negotiating Behaviour*, p. 242–3.

62 Memorandum for Admiral Leahy. The White House, Washington, 16 July 1948. Truman Papers.

63 *FRUS*, 1948, Vol. II, p. 1195.

64 Joint Intelligence Committee, 'Soviet Intentions and Capabilities, 1949', 2 December 1948. Quoted in M. A. Evangelista, 'Stalin's Postwar Army Reappraised', *International Security*, no. 3, winter 1982–83, p. 10.

65 CIA, National Intelligence Estimates, NIE-3, 'Soviet Capabilities and Intentions', 15 November 1950, p. 5. Quoted in M. A. Evangelista, 'Stalin's Postwar Army', p. 12.

66 JIC Report, 2 December 1948. Ibid.

67 Ibid.

68 Ibid.

69 T. Wolfe, *Soviet Power and Europe*, p. 39.

70 CIA Report, 27 October 1948, pp. 39–41. Quoted in M. A. Evangelista, 'Stalin's Postwar Army'.

71 H. Adomeit, *Soviet Risk-Taking*, p. 143.

72 D. A. Rosenberg, 'American Atomic Strategy and the Hydrogen Bomb Decision', *Journal of American History*, Vol. 66, no. 1, June 1979, p. 65. Cited in H. Adomeit, *Soviet Risk-Taking*, p. 142.

73 Ibid.

74 Meeting with the President, 13 September 1948. Forrestal Papers, Princeton Library. I am grateful to Dr Avi Shlaim for this quote.

75 R. J. Levin, *Sovetskoe gosudarstvo i pravo*, no. 9. Cited in *Current Digest of the Soviet Press*, Vol. 1, no. 2, 8 February 1949, p. 2.

76 See G.F. Kennan, *Memoirs*, pp. 327–51.

77   M. Djilas, *Conversations with Stalin* (New York: Harcourt Brace, 1962), p. 153.

78   See W. O. McCagg, 'Domestic Politics', p. 292.

79   *FRUS*, 1948, Vol. II, p. 915.

Chapter 5

Strategies of opposition

The Soviet Union and Western military and political integration, 1949–50

At the end of 1948 and the beginning of 1949, it was apparent that Soviet strategy towards Western Europe, particularly with regard to Germany, had suffered a notable setback. The Soviet blockade of Berlin had been undermined by the success of the Western airlift. The West appeared to be moving inexorably towards the creation of a West German state, and Western efforts to form a new integrated military alliance in Europe continued apace.

Marshal Shulman has described Soviet foreign policy in 1949 as 'dominated by two waves of effort, one against NATO and the other against the formation of a West German government'.[1] This idea of Soviet differentiation between the two issues is misconceived. From the Soviet perspective the two appear to have been integrally interwoven. Moscow's activities, in 1949, were directed simultaneously against the idea of Western military integration and against the role of a new Western Germany within an integrated organisation. The Soviet Union sought to limit the extent of Western military cooperation and also attempted to prevent the utilisation of West German power within new defence structures.

During late 1948 and early 1949, the negotiations to set up a West German government in the Western zones of occupation intensified. On 8 April 1949, it was announced that the United States, Britain and France had agreed 'on all questions relating to the establishment and control of a West German Federal Republic'.[2] As soon as the republic was established, it was agreed that occupation troops would remain for security reasons under a new and simpler occupation statute.[3] Coincidentally with this, in April 1949, the defence ministers of the five Brussels Treaty powers, with American and Canadian participation, announced their agreement on a sweeping plan for the defence of Western Europe.[4] On 12 April the United States and Britain reported their agreement establishing facilities in England to station American atomic bombers.[5] On 13 April, Britain, France and the United States announced they were revising their attitude towards German industry. Dismantling in the Western zones was reduced and restrictions were lifted from some types of industrial production.[6]

During 1948, the USSR had attempted to follow a dual strategy towards Germany. Soviet strategies had been directed at persuading the West to agree to a demilitarised regime for Germany whilst simultaneously securing communist rule for the Eastern zone. The efforts to influence Western aims in Germany intensified in early 1949. The Soviet Union insisted that, in any settlement, Germany should be treated as a single military, political and economic entity. Throughout the spring and summer of 1949, the USSR advocated the settlement of the German question on the principle of unity with a central government. In January 1949, Stalin advanced a proposal to resolve the Berlin crisis on 'condition that a session of the Council of Foreign Ministers be convened to consider the entire German question'.[7]

The USSR presented itself as the champion and protector of German unity. In June 1949, *Pravda* summarised Soviet behaviour at the Council of Foreign Ministers as 'adherence to German unity as opposed to the splitting tactics of the USA, Great Britain and France'.[8] Throughout February 1949, the Soviet press and its spokesmen accused the West, particularly the United States, of seeking to split Germany irrevocably.[9] Soviet commentators called for a peace treaty and for the whole of Germany to be united.

Vyshinsky, the Soviet Foreign Minister, characterised the Soviet position in June as 'one of consistent struggle for the unity of Germany, for the cooperation of the four powers on the German question, for the most speedy conclusion of the peace treaty with Germany'. Soviet proposals for a peace settlement envisaged the withdrawal of occupation forces from the new unified Germany a year after enactment.[10] This was a more explicit expression of previous Soviet calls for the demilitarisation of Germany. The USSR professed itself eager for all foreign troops to withdraw from Germany. During the Foreign Minister's conference, Vyshinsky contrasted the attitudes of the East and the West on this issue:

But in any event, must not a clear reply be given in the peace treaty to the question of how much time the occupation forces will spend in Germany? The other delegations consider that the draft peace treaty should not stipulate the period for the presence of the occupation forces in Germany. Neither is such a period laid down in the occupation statute. Evidently the American, British and French delegations are trying to prolong the occupation of Germany for a long time.[11]

These 'new' Soviet proposals for Germany, had they been accepted by the West, would have precluded the creation of a West German state and deprived the West of a military and political stronghold in Central Europe, a concern that was particularly urgent as the Western powers continued to rebuild German industry. The proposals also allowed the USSR, as the champion of German unity, to appeal to a strong nationalist vein in German opinion, a factor recognised by the West,[12] and one which the USSR hoped would retard the creation of a new West German entity.

In March, *Pravda* revealed Soviet concern over the linkage between Western activities in Germany and a new integrated military alliance. In an article entitled 'Preparation for the Inclusion of Western Germany in the System of the North Atlantic Pact' it stated that 'the more active policy of the three countries on the German question has a direct connection with the concluding of the Atlantic Pact'.[13]

From Soviet writings, there appears little doubt that the USSR considered it a *sine qua non* of the new West German state that it would be integrated into the North Atlantic Treaty Organisation. On 30 August an article in *Pravda* commented angrily that:

... the Anglo-American bloc regards the German militarists as allies. The heart of the anti-Comintern Pact was a bloc of two of the principal aggressive forces in the post-war era. The heart of the Atlantic Pact is a military alliance of the two basic aggressive forces of the post-war period.[14]

Soviet concern in 1949 over Western military integration in the North Atlantic Treaty Organisation had been preceded by similar anxiety over other defence structures, such as the Brussels Pact. Soviet perceptions of and objections to NATO were, however, distinct from those expressed in relation to the Brussels Pact. Soviet objections to the Brussels Pact appear to have been primarily concerned, not with the fact that the British and French were forming a joint military structure, but with the fear that an Anglo-French alliance, with German participation, would not be capable of controlling German militarism and preventing German domination of Europe.[15]

Soviet commentaries on the formation of NATO in 1949 were rather different in nature. A critical Soviet concern was that NATO would ensure American involvement in European affairs, and that American influence would be used to mobilise Western European defence efforts against the USSR. The second Soviet fear was that a Western Germany within NATO would be a strategic redoubt for the United States against the Soviet Union. Thus Soviet views appear to have progressed from anxiety over German militarism to concern about American domination of Germany and Europe. One analyst, in an article published in *Pravda*, commented that the Atlantic Pact backed the revival of a militarised Germany and was directed against the USSR.[16] This implies that the Soviet Union suspected that the United States would draw West Germany into its operational planning against the Soviet Union on an integrated basis, and that American contingency plans would incorporate West German military assets.

Yet there remained an alternative outcome which the Soviets neglected to consider in their public statements: the United States could impose a stranglehold upon Germany, blocking German revanchism.

During 1949, the Soviet Union made numerous suggestions that appeared destined to deny the future West German state any involvement in NATO.[17] This was particularly apparent in the proposals concerning the withdrawal of troops from Germany, which presumably would have included the Eastern zones. Had they been accepted, the Western zones of Germany would not have been included in NATO. It is difficult to evaluate the sincerity of these proposals; nevertheless, they raised the possibility of the loss of Soviet control of East Germany.

An examination of the Soviet offers is instructive. At the conference of Foreign Ministers in May and June 1949, Vyshinsky made several suggestions. First, he wished to re-establish the activity of the Control Council in Germany, on its former basis, as the organ exercising supreme power, and he wished to re-establish the inter-Allied *Kommandatura* of Berlin for the coordination of the civic management of Berlin as a whole to ensure normal life within the city. Second, he favoured the creation of a single German central organ which would be charged with determining the economic and political structures of Germany as a whole.[18] Vyshinsky alleged that the Soviet position on German questions had always been well known and that the Soviet government reaffirmed its position on reparations and the Ruhr.

In essence these proposals envisaged a return to the 1945 position. They may be interpreted on several levels. On the one hand, they may have represented a genuine attempt by the USSR to open up the German issue for reunification; on the other, they could have been intended to dilute progress towards integration and reconstruction within the Western zones. The first possibility should not be discounted, but the second interpretation of Vyshinsky's proposals is implicit in the Soviet terms for reunification, German unity on a Soviet basis. As a mechanism for unity, for example, the USSR advocated one currency for the whole of Germany – the East German mark.[19]

The Soviet provisions were unacceptable to the Western powers, which perceived them as an attempt to gain influence over the Western zones; they responded by offering parallel terms on the basis of Western currency. Adam Ulam has claimed that, in view of the Western moves towards defence integration, Stalin may have been willing to betray his East German allies and accept a united Germany in pursuit of broader European aims.[20] The USSR was only prepared to countenance a united Germany on its own terms, for example the use of Eastern zone financial structures, terms which would not have betrayed the East German leaders, but which would perhaps have eventually extended the East German model.

In 1949, Soviet officials repeatedly called for a return to the situation which had existed in Germany during 1945, and demanded a reinvigoration of the Potsdam decisions, which they alleged the United States had violated. This appears again to have been an attempt to whittle away advantages which the USSR perceived the West to have accrued. A *Pravda* correspondent was very frank about Soviet aims in Germany when he spoke to an American correspondent during the Foreign Ministers' conference. He claimed that the

chief objective of the Soviet Union at this conference was to obtain a renewal of trade between Western and Eastern zones; that the Soviet

government did not believe and did not desire the political unification of
Germany but the maintenance of *status quo* in the political sphere.[21]

A return to the *status quo* of 1945 would have represented a
triumph for the USSR, prohibiting further defence collaboration in
the Western zones of Germany.

Both the United States and the Soviet Union publicly professed
their interest in a united Germany. However, their approaches to the
issue differed. The United States saw the German issue in broader
European terms and maintained that so long as Europe remained
divided so too would Germany. For the United States, the German
question could be resolved only within the context of a broader
settlement. A memorandum in April 1949 made this point explicitly:
'It would be to our advantage to end the division of Germany
provided that the division of Europe could be ended at the same
time.'[22] In contrast, the USSR seemed prepared to accept a united,
neutral Germany within a divided Europe.

Soviet diplomatic efforts to avert the military integration of the
West German zones into NATO were accompanied by a press campaign throughout 1949 which sought to convey the impression that
the processes under way for West European integration were, despite
legitimate Soviet concern, fragile and contradictory. Numerous
articles asserted that, despite the apparent agreement between the
Western European nations, there remained issues on which countries
were diametrically opposed, and Soviet commentators pointed to
differences between the Western countries.[23]

The Soviet press characterised the United States as bent on
imposing a hegemonic order upon the economically insecure states
of Europe, an effort which, they insisted, would generate intra-bloc
conflict.[24] Secondary Soviet sources on this period raise the same
themes: they depict West European integration in NATO as the
result of American economic dominance, and identify contradictions
among the Western powers.[25] Soviet economists and social scientists
expressed similar views. Soviet writings revived the orthodox view
that the West would undergo a severe economic crisis, and
reaffirmed the inherently superior nature of the socialist system.[26]

Ideological orthodoxy was reflected in the reopening of the debate
on the work of Eugene Varga. His contention that the crisis of
capitalism might be delayed as a result of certain elements of
centralised planning being adopted by the Western powers during

the war years, and his belief in the peaceful development of capitalism in the post-war era, were severely criticised.[27] In April 1949, *Voprosy ekonomiki* printed transcripts of a session of the Learned Council of the Economics Institute of the USSR Academy of Sciences which severely criticised Varga. It was noted that 'one of the radical mistakes of Comrade Varga and of almost all the work issued by the former Institute of World Economy and World Politics . . . is the reformist notion of the peaceful development of capitalism after the war'.[28] L. Ya Eventov, a fellow economist, was forced to recant his views and did so in characteristically orthodox terms: 'my basic error consists in the fact that in analysing the problems of the war and post-war capitalist economy I did not use the struggle between the two systems as the starting point'.[29]

Soviet ideology, depicted in terms of open struggle between East and West, maintained that conflicts existed within the Western bloc. Such apparent theoretical confidence in intra-Western bloc conflict appears at variance with the reality of progressively closer military and economic cooperation between the Western states. During 1949, Soviet efforts to deny Western integration and collaboration were determined by belief in the structural weakness of the capitalist system. This weakness, it was thought, would enable the Soviet Union to manipulate the 'contradictions' of the West. The denial of Western integration was also regarded as essential in a period when intra-bloc conflict would stimulate a more belligerent approach by Western elites to their systemic adversary, the Soviet Union.

At the beginning of 1949, in a statement by the Ministry of Foreign Affairs on the North Atlantic Pact, Molotov stated that: 'The Soviet Union is compelled to take into consideration the fact that the ruling circles of the United States and Great Britain have gone over to a frankly aggressive political course . . .'[30] This statement reflected the ideas initially propagated by Zhdanov, at the first Cominform meeting in September 1947, to the effect that the world was divided into two hostile camps ,with the division running horizontally through societies and based upon class lines.[31] The elaboration of this theme by Soviet social scientists at the beginning of 1949 helped provide the theoretical underpinning to support the Soviet belief in the value of attempts to manipulate West European opinion.

Attempts to utilise progressive Western opinion began in January 1949 when P.N. Pospelov, the editor of *Pravda*, announced that 'peaceful coexistence' was the order of the day, and the USSR began to advocate a strategy designed to appeal to elements in the West opposed to nuclear weapons and remilitarisation in Europe. The Peace Movement was designed to gather popular support for such issues.[32] The instruments of this campaign were the Cominform and the indigenous Communist Parties within Europe. On 11 January, leading French communist Marcel Cachin talked of the possibilities of peaceful coexistence.[33] Three days later he visited Italy and P. Togliatti, the leader of the Italian communists, began to talk of socialism 'winning' by peaceful means.[34] As Marshal Shulman has pointed out, this appeared to indicate a change of strategy by the Communist movement at large.[35]

The first peace offensive was a brief affair, launched by Cachin in January, and was followed by a declaration by the leading French communist, Thorez, of full support for the Red Army in the event of war.[36] This radical pronouncement apparently alienated many and was judged too extreme.[37] The second wave of the peace offensive had more success. On 24 February the International Liaison Committee of Intellectuals for Peace, appointed at the Wrocław Congress, met in Paris and announced a series of meetings to be held in several major cities. A World Peace Congress would take place in Paris in April and a Cultural and Scientific Congress in New York in March.[38] At first, the Peace Movement adopted a fairly moderate tone towards the United States, with a view to securing the broadest possible base for support in the West.[39] The motives of the Peace Movement were explicitly outlined in an *Izvestyia* editorial:

> The Soviet emphasis on the cleavage between the ordinary people of the United States and Britain and the warmongers does not necessarily mean that the government has abandoned hope of reaching a peaceful settlement with the West. Rather, it has been a reflection of the hope that popular resentment against war will cause the Western governments to modify their programmes.[40]

After the signing of the NATO treaty, the Cominform *Bulletin* noted that: 'The struggle for peace has entered a new sharper phase.'[41] In mid-1949, the Peace Movement became more militant, particularly over the issue of German remilitarisation.

Thus it sought to take advantage of perceived divisions in Western opinion and to deny the West, in particular the United States, support for its military-political strategies. Simultaneously, the Soviet peace offensive appeared designed to reduce international tension and promote the image of the USSR as a peace-loving nation dedicated to outlawing atomic weapons.

Soviet statements, in 1949, convey the impression that the USSR was eager to achieve some form of prohibition of nuclear weapons. This public position may be interpreted as another attempt to deny the United States the advantages which accrued from monopoly possession of such weapons. Despite this rationale, elements in the Soviet leadership, especially the military command, may have been less than wholly convinced of the revolutionary effect of nuclear weaponry on the conduct of war. Throughout 1949, the Soviet Union went to great lengths to publicly denigrate the utility of atomic weapons. In July 1949, Air Marshal K. Vershinin wrote:

> The experience of the Second World War completely refutes the doctrines of Douhet, Fuller and their German supporters, to the effect that it is possible to win a war with a highly developed and equipped air force alone or land forces alone or both taken together. ... Today Anglo-American strategy emphasises air power in conjunction with the atom bomb in an attempt to convey to their people that their participation in a new war would be small; and at the same time strives to intimidate the peoples of the USSR and the people's democracies with the threat of an 'atomic' or 'push button' war. These ideas proceed from the perverted conception that the outcome of a war can be decided by one type of arms alone. History has proved the reverse more than once.[42]

In August, an article in *Voprosy Filosofii* applauded the English physicist, P. M. S. Blackett, for disclosing 'the complete lack of foundation' for the 'atomic blitzkrieg' strategy: 'Although atom bombs are weapons of mass killing, inhuman and barbaric weapons of aggression, Blackett comes to the sharp and definite conclusion that they cannot decide the outcome of a war.'[43]

The Soviet military repeatedly affirmed the idea that a state could not rely upon one type of weapon alone, and criticised the Western powers for reliance upon air power and for ignoring the use of mass armies: 'Evidently the imperialists did not profit from the lessons of the last war, which ended in the collapse of a number of major capitalist powers and showed the bankruptcy of bourgeois military science based on the theory of single-arm military participation.'[44] Admiral I. Yumashev accused the Anglo-Americans of a 'bourgeois fear of mass armies'.[45] The Soviet press dwelt on the success of the Soviet army in World War II and pointed to the constantly improving tactics of the Soviet tank troops.[46] Marshal Sokolovsky also pointed to another consideration which prevented a state from relying on a single weapon strategy. He maintained that factors other than purely military ones were decisive in warfare:

> only a state which is stronger than its opponent economically, militarily and in a moral political sense, a state which is superior to its opponent in the endurance and unity of the people throughout the war, is capable of winning a modern war. . . . Only the Soviet army, an army of a new type, is capable of resolving all the tasks of contemporary warfare.[47]

These views could all be set in the framework of Stalin's renowned (and later much scorned) 'permanently operating factors' governing the outcome of wars independent of new technologies and weapons systems.

This denigration of atomic power and the constant emphasis upon Soviet conventional superiority may have been a strategy of bluff by Soviet leaders seeking to conceal their vulnerability to a militarily superior opponent. There is little doubt over the relief that the Soviet leaders felt in September 1949 when they achieved their first atomic explosion. One Soviet commentator openly stated that the United States could no longer blackmail the USSR.[48] Indeed, in a speech in November 1949, Malenkov included the possession of the atomic secret as a contributory factor to the strength of the Soviet position.[49] In this major speech, Malenkov proclaimed that the global balance was now tilted in favour of socialism and the Soviet state. The Soviet Union not only had the atomic bomb:

> In the tremendous contest between the two systems – the system of Socialism and the system of Capitalism – the superiority of the Socialist system is distinctly apparent. . . . We are living in an epoch when the movement of the masses towards democracy and Socialism is gaining strength each day.

Malenkov listed factors which had contributed to this favourable trend, in particular the communists' success in China, the success of the Peace Movement and the state of the Soviet economy. The Soviet economy, he claimed, was expanding substantially: 'our national economy has not only attained its pre-war level but surpassed it'. The West, in contrast, Malenkov affirmed, was in a sorry state of economic stagnation and industrial crisis.[50]

Malenkov's position in 1949, and his influence on foreign policy, deserve some clarification. Malenkov had been the major beneficiary of Zhdanov's demise in late 1948–49. In early 1949, Malenkov had moved to erase Zhdanovite influence, most notably in the Leningrad purge. During this purge many of those associated with Zhdanov were removed and then executed, among them N.A. Voznesensky and Kuznetsov.[51] In his memoirs, Khrushchev reveals that the charges against these two men were connected with treason and suggests that their connections with Tito and Djilas came to be regarded as rather suspect, especially in the wake of the Stalin–Tito rift.[52] Both Beria and Malenkov appear to have been the primary instigators of the Leningrad purge, with the apparent motive of destroying the power base of the Zhdanovites.[53] From early 1949, this strategy appears to have been successful: Malenkov and Beria shared the third position in the party hierarchy, exercising considerable influence over policy formation.

Marshal Shulman identifies two major strands in Soviet thinking on foreign policy during this period. One, the Malenkov line, was characterised by exuberant confidence in historical forces that would lead socialism to prevail, together with a belief in the strength of the Soviet position. Shulman argues that this implied an optimistic, restrained and indirect Soviet strategy working through the Peace Movement.[54] He identifies a contrasting school of thought associated with Molotov and M.A. Suslov. Shulman argues that their views were governed by a belief in the inevitability of war and, consequently, the necessity for militant action. Shulman characterised this view as 'defensively militant'.[55] Shulman demonstrates that both schools of thought relied on the use of similar tactics, such as using the Peace Movement and foreign Communist Parties as weapons in the struggle against the West, and that both employed the term 'peaceful coexistence' and 'struggle for peace' to describe their aims.[56]

The distinction between the two groups is useful in identifying different perceptions of how aggressive the West was and how the Soviet leadership perceived the timing of a predicted Western onslaught. Malenkov appears to have been confident that the strength of the Soviet position would act to restrain the West and that the disintegration of the Western bloc was historically inevitable. Molotov and Suslov, in contrast, believed that Soviet strength would provoke the West to launch a war. In Malenkov's 7 November speech on the thirty-second anniversary of the Great

October Socialist Revolution, he stated that: 'The Soviet people are not afraid of peaceful competition with capitalism. Therefore they speak out against a new war and in defence of peace.'[57] However, in a speech in March 1950 Molotov argued that

> Although the positions of imperialism after the Second World War proved to be undermined in many ways and the destinies of the rotten outworn capitalist regime have been conclusively predetermined, imperialism does not intend voluntarily to join its forefathers in the realm of history ... we are well aware of the truth that, so long as imperialism exists, there also exists the danger of fresh aggression ... wars are inevitable.[58]

In 1949–50, Suslov's two main responsibilities were ideology and the oversight of foreign Communist Parties. He appears to have orchestrated a more militant line through his links with the Communist Parties. At a Cominform meeting in November 1949, he called for militant action by the member parties under the 'struggle for peace'. Suslov argued at this meeting that Soviet successes had increased the probability of war: 'Historical experience teaches that, the more hopeless things are for imperialist reaction, the more it rages and the greater the danger of military adventures.'[59] Suslov ordered a greater struggle for peace, through the parties, the Peace Movement and the working classes.

The Malenkov–Suslov difference over foreign policy is of material significance because it signalled a realignment within the top echelons of the Soviet leadership. Suslov had actually been regarded as within the Malenkov camp, and rose to prominence alongside both Malenkov and Beria upon the demise of Zhdanov in 1948.[60] Suslov gradually assumed control of ideological affairs and the reorganisation of Agitprop, and during the 1949 purge of Zhdanovites from the administration, he became the new editor of *Pravda*. He was also Central Committee Secretary.[61] As Hahn has pointed out, Suslov was 'a key beneficiary of the purge of Zhdanov's faction and must have had a personal hand in purging the ideological apparatus'.[62]

Malenkov was clearly in a powerful position throughout 1949, but there is evidence that towards the end of the year Stalin began to be suspicious of his power and started to make moves to check his influence. Most notably, Khrushchev, the Ukrainian First Secretary and Politburo member, was transferred to Moscow in December

1949, and quickly emerged as the principal opponent of Malenkov in agriculture. In his memoirs, Khrushchev wrote that: 'I even began to suspect that one of the reasons Stalin had called me back to Moscow was to influence the balance of power in the collective and to put a check on Beria and Malenkov's plans.'[63] The fact that Suslov had begun to distance himself from Malenkov is not without significance, since it was precisely during this period, late 1949 to early 1950, that Suslov began to exhort foreign communists to greater efforts.[64] It was almost as if the Suslov strategy had taken precedence over the more restrained Malenkov line in foreign policy.[65] This culminated in the Stockholm Declaration of 1950. The peace offensive, however, failed to obstruct Western integration, and in early 1950 the Soviet Union had to develop new strategies in Europe.

The Soviet Union, the Korean War and Europe

Soviet–American relations were dominated during 1950 by events in Korea. The Korean War was important for several reasons, not least because it led to a fundamental reassessment on the American side of the Soviet threat and what was necessary to defend US interests in the Far East and in Western Europe.[66] This section is not concerned with the details of the military conflict in Korea, but rather with the relationship between the conflict in Korea and the effect it had on Soviet behaviour in Europe.

The North Korean attack on South Korea led many in the West to assume that it was the opening salvo of a widespread communist campaign to extend influence.[67] Others interpreted Soviet conduct as a probe, designed to draw American attention away from Europe.[68] Historians have advanced numerous interpretations of the origins of the Korean War and the Soviet role in it.[69] Whilst there is a whole body of literature on the American reaction to, and behaviour in, Korea, there is little on the Soviet side. Using such sources as are available upon and a careful reading of Soviet actions, it appears that Soviet leaders used the Korean conflict to further political-military aims in the East, and also as the war progressed hoped to use it to put pressure on the process of consolidation in the West.

Primarily, the Korean conflict arose out of local conditions in the Far East. At the Cairo meeting in 1943, Korea had been promised independence, but had been divided into two occupation zones.[70]

Moscow controlled the North and Washington the South. Soviet troops were withdrawn in January 1949. US troops left a few months later. Both, however, left in place separate regimes. The major characteristic of the North Korean regime was its dependence on Moscow, certainly for military supplies.[71] Recent research in the Moscow archives clearly demonstrates that Moscow continued to maintain close supervision over events in the North even after Soviet troops had withdrawn. There are a considerable number of documents revealing the nature of the Soviet–North Korean relationship, but one written on 19 March 1949 is worthy of particular note. The letter, from the Soviet ambassador to Pyongyang, outlined the measures that Moscow considered should be carried out in North Korea to maintain the communist state.[72] Moscow wanted to establish and reinforce a communist presence on the Korean peninsula. This aim was primarily inspired by a desire to counteract the growth of US influence in the region and maintain a watchful eye on possible Japanese territorial ambitions.[73]

In this period the Americans were consolidating their strategic power in Asia, were moving towards the conclusion of a peace treaty with Japan, and were generally strengthening their chain of military bases in the East.[74] Moscow had been cut out from influence in the settlement of the Japanese question despite its protests. This 'exclusion' and the Soviet preoccupation with a future threat from either Japan or indeed China hold the key to an understanding of the Soviet role in the start of the Korean War. There is little doubt that Stalin armed and supplied the North Korean invasion but the question is how far he instigated it and what ambitions he hoped to satisfy.

The first point is that Stalin did not seek to confront the United States over Korea. Stalin's support for the North Korean invasion is, in part, explained by the fact that he thought that it would indeed be accomplished easily. Kim-il Sung appears to have reassured Stalin, during discussions,[75] that the invasion of the South could be easily achieved with the predicted support of at least some of the South Korean population.[76] Kim, although the original proponent of the plan to invade, waited until he had Stalin's support before launching the attack.[77] According to Khrushchev's memoirs, which record the discussions between Stalin and the North Korean leader,[78] Stalin did not wholly believe Kim-il Sung, that the war would provide an easy victory, but was willing to take a risk. Volkogonov's recent biography of Stalin also mentions the discussions between the Soviet and Korean leaders, stating that Stalin knew of the North Korean plan but made many attempts to distance himself from the attack: 'From the outset (he) made every attempt to avoid direct confrontation between the USSR and the USA.'[79]

Stalin's calculation in early 1950 was cautious. There seemed little chance that Washington would make South Korea a major bone of contention.[80] It had signalled its lack of interest in Korea very clearly. In mid-1949, the bulk of US forces had been withdrawn from Korea.[81] American spokesmen had defined their strategic interests in the region in such a manner as to exclude Korea.[82] Senator Tom Connally, the chairman of the Senate Foreign Relations Committee, for example, had, during an interview on 5 May 1950, stated that Korea was not an essential part of the defence strategy of the United States: 'I don't think it is greatly important. It has been testified before us that Japan, Okinawa and the Philippines make the chain of defense which is absolutely necessary.'[83]

The American military reaction to North Korean aggression was, however, rapid. On 27 June, the UN Security Council, from which the Soviet delegation had absented itself, condemned the invasion of South Korea, and called upon the North Koreans to withdraw. On 30 June, US ground units were ordered into action.[84] The Americans developed a double-pronged response to the Korean conflict: a military response in the East and a build-up of defences in Europe.[85] There was recognition within the US administration that the European allies were anxious that the war was an attempt by the Kremlin to probe US resolve in Europe.[86]

Moscow sought to limit its overt involvement in the conflict and to minimise the risks to itself. Shortly before Kim-il Sung began the invasion, Moscow withdrew its military advisers.[87] Throughout the summer of 1950, Soviet spokesmen portrayed the war as a local conflict in which 'foreign troops' should not be used. On 7 August, *Pravda* commented that 'a civil war is taking place between the Northerners and the Southerners, between two parts of the Korean people, temporarily split into two governmental camps'.[88] The 'local conflict' approach was an attempt to undermine the basis of American involvement. This was reflected not only in Soviet rhetoric but also in diplomatic behaviour.

After boycotting the Security Council for months, the Soviet representative, Jacob Malik, returned to it on 1 August and utilised Indian proposals to try to end the war in Korea, calling for the withdrawal of all foreign troops.[89] The decision by the Soviet Union not to send a representative to the Council earlier is recorded in Gromyko's memoirs as a matter of some contention between himself and the Soviet leader. Gromyko recalls that he advised Stalin to send a representative as soon as the North Korean invasion occurred because, he feared, the United Nations would unite against Moscow.[90] Kirk, the American ambassador in Moscow, commented that Malik's return 'showed that the Soviets were disturbed by the possible consequences of the Korean conflict and were trying to limit them, particularly by halting rearmament of the West'.[91] This evaluation appears to have been partially correct; but it was also an attempt by Moscow to influence the proceedings of the Security Council, the return of the Soviet representative coinciding with Moscow's assumption of the chairmanship of the Council.[92]

Soviet policy during the Korean War itself was complicated. It consisted in support for Kim-il Sung.[93] This promised the opportunity for a quick victory to secure some advantages *vis-à-vis* the strength of the Americans in Japan. A linkage did not appear to have been made by Stalin between Soviet actions in the East and American reaction in Europe. Once the war had begun, however, this very quickly became an important feature of Soviet foreign policy. When the war in Korea was prolonged through UN intervention, Moscow linked the situation in the East with that in Europe and sought to exploit US involvement in Korea to the detriment of its role in military integration in Europe.

As the Korean crisis deepened, with the entry of communist Chinese forces in November,[94] Moscow started to protest against the rearmament of Germany. On 3 November, Moscow proposed a four-power Foreign Ministers' conference to discuss the issue of the demilitarisation of Germany. This proposal coincided with the rout of General McArthur's forces in Korea, and with public Western differences on the wisdom of the drive to the Yalu river.[95] On 30 November, the head of the government of the DDR, Otto Grotewohl, wrote to West German Chancellor Adenaeur taking up the Eastern bloc suggestion for the creation of an 'All German Consultative Council' which, he suggested, might eventually form the basis for a provisional government for the whole of Germany.

Soviet analysts in this period appeared to want to exploit what they saw as policy differences in the Western alliance over the rearmament of Germany and over Western policy in Korea. This was noted by one American analysis which commented that

> the rearmament of Western Germany gives a propaganda weapon to
> the Soviets regardless of the *Bereitschaften* of the Soviet zone . . . it
> could well strengthen 'neutralist' opinion by accrediting the notion of a
> 'belligerent attitude' on the part of the US and the West.[96]

Again, this contemporary evaluation seems accurate. The Soviet
press appeared to believe, or at least put forward, the idea that the
conflict in the East would provoke intra-bloc discord in the West. On
27 November 1950, *Pravda*, paraphrasing the US press, posed the
question: 'Will not the war in Korea lead to the complete disintegration of the Atlantic alliance?'[97] On 1 December, it was noted in
Moscow that the reaction in Western Europe to the UN military
reverses in Korea revealed a European desire for a diplomatic, not a
military, solution.[98] As if to add to the pressure, on 15 December, the
Soviet government sent the British and French notes protesting
against West German rearmament, calling it a violation of Anglo-
Soviet and Franco-Soviet treaties.[99]

These notes were designed to play upon French fears of a
revanchist Germany. They seem to have been well targeted. The
French government had expressed concern about the rearming of
German troops.[100] For the French, German manpower in any
defence scheme was controversial. The French felt the costs of World
War II far too closely to accept German rearmament easily. It was
this concern over German ambitions that had inspired the French
Defence Minister, René Pleven, to suggest a European army as an
alternative to a West German army in NATO. The original French
scheme for a European Defence Community (EDC) called for an
organisation in which German forces were firmly tied into a supra-
national force.[101] The French Communist Party was mobilised by
Moscow to campaign against the idea of German rearmament and
led a campaign directing attention to what it termed the 'struggle
against the Wehrmacht'.[102] The Soviet-inspired Peace Campaign in
Europe was also directed to preventing the inclusion of Germany in
any West European defence initiative.

At this stage, the East Germans were mobilised to form a bridge
between East and West Germany to try to impede the inclusion of the
Western part into an anti-Soviet alliance. At an extraordinary meeting, on 2 March 1951, of the GDR Volkskammer, a resolution was
passed to send to the Federal Bundestag to press the four Great

Powers to conclude a peace treaty with a Germany that had been unified, democratised and *demilitarised*. All occupation forces should then withdraw after the signing of the treaty.[103]

Throughout the spring of 1951, Moscow constantly reiterated its idea of 3 November that a conference should be convened to discuss the issue of Germany and areas of East–West tension. During the preliminary talks, Moscow made its agenda very clear. It wanted to discuss three issues: first, the demilitarisation of Germany; second, the withdrawal of occupation forces; third, the reduction of the armed forces of the four powers.[104] The Soviet delegation continually raised the issue of the future of Germany, but also protested against NATO and US bases abroad.[105] The Soviet delegation made it clear that it would not participate in further meetings unless there was discussion of NATO and the overseas military bases of the United States.[106] It even linked the issue of a German settlement with the question of Trieste.

It is interesting that Western historians have, on the whole, ignored the details of the negotiations that took place in this period in 1951–52. It is here that we see the genesis of Soviet suggestions for neutralisation and demilitarisation in Central Europe. On 4 February 1951, for example, Moscow suggested, in a telegram to Washington, that it might be possible to limit NATO forces. This implies acceptance of the existence of NATO, albeit in a scaled down form.[107] One member of the Truman administration saw it as an opportunity for bargaining with Moscow over Central Europe. Washington could offer to maintain the same number of troops as the USSR and its satellites east of the 'Bug River'.[108] This tentative exchange appears to have been lost in the momentum, on the Western side, towards military-political integration in Europe. The point remains that Moscow was suggesting some limitation of NATO forces rather than completely opposing the organisation.[109] Nothing came of the Soviet idea, and the negotiations in Paris degenerated into statements of opposing positions on the question of the future of Germany. Soviet diplomacy, at this point, seemed to have broken down in the face of the Western refusal to concede ground over the future of West Germany.[110]

The situation in Korea had worsened considerably in the spring of 1951. The Chinese forces had been halted, and Seoul retaken by UN forces. A second Chinese offensive failed to make any real impact on the UN forces, and a line had been established near the 38th parallel.

It was at this point that Moscow suggested a cease-fire.[111] On 23 June 1951, Malik called for mutual withdrawal from the 38th parallel. Cease-fire negotiations took place, but the fighting continued. What this signalled on the Soviet side was acceptance that an armistice could be arranged in Korea without the settlement of the issues which had originally formed an integral part of the conditions for peace – the withdrawal of US troops.[112] In the summer of 1951, Moscow had to face the fact that the Western alliance had not only remained united over Korea but was irrevocably moving towards a coherent military-political unit in Western Europe which would include West Germany.

Soviet initiatives to block the full integration of West Germany into a Western alliance failed. In the autumn of 1951, the British decided that West Germany should no longer be regarded as a threat.[113] For the rest of 1951, Soviet diplomacy consisted of a constant reiteration of the arguments against the incorporation of Germany into NATO. This was, again, the major theme of a Soviet initiative in early 1952. On 10 March, the Soviet government proposed a peace treaty with Germany and once more outlined conditions for peace that would have meant the withdrawal of US troops and the demilitarisation of Germany. It put forward a draft which proposed that Germany should be re-established as a unified state, and that all armed forces of the occupying powers should be withdrawn from Germany within one year. Another clause explicitly banned the new Germany from entering into 'any coalition or military alliance' directed against any power which took part with its armed forces in the war against Germany. A further clause insisted that all military bases on German soil be liquidated.[114]

The Americans turned the proposal down for a variety of reasons. There was a feeling that after the arduous negotiations to persuade the European allies, particularly the French, of the virtues of defence integration, Washington was not prepared to give up the hard won political-military gains. The Soviet initiative was dismissed as yet another attempt by Moscow to divert Western military integration. In its response, Washington made it a condition of the unification of Germany that the United Nations should supervise general elections throughout the whole of Germany.[115] This was unacceptable to Moscow.

The Western allies did not really take the Soviet initiative seriously. A key question is whether Moscow intended it seriously.

This is a difficult issue to judge. It certainly does not seem to have been a move to relieve East–West tensions. Ideological hostility in the Soviet press towards both the United States and German remilitarisation had not abated. The Soviet proposal, which conceded a unified, neutral Germany, seems to have been in direct opposition to all post-war Soviet plans for Germany.

There are, however, several reasons why Soviet leaders may genuinely have been prepared to concede a unified, demilitarised Germany in 1952. One was that a unified, demilitarised Germany was actually a preferable alternative to a West German state locked into a military alliance predicated upon an anti-Soviet bloc. Soviet leaders, in this scenario, had to fear the rebirth of German militarism and German power reinforced by Western nuclear capacity. A West German army sitting on the borders of the Soviet empire was not something that the Soviet leadership can have viewed with equanimity. There was a fear that Germany would dominate the Western bloc, and utilise its technological resources for the fulfilment of what Moscow perceived to be historic territorial ambitions. This belief was frequently propagated in the Soviet press of the period. While Western historians have treated Soviet statements against the rebirth of German militarism as merely propaganda ploys, in Moscow there was still a genuine and deep-seated concern over German ambitions. There was also the ever present fear of US power augmented by German manpower in Central Europe. Demilitarisation would, at a stroke, have removed the German threat and prevented the establishment of US bases in Central Europe.

A primary concern of the Soviet Union at this stage was to keep Austria neutral. Moscow was concerned over the future composition of the Austria army. On 13 March, Washington had proposed a draft treaty of settlement for Austria,[116] but Moscow insisted that the Great Powers should share responsibility for the democratisation, denazification and demilitarisation of Austria. The Soviet priority was to prevent Austria being pulled into the Western camp.[117]

There are also suggestions that there was a concern that the East German state might be pulled Westwards. Historians in the West have tended to ignore the concern of the Soviet leadership over the maintenance of bloc cohesion in the East. From what we know of the Soviet–Yugoslav dispute, and from the evidence emerging from the

Party Archive in Moscow,[118] the predominant concern of the Soviet leadership was to maintain its grip upon the Communist Parties in the East.[119] While neutralisation did not offer control of East Germany, it did at least mean that the East German camp would not be drawn away into a Western bloc. Demilitarisation under four power control was a better option. Indeed, this emphasis upon four power supervision of Germany was consistent with at least part of the pattern of Soviet thinking about Germany in the post-war period. Four-power control, as suggested in the Soviet note of 1952, offered Moscow a say in the control of the whole of Germany.

The initiative of 1952 illustrate the ambivalence in Soviet thinking about Germany. There was concern not to have a revived Germany in any form near Soviet borders, and American troops at least offered the hope of subjugation. From a different perspective, American forces also offered the vision of a powerful anti-Soviet alliance, armed with nuclear weapons centred around the historic enemy. Again, a divided Germany offered the advantage of, at least at some level, legitimising Soviet control in the east. This theme comes through much more clearly in the period 1953–55.

The American reaction guaranteed that the Soviet initiative sank without trace. Historians have, on the whole, either ignored the initiative altogether,[120] or taken it merely as a propaganda ploy.[121] It occurred at an interesting moment in Soviet history. In 1952, Stalin's health was ailing and he appears to have been absent from the forefront of decision-making for most of the year. He died on 5 March 1953. It is difficult to make the case that the Soviet initiatives represented a radical departure in thinking about foreign policy merely on the grounds that the dictator's personal power had waned, but it is certainly true that, after his death, his successors placed greater weight upon the idea of a unified Germany.

Conclusion

Stalin left his successors a complicated legacy. On the one hand, Soviet power had undeniably grown: control over Eastern Europe, albeit marred by the dispute with Yugoslavia, had been secured; the country had succeeded in making vast technological strides to explode an atomic bomb in 1949; and some form of control over Germany had been asserted. The cost of these achievements, on the other hand, had been the preclusion of cooperation with the United

States and Western Europe. Stalin's successors faced an increasingly integrated and hostile Western alliance with a West German state at its centre.

Notes

1 M. Shulman, *Stalin's Foreign Policy Reappraised* (Cambridge, Mass: Harvard University Press, 1963), p. 51.

2 *New York Times*, 9 April 1949.

3 M. Shulman, *Stalin's Foreign Policy*, p. 51.

4 Ibid.

5 Ibid.

6 Ibid.

7 The allegation was that Washington was dividing Germany. See 'Statement of the Ministry of Foreign Affairs of the USSR on the North Atlantic Pact', *Pravda*, 29 January 1949, p. 2. Quoted in the *Current Digest of the Soviet Press*, 1, no. 5, 1949, pp. 9–19.

8 *Pravda*, 4 June 1949.

9 See articles in *Pravda* and *Izvestiya*, 17 February 1949. Quoted in *CDSP*, Vol. 1, no. 7, 1949, pp. 32–7.

10 'At the Paris Session of the Council of Foreign Ministers', *Pravda*, 14 June 1949. Quoted in *CDSP*, Vol. 1, no. 24, 1949, p. 31.

11 Ibid.

12 See the memorandum by Mr Ware Adams of the Policy Planning Staff to the Director of the Policy Planning Staff (Kennan), Washington, 7 March 1949. It states that 'the Germans have refused to participate in any arrangement that would imply a separate "state" or prejudice the eventual achievement of German unity.' *Foreign Relations of the United States*, 1949, Vol. 3, Council of Foreign Ministers, Germany and Austria, pp. 47–9.

13 See 'Preparation for the Inclusion of Western Germany in the System of the North Atlantic Pact', *Pravda*, 29 March 1949. Quoted in *CDSP*, 1949, Vol. 1, no. 13, p. 34.

14 M. M. Marinin, 'Preparations for Drawing Western Germany into the North Atlantic Bloc', *Pravda*, 30 August 1949. Quoted in *CDSP*, Vol. 1, no. 36, p. 15.

15 N. N. Sofinskiy, *Bonn i Washington* (Moscow 1969), glava 1.

16 M. Marinin, 'On the Atlantic Treaty', *Pravda*, 1 July 1949, p. 3. Quoted in *CDSP*, 1949, Vol. 1, no. 27, pp. 18–19.

17 As noted above.

18 For Soviet demands see *FRUS*, 1949, Vol. 3, p. 917.

19 How serious these Soviet proposals were is a difficult question. However, it should be noted that the building up of the Soviet zone in Germany continued even as these offers were being made. For example,

Vneshnyaya Torgorlya in May 1949 published an article by V. Pashukin on future developments building up the Eastern zone; see 'The Two Year Plan for Reconstruction and Development of Peaceful Economy in the Soviet Occupation Zone of Germany', quoted in *CDSP*, Vol. 1, no. 24, 1949, pp. 12–15.

20   A. Ulam, *Expansion and Coexistence. Soviet Foreign Policy 1917–1973* (New York: Praeger, 1974), p. 507.

21   'The U.S. Delegation at the Council of Foreign Ministers to the Acting Secretary of State.' Paris, May 18, 1949. *FRUS*, 1949, Vol. 3, p. 929.

22   'Memorandum by the U.S. Ambassador at Large (Jessup) to the Secretary of State.' Washington, April 19, 1949. *FRUS*, 1949, Vol. 3, p. 59.

23   See, for example, the series of articles in *Pravda* and *Izvestiya* during March 1949 outlining Italian and Canadian protests against the bloc. *Pravda*, 17 March, p. 6; 18 March, p. 8. Quoted in *CDSP*, Vol. 1, no. 11, 1949, pp. 42–3.

24   See Ya. Viktorov, 'One More Aggressive Bloc', *Pravda*, 28 February 1949, p. 4. Quoted in *CDSP*, Vol. 1, no. 8, 1949, p. 23.

25   P. A. Nikolaev, *Politika Sovetskovo Soyuza v Germanskom Voprose* (Moscow: 1966), p. 123.

26   *Pravda*, 19 May 1949.

27   *Voprosy Ekonomiki*, no. 8, 1949.

28   Ibid.

29   *Voprosy Ekonomiki*, no. 8, 1949.

30   'Statement of the Ministry of Foreign Affairs of the USSR on the North Atlantic Pact', *Pravda*, 29 January 1949; *CDSP*, Vol. 1, no. 8, p. 9.

31   *For a Lasting Peace*, no. 1, 1947, p. 1.

32   *Pravda*, January 22 1949.

33   *L'Année Politique, 1949* (Paris, 1950), pp. 2–3. Quoted in Shulman, *Stalin's Foreign Policy*, p. 55.

34   Speech at Bologna, 15 January 1949. Quoted in Shulman, *Stalin's Foreign Policy*, p. 55.

35   Shulman, *Stalin's Foreign Policy*, p. 55.

36   *L'Humanité, 23 February 1949, p. 1.* Quoted in R. Tiersky, *French Communism 1920–1972* (New York: Columbia University Press, 1974), p. 207.

37   Ibid.

38   The call was issued jointly by the Peace Organisation and the Women's International Democratic Federation, one of the oldest and most active of the communist-controlled front organisations.

39   Shulman, *Stalin's Foreign Policy*, pp. 93–4.

40   *Pravda*, 24 April 1949

41   *Pravda*, 11 March 1949.

42   Air Marshal K. Vershinin, *Pravda*, 17 July 1949. Quoted in *CDSP*, Vol. 1, no. 29, 1949, pp. 20–1.

43   O. V. Trakhtenberg, 'The Sociology of the Atom Bomb', *Voprosy Filosofi*, no. 3, 1948 (published June 1949).

44   Admiral I. Yumashev, *Pravda*, 24 July 1949. Quoted in *CDSP*, Vol. 1, no. 30, 1949, p. 15.

45   Ibid.

46   *Pravda*, 11 September 1949.

47   Order of the Minister of Armed Forces of the USSR, *Pravda*, 9 May 1949. Quoted in *CDSP*, Vol. 1, no. 19, 1949, p. 25.

48   *Pravda*, 23 February 1949.

49   *Pravda*, 7 November 1949.

50   Ibid.

51   W. Hahn, *The Fall of Zhdanov and the Defeat of Moderation 1946–1953* (London: Cornell University Press, 1982), pp. 122–9.

52   Hahn, *The Fall of Zhdanov*, p. 127.

53   Hahn, *The Fall of Zhdanov*, pp. 124–5.

54   Shulman, *Stalin's Foreign Policy*, pp. 111–23.

55   Shulman, *Stalin's Foreign Policy*, p. 118.

56   Shulman, *Stalin's Foreign Policy*, p. 123.

57   *Pravda*, 7 November 1949.

58   *Pravda*, 11 March 1949.

59   *Pravda*, 29 November 1949.

60   Hahn, *The Fall of Zhdanov*, pp. 108–13.

61   Hahn, *The Fall of Zhdanov*, p. 112.

62   Hahn, *The Fall of Zhdanov*, pp. 112–13.

63   E. Crankshaw, ed., *Khrushchev Remembers* (Boston: Little Brown, 1971), p. 250.

64   Hahn, *The Fall of Zhdanov*, pp. 112–13.

65   Some circumspection is necessary, however, as it is possible that Suslov may have been aware of Stalin's suspicions of Malenkov and therefore may have decided to dissociate himself from his former ally not on account of disagreements over foreign policies but to avoid demotion or indeed liquidation. The reasoning is supported by the climate of fear prevalent at the time: there were immediate grounds for this in view of what had happened to Molotov earlier in 1949. Although Molotov was formally ranked second after Stalin, in 1949 he does not appear to have exercised any real power. On 4 March 1949 he was removed from his post as Foreign Minister and at the same time his Jewish wife was arrested and sent into exile. Khrushchev reveals that from this time onwards Stalin excluded Molotov from informal meetings.

66   The Joint Chiefs of Staff, Memorandum for the Secretary of Defense, Papers of the Department of State. 59 795 00/7–1050.

67   See Dean Acheson, *Present at the Creation. My Years at the State Department* (London, Nation, 1969), pp. 355–7.

68   At a meeting at the Pentagon in December 1950, Acheson stated his belief that 'the Soviet Union would like to see us tangle with the Chinese. If our resources are devoted there, we cannot build up strength in Europe.' Department of State, Memorandum of Conversation, 795.00./12–350.

69 See A. Ulam, *Expansion and Coexistence*, M. Shulman, *Stalin's Foreign Policy*, and Rosemary Foot, *The Wrong War, American Foreign Policy and the Dimensions of the Korean Conflict 1950–1953* (Ithaca: Cornell University Press, 1985), who all have varying degress of doubt about the precise role of the Kremlin in starting the conflict. Dean Acheson had no such doubts. He writes that 'the attack had been mounted, supplied and instigated by the Soviet Union' and that 'it would not be stopped by anything short of force'. Dean Acheson, *Present at the Creation*, p. 405.

70 Stephen S. Kaplan, *The Diplomacy of Power. Soviet Armed Forces as a Political Instrument* (Washington: Brookings Institution, 1981), p. 316.

71 Stephen S. Kaplan, *The Diplomacy of Power*, p. 326.

72 AVF RF, Fond 17, opis 22 Delo 238, papka 37. p. 22. Quoted in Kathryn Weathersby, Working Paper no. 8, Cold War International History Project, Woodrow Wilson International Centre for Scholars, p. 22.

73 For a general discussion of Soviet aims in the Far East, see Kathryn Weathersby, note 72.

74 See *Otnosheniya Sovetskogo soyuza s narodnoy Koreey 1945–1980. Dokumenty i meteririly* (Moscow: Nauka, 1981).

75 See Khrushchev's comment that Kim-il Sung had told Stalin that: 'He was absolutely certain of success. I can remember Stalin had his doubts.' E. Crankshaw, *Krushchev Remembers*, pp. 33–4.

76 The official Soviet version was that the South Koreans had invaded the North. See note 73.

77 Foreign Ministry Background Report. (Authors not indicated) 'On the Korean War, 1950–53, and the Armistice Negotiations', 9 August 1966. Storage Centre for Contemporary Documentation (Post-1952 Central Committee Archive) Fond 5, opis 58, Delo 266, 1.122–131. Quoted in Weathersby, (note 72), p. 25. See also Kathryn Weathersby, 'New Findings on the Korean War', *Cold War International History Bulletin* 3, fall 1993.

78 E. Crankshaw, *Krushchev Remembers*, pp. 33–4.

79 D. Volkogonov, *Stalin. Triumph and Tragedy* (London: Weidenfeld and Nicolson, 1990), pp. 540–1.

80 In a memorandum for the Secretary of Defence in July 1950, the Joint Chiefs of Staff described Korea as an area of 'slight strategic importance'. See US Department of State, 795.00/7–1050.

81 For the reasons for US withdrawal from Korea, see *FRUS*, 1948, Vol. 6, pp. 1094, 1155, 1180.

82 For the linkage between American statements of disinterest in Korea and North Korean military mobilisation, see J. M. Mackintosh, *The Strategy and Tactics of Soviet Foreign Policy* (London: Oxford University Press, 1962). He points out that it was after Acheson's speech, that a fifth

infantry division was activated in North Korea on 1 March 1950 and a sixth formed in Sariwan on 17 April 1950 (pp. 46–7).

83 Excerpt from 'US News and World Report' May 5 1950. Article: World Policy and Bipartisan. An Interview with Senator Tom Connally. *FRUS*, 1950 Vol. VII, Korea, p. 65.

84 J. L. Gaddis, *The Long Peace* (New York: Oxford University Press, 1987), p. 79.

85 In July, the Americans were considering how best to utilise German manpower. From Frankfurt, McCloy to Secretary of State, no. 461, July 18, Papers of the Department of State, 1950740.5/7–1850.

86 US Department of State Memorandum for Secretary Marshall, 795.00/11–2850.

87 Khrushchev wrote, 'It was incomprehensible to me but as Kim-il Sung was preparing for his march, Stalin called back all our advisers' (p. 370). Quoted in Stephen S. Kaplan, *The Diplomacy of Power*, p. 326. This data is reinforced by R. Simmons. He states, 'In 1948, there were 150 advisers in each North Korean army division; in 1949 the number was reduced to 20 per division; by the spring of 1950 there were between 3–5 with each division.' See R. Simmons, *Strained Alliance*, p. 120, citing *North Korea: A Case Study in the Techniques of Takeover* (Washington DC), Government Printing Office, 1961, p. 114.

88 'Ignorance in Question of International Law', *Pravda*, 7 August 1950. See also 'On Definition of Aggression', *Pravda*, 13 August 1950. Quoted in *CDSP*, Vol. 2, no. 31, 1950.

89 See M. Shulman, *Stalin's Foreign Policy*, pp. 150–1.

90 A. Gromyko, *Memoirs* (London: Hutchinson, 1989), p. 102.

91 398.43 UNESCO/8–150 Telegram, US Ambassador to the Soviet Union (Kirk) to the Secretary of State, Moscow, 1 August 1950, *FRUS*, 1950, pp. 512–13.

92 Malik returned to the Security Council, on 1 August, the very day that Moscow assumed the chairmanship of the Council.

93 One of the major works on the Korean War makes the point that Stalin kept supplies, especially petrol, from the Soviet Union to the Korean forces strictly limited. See Allen S. Whiting, *China Crosses the Yalu. The Decision to Enter the Korean War* (Stanford: Stanford University Press, 1960), p. 43.

94 The exact relationship between Stalin and Mao remains a major bone of contention between scholars of this period. Some analysts assert that the Chinese intervention should be seen as arising out of indigenous Chinese aims, while others believe that Stalin actively encouraged Mao's intervention to prevent the Americans taking over either North Korea or Manchuria. In an informal discussion with Dr Kudryashov (see unpublished papers) he told me that he has seen documents which directly link the Central Committee with the decision to urge the North Korean invasion.

95 For example, in November and December the Soviet press commented on the US military reverses; see, for example, the comment in *Pravda*, 25 December 1950, on the grave crisis in US foreign policy aroused by the failure of the American military adventures in Korea.

96 Department of State, 740.5/12–1150, Office Memorandum, US Government, to Ridgeway B. Knight, 11 December 1950.

97 *Pravda*, 27 November 1950.

98 *Pravda*, 1 December 1950.

99 See M. Shulman, *Stalin's Foreign Policy*, p. 167.

100 See Douglas MacArthur, Joseph J. Wolf. French concern with using German Troops in NATO, November 2, 1950, 740.5/11–250.

101 John W. Young, *Britain, France and the Unity of Europe 1945–51* (Leicester: Leicester University Press, 1984), p. 171.

102 For the workings of the French left, in the early post-war period, see Shulman, *Stalin's Foreign Policy*, pp. 213–18.

103 Discussed in Department of State, Message from Berlin to the Secretary of State, March 3, 1951. Department of State, 396.1. /3–351.

104 The US Representative at the Four Power Exploratory Talks (Jessup) to the Secretary of State, 5 March 1951. RG 396,1-PA/3–551, *FRUS*, 1951, Vol. 3, pp. 1087–9.

105 The Government of the Union of Soviet Socialist Republics to the Government of the United States of America, 396.1-DA/6–2051, *FRUS*, 1951, Vol. 3, pp. 1159–60.

106 Ibid.

107 The reference to this telegram is made in Secretary's Memorandum, lot 53D444, no. 764, Memorandum by Lucius D. Battle, Special Assistant to the Secretary of State, Washington, 7 February 1951, *FRUS*, 1951, Vol. 4, p. 1530. There is, however, no record of the telegram itself.

108 Ibid.

109 A similar offer made by the Americans had actually been refused by Moscow in 1946. Secretary Byrnes had offered to confine US, French and British occupation forces in Germany to 300,000. The total USSR occupation forces were to be 200,000. See *FRUS*, 1946, Vol. 2, pp. 1466–7.

110 This frustration was aired in the Soviet press. See Ya. Zhukov, 'A legitimate question, Why are the Western powers' representatives prolonging negotiations?' *Pravda*, 25 April 1951. Quoted in *CDSP*, 26 June 1951, Vol. 3, no. 17, p. 13. M. Kharlamov, 'For Peaceful Solution of the Korean Conflict', *Pravda*, p. 4. Quoted in *CDSP*, Vol. 3, no. 21, p. 12.

111 A. Ulam. *Expansion and Coexistence*, p. 533.

112 Ibid.

113 CAB 128/18, C.M. (50) 55. Cited in John W. Young, *Britain, France*, p. 169.

114 See 'Draft of Soviet Government of Peace Treaty with Germany', Diplomatic Correspondence Relating to Germany. Soviet note to the United

States, the United Kingdom and France, 10 March 1952. Council on Foreign Relations, C. W. Baier and R. P. Stebbins, eds., *Documents on American Foreign Relations 1952* (New York: Harper and Brothers, 1953).

115   Department of State *Bulletin*, XXVI, 7 April 1952, pp. 530–1. Quoted in C. W. Baier and R. P. Stebbins, *Documents on American Foreign Relations*, pp. 580–631

116   Diplomatic Correspondence Relating to Austria. United States Note Enclosing New Tripartite Treaty Draft, 13 March 1952. Quoted in C. W. Baier and R. P. Stebbins, *Documents*, pp. 262–6.

117   Soviet Note of Reply. Quoted in C. W. Baier and R. P. Stebbins, *Documents*, p. 267.

118   See S. Kudryashov, 'The Central Committee of the All-Union Communist Party and Eastern Europe 1945–1953. New Documents', paper prepared for the British International History Conference, 1992, University of Leeds. Having gained access to some of the documents of the Central Committee, Dr Kudryashov believes that control in the East was the Kremlin's primary consideration in the period under review.

119   Ibid.

120   A notable exception is A. Ulam, who writes that: 'In refusing to enter into what would have been long and exasperating negotiations, the Americans overlooked the truth that patience and a sense of timing are major ingredients in the art of diplomacy.' See A. Ulam, *Expansion and Coexistence*, p. 537.

121   For a discussion of Stalin's mental health at the end of his dictatorship, see Anthony D'Agnostino, *Soviet Succession Struggles. Kremlinology and the Russian Question from Lenin to Gorbachev* (Boston, Mass.: Allen and Unwin, 1988), pp. 179–82.

Chapter 6

Strategies of stabilisation

At the beginning of the period 1953–56, the Soviet Union was faced with a defence dilemma. The historic enemy, Germany, a power which had attacked the USSR twice within the past forty years, appeared to have been rejuvenated by the Western powers. Germany had always been perceived as a threat; that threat was now coming into focus. It was crucial for Moscow to stabilise the European theatre in some way that would constrain potential German aggression. United States power remained an option. The option was, however, dangerous itself. A European bloc led by the United States formed the second horn of the security dilemma. Moscow was faced with a choice. Should it adopt policies to encourage US involvement, from which it could hope to benefit from the restriction of German ambitions, or should it attempt to create a stable European environment free from US interference?

Two themes emerge clearly in Soviet foreign policy behaviour in Europe during the period 1953–56. The first is a continuation of the Soviet attempt to 'manipulate' what were perceived as policy differences between the Western powers over the integration of the Federal Republic into defence organisations. Moscow wanted to prevent the rearmament of Germany. The second is a newer theme: an attempt to stabilise the central strategic relationship with the United States through an acceptance of bloc structures in Europe and a wide-ranging programme of detente. These ambitions were not pursued in a straightforward manner after Stalin's death. Soviet external politics was moulded by the disagreements among the leadership over both strategic and foreign affairs.

Detente in foreign affairs

Immediately after the dictator died, a reallocation of political power took place within the walls of the Kremlin.[1] Malenkov became First Secretary of the Party and Premier; Beria became Minister of Internal Affairs and took control of the organs of state security; and Molotov once more took over the Ministry of Foreign Affairs which he had surrendered in 1949.[2] Khrushchev quickly succeeded Malenkov as First Secretary of the Party and thus assured for himself a place in the ruling oligarchy.

The new leadership moved rapidly to try to secure some form of detente with the Western powers. From the Kremlin's perspective, in March 1953, the Stalinist legacy in foreign policy was not a promising one. The Western Allies seemed to be moving inexorably towards an integrated defence alliance which included West Germany; negotiations on the future of Germany and Austria were deadlocked; and the settlement in Korea was still unresolved. In addition, the relationship with Tito remained acrimonious; relations with Israel were non-existent;[3] and Moscow took little part in the United Nations. While the situation at home was uncertain, Moscow sought to stabilise the situation abroad.

The Western powers seemed inclined to negotiate with the new Soviet leaders. Churchill, for example, spoke of the need for an early conference of the Great Powers to discuss issues of East–West tension, and he raised the possibility of agreement over Korea and Austria.[4] The new administration in Washington, under President Eisenhower, also appeared prepared to cooperate with Moscow.[5]

Soviet initiatives took place to achieve a detente almost immediately. Upon his return from Stalin's funeral in Moscow, Chou En-lai, the Chinese Prime Minister, announced his willingness to break the deadlock of the Korean settlement and to discuss one of the major issues of contention – the return of POWs. In July, an armistice was announced. Moscow's attempts to improve relations with other states continued throughout the spring and summer. They included the relinquishing of claims to Turkey, the re-establishment of relations with Israel, and moves to heal the rift with Tito.[6]

In the midst of this programme to establish a less hostile external environment, the new leadership was shaken to its core by the uprisings in East Germany during June 1953. A series of workers' demonstrations in East Berlin and in several other cities threatened to overturn the regime. The East German Communist Party, under Ulbricht, had assiduously pursued a cult of Stalin, with a series of show trials and purges directed mainly against the German middle classes.[7] Immediately after Stalin's death, the Kremlin had demanded a certain relaxation within East Germany, and a number of measures had been taken towards reform, albeit in a limited fashion. There was a partial adjustment of the tax system and some political amnesties. These moves seemed designed to reconcile the middle classes to the regime. They were officially justified as providing the grounds for bringing about the unification of Germany.[8]

The East German reforms appears to have been an attempt by Beria to prepare the ground for an offer of unification to the West. It was he who apparently ordered the SED to make the political concessions, precisely in a bid to bring about negotiations on the issue of Germany with the West.[9] The concessions were designed to cultivate support among the middle classes for the SED, which would render it capable of taking power at a later stage in Germany.

This strategy was not universally endorsed within the Soviet leadership. Khrushchev later accused Beria of having been willing to give up East Germany in return for preventing the formation of the EDC, and to have been prepared to release a united Germany from Soviet control.[10] If this evidence is reliable, it points to a major divergence of opinion within the Kremlin on the future course of Soviet strategy in Europe. Beria had been involved in debates about Soviet policy in Germany in 1946–47[11] and had been associated with the belief that East Germany would have to be given up into a unified Germany.[12] In 1953, he appeared willing to negotiate with the West on the future of Germany.[13] Beria's association with Malenkov also indicates that the new leader endorsed this line. This is also some evidence that most of the ruling Soviet elite went along with Beria's schemes for East Germany, if somewhat reluctantly. Gromyko, for example, relates that at one meeting of the Presidium he and Molotov resented Beria's 'cavalier attitude' towards the East and for not accepting its existence as a separate state,[14] but the idea was overtaken by the events of June.

Inspired by the relaxation of political repression and encouraged by the death of Stalin, East German workers staged large-scale demonstrations and attacked communist officials. Soviet troops intervened and three mechanised divisions sealed off the streets and ended the insurrection by force.[15] The collapse of the East German regime underlined, for the Soviet leaders, the fragility of their control in Eastern Europe. Although Ulbricht was restored to power, this was only achieved with the aid of Soviet military force.[16]

Beria's activities in Germany, followed by the uprising, provided the rest of the Soviet leadership with a pretext for removing him from power. Recent work on Beria depicts him as a fairly committed reformer of the system after the death of Stalin. Beria, it is claimed, initiated several radical reforms in domestic as well as international affairs[17]. For example, on 4 April the Soviet leadership announced the repudiation of the Doctors' Plot and the rehabilitation of the doctors themselves, an initiative traced direct to Beria.[18] Beria's activities in East Germany can be ascribed to his desire to reinvigorate not only the Soviet system but also the ailing and politically tense situation in the Eastern bloc. His failure in East Germany strengthened the position of Khrushchev within the ruling group. Khrushchev relates that he had tried to form an alliance against both Malenkov and Beria. The execution of the latter meant that Khrushchev's position within the ruling elite was considerably enhanced, but, at this stage, he did not have the necessary power to challenge Malenkov for the leadership. The removal of Beria and the instability in East Germany seemed, however, to have closed off any real hope that Moscow would seriously contemplate a neutralised Germany. Nevertheless, Moscow still hoped to prevent the incorporation of West Germany into a Western defence alliance.

Moscow and Western integration

Immediately after Stalin's death, Malenkov had continued to propound the Stalinist line by issuing warnings against the incorporation of West Germany into organisations such as the EDC. The Soviet leadership continued explicitly to target the French government, which had not yet ratified the treaty, as the most sensitive ear to Moscow's claim of a revival of German militarism.[19]

In the three years following the initial French plan for the EDC, the West Germans, under the influence of Konrad Adenauer, leader of the Christian Democrats (CDU), had managed to turn plans for West European defence integration into part of the campaign to have sovereign status granted to the Federal Republic.[20] Adenauer insisted that West German soldiers could only be assigned to the West European army if the Federal Republic was accorded equal political status to other participating powers.[21]

Adenaueur feared a second 'Potsdam' where the wartime Allies might settle the future of Germany without the participation of the Germans.[22] He believed that, in this situation, France and Britain would prefer detente with Moscow; that Washington would return to its historic isolationism; and that a unified Germany would succumb to communism.[23] These perceptions were not entirely well founded. Dulles, Eisenhower's Secretary of State, was committed to the rehabilitation of West Germany. While aware that Germany had to be seen to be incapable of launching another war, Dulles also considered it imperative to use German economic potential to reinvigorate the rest of West Europe.[24] For the Eisenhower adminis- tration, West Germany was the key to its European strategy, and it had found, in Adenauer, a German leader who shared a similar vision of a strong, economically vibrant West German state locked into a Western alliance.

Adenaueur was committed to what has been termed *Westbindung,* that is, alignment with the West. His commitment to integration with the West European democracies coincided with the Eisenhower administration's view of the future of West European politics. Dulles believed that the EDC was the instrument through which this could best be achieved. It would, in his vision, combine West Germany and France in a manner that would be more reliable than a treaty relationship.[25] While paying lip-service to the idea of a united, neutralised Germany, the Eisenhower administration sus- pected that it would merely be open to Soviet economic and political penetration. Neutrality would only be discussed by Washington on the basis of free elections, a term it knew would not be accepted by Moscow.[26]

The French regarded Adenauer's ambitions with increasing alarm. By February 1953 they had proposed a series of changes to the structure of the EDC which would have altered the treaty substan- tially and placed controls upon the German role within it. Paris demanded that US troops should be made part of the EDC, formed as a supra-national structure. It did not want them merely to be stationed in Germany, with the concomitant risk that a bipartite US–German power bloc would dominate the continent.[27]

Moscow was aware of the public debate in the West and attempted to use the differences amongst the Western allies to foster dissension over the EDC. The Soviet press continually drew attention to the concerns of the French people,[28] and numerous articles were published on the nature of West German domination within the EDC.[29] Soviet commentators linked future West German political dominance with its rapidly flourishing economy.[30]

At the Berlin conference in early 1954, the Soviet delegation proposed that Germany should be united and neutralised. The Soviet note suggested that both East and West should withdraw their occupation forces, and that Germany should be prohibited from entering into any military alliances.[31] The Soviet suggestion did not, however, envisage neutrality without external control. It proposed that the Great Powers should retain the right to intervene in German affairs if necessary.[32]

In essence, Moscow sought guarantees over the political composition of any future Germany. This was evident in discussions over the British proposals made at the conference. Eden suggested that an all-German government could be formed, but only on the basis of free elections.[33] Molotov rejected the idea, on the pretext that the East German people would not accept such an arrangement. It seems far more likely that Moscow's concern, reinforced by the events of June 1953 in East Berlin, was that a unified Germany might, on the basis of a popular vote, incorporate itself into a Western bloc.[34]

Soviet proposals at the conference for a settlement in Austria seem, equally, to have been inspired by the desire to 'deny' the West political and military influence in Central Europe. At the conference, the Soviet delegation proposed that all foreign troops should be removed from Austria on condition that Austria undertook not to enter into 'any coalition or military alliance directed against any power which participated with its armed forces in the war against Germany and in the liberation of Austria'.[35] Soviet initiatives were aimed at trying to keep Austria neutral. No agreement was reached on the future of either country at the conference.

The Soviet hope that Western moves towards European military integration might be slowed down were encouraged, during 1954, by the collapse of the EDC. The French had resisted pressure to be drawn into what they increasingly perceived as an instrument for the revival of Germany, backed by Washington. During the spring of 1954, Dulles had tried to make ratification of the EDC a *sine qua non* of continued American cooperation in Europe.[36] At one point, he even threatened directly to include the Federal Republic in NATO in the event of the EDC failing. This was the very thing which the

French had objected to in 1950.[37] US pressure made Paris extremely wary. The Franco-American relationship was under additional strain at this point because of Washington's refusal actively to support the French in the war in Indo-China. Indeed, Paris linked cooperation on the issue of an EDC with American aid in that theatre.[38] The Americans partially acquiesced and agreed to add Indo-China to the issues to be discussed at the conference in Geneva.[39] Moscow was well aware of this particular tension in the Western alliance and attempted to exploit it by offering to use its influence in Indo-China if Paris were to reject the EDC.[40]

The French refused to ratify the EDC treaty.[41] It was defeated by the opponents of German rearmament, who came from across a broad span of French politics. The Communist Party obviously opposed it,[42] but it was aided by the Gaullists, who believed that France had a special and independent role to play on the continent. Soviet triumph at the failure of the EDC was short-lived. Although the EDC had died in a quagmire of national interests, an alternative arrangement was provided by the British. Churchill and Eden suggested the formation of a West European Union. This proposal involved reviving the idea of the Brussels Treaty of 1948; including Italy and the Federal Republic; and transferring key security decisions to NATO, rather than leaving them in the hands of national governments. Several concessions were made to French concern over German power. The British and the Americans extended guarantees of a troop presence to the continent. Force structures and strategy would be decided by NATO. West Germany would have to accept restrictive measures on its naval and air build-up and, in particular, relinquish the ownership or build-up of nuclear weapons. In return, the West Germans were granted sovereignty and membership of the Atlantic alliance. French fears were, to some extent, mollified by these moves, particularly by the British guarantee, which the French believed would act as a European counterweight to German power.

Stabilisation of the blocs

The Paris treaties, which incorporated these agreements, were signed on 23 October 1954 but not without further opposition from several quarters. The formalisation of the division of Germany, which placed the West German Republic firmly in the Western camp and seemed to relinquish all real hope of unity, aroused hostility in Germany itself. The SPD[43] demanded another conference on the issue, and a series of strikes were organised in favour of at least keeping open the possibility of a unified Germany. This became another avenue along which Moscow pursued its bid to engender opposition to the creation of a Western bloc involving the historic enemy.

Just before the treaties were signed, Moscow suggested that a conference be held to discuss the future of Germany. The Kremlin held out the prospect of discussing the previous Western suggestion of all-German elections, an Austrian peace treaty and atomic disarmament. This seemed to have been designed to appeal to both the French and the West German peoples. The Western governments were not, however, after the exhausting and tortuous negotiations of the previous three years, prepared to open the debate again. Moscow had failed. It faced an increasingly powerful West Germany in a united Western military bloc.

Earlier in the year, Moscow had itself offered to join NATO.[44] After the failure of the Berlin conference, it proposed that a new collective security arrangement for Europe should be considered and stated its readiness to participate in the Treaty Organisation. This suggestion has been dismissed out of hand by many historians, but it is worthy of some consideration. Whilst it was obviously an attempt to delay West European defence integration, it may also have had another purpose. It is possible to speculate that the Soviet leadership differentiated in this period between purely European defence institutions and NATO, with its powerful American component.[45] The latter offered some guarantees on German militarism in a way that the EDC did not. It is noticeable, for example, that, throughout 1953 and 1954, the Soviet press pointed to the inevitability of a German-dominated EDC. It stressed the economic strength of the Federal Republic. If this was indeed a concern for Moscow, a solution might have been to participate in NATO, to operate a stranglehold on Germany and nullify the American strategic threat in one go. Allies could not target each other. The EDC on the other hand, as a solely European body, would be dominated by the most economically powerful European state, West Germany. In the Soviet view, as a military organisation it could only engender German revanchism.[46]

Membership of NATO would, it might be argued, have been the best response to Soviet security requirements. It would have resulted in a pan-European organisation on which both the Americans and the Russians had a firm grip. As this was not achieved, Moscow attempted to manage its security in another way, through acceptance of the bloc structure.

Moscow had to settle for the division of Germany, consolidation of the Eastern bloc and new attempts to harness US power. After the failure to prevent the rearmament of the Federal Republic within NATO, it appears as if those in the Kremlin not closely associated with the proposals for the neutralisation of German power assumed greater influence. On 25 January, Moscow ended its state of war with Germany and announced an intensification of its links with the GDR; the powers of the SED were consolidated.[47]

On 8 February, Malenkov was forced to resign from the office of Prime Minister.[48] Khrushchev's assertion of power, backed by the military, seemed to mark a new period in Soviet foreign policy in Europe. Immediately, he set about the consolidation of control in the east. Stalin had depended upon bilateral relations with the separate East European Communist Parties, and the ties between the eastern states and the Soviet Union essentially rested on the informal understanding of the subordinate role of the satellites to Moscow, backed by the tacit threat of Soviet military power. Khrushchev developed the idea of different 'Roads to Socialism'. This was a move to grant some autonomy to the Eastern bloc states; but it also represented an attempt to make Soviet rule seem more tolerable and sustainable.

Moscow tried to ensure control in the east through the adoption of a formal military structure for the East European armies. Moscow had threatened, in November 1954,[49] to create a defensive organisation in the east if the Paris Treaties went ahead. The Paris agreements were ratified on 26 March 1955, and, a few days later, Moscow invited the other communist states to set up the Warsaw Treaty Organisation. The WTO was formally established on 14 May 1955, to include the Soviet Union, Poland, Czechoslovakia, East Germany, Hungary, Romania, Bulgaria and Albania, just a few days after the Federal Republic became a member of NATO.[50]

According to most Soviet sources, the WTO was founded in response to the Western refusal to accept Soviet proposals for a general European security system that would neutralise Germany.[51] The West had, instead, incorporated the Federal Republic into NATO. Officially, the *raison d'être* of the pact was the threat from German revanchism.[52] Moscow justified the new organisation as a response by the East Europeans to the possibility of German militarism.

The creation of the Warsaw Treaty Organisation provided Moscow with several advantages. The first was that it formalised and controlled military relations among the East European states. During World War II, it is true, regimes subservient to Moscow had been set up throughout the east. But the security relations had been of a bilateral nature, between Moscow and the separate East European capitals, and there had been no systematic attempt to integrate the indigenous forces with those of the Red Army, or, indeed, with each other. The new pact placed the armed forces of the satellite states under the *de facto* control of the Red Army.[53] A joint command of Soviet and East European Armed Forces was set up, which oversaw the defence arrangements within each of the East European states.[54]

The second benefit that Moscow accrued from the setting up of the Warsaw Pact was that it provided Moscow with a new rationale for stationing troops in Eastern Europe. This was particularly useful with regard to both Hungary and Romania, because, when the peace settlement with Austria was signed on 15 May,[55] the original pretext of needing to have troops in those countries to supply the Soviet occupation zone had been removed.

A third, and not insignificant, benefit was that the problem of Germany, at least in one sense, had been resolved. The threat of a unified Germany sitting in the heart of Europe with territorial ambitions had been vanquished under the terms of the Paris agreements. It did not appear likely that the two Germanies would attempt to unite, or, indeed, be permitted to unify. Territorial emasculation, alongside the formal prohibitions on West German military forces, removed one of the historic concerns of Soviet thinking about security. On 7 June, Moscow signalled its acceptance of the new status of the Federal Republic by inviting Adenauer to Moscow for talks.[56] The position was subsequently confirmed when the Soviet Union demanded that the Western powers recognise the sovereign status of the GDR.

Yet while the old threat of German revanchism had been removed, Moscow was now faced with the fact that US troops were permanently located on the continent and represented the mainstay of an anti-Soviet alliance. On the one hand, the very presence of US troops enabled Moscow to claim legitimacy, at least in its own eyes, for its occupation of the Eastern zones and still, in one sense, provided guarantees against revanchism. But, it also meant the permanent stationing, close to Soviet borders, of US ground and air forces and nuclear weapons.[57] This was not regarded with equanimity in Moscow. If the problem of Germany had been managed, the threat of US strategic and tactical power was growing. This concern fed directly into a debate, which had been going on since Stalin's death, over the nature of international relations in the nuclear age and, indeed, over the best options for Soviet security in Europe.

Towards stabilisation: the Soviet debate over strategy and the origins of Soviet thinking about deterrence

One of the major areas of contention between Khrushchev and Malenkov, during the period 1953–55, had been the impact of nuclear power upon military doctrine and foreign affairs. After the explosion of the Soviet hydrogen bomb, in August 1953, Malenkov had propounded radically new ideas for Soviet defence.[58] He argued that the recent Soviet success in exploding a fusion weapon meant that a state of deterrence existed between East and West. That is, that stabilisation had been achieved with Washington. He stated that, because of the Soviet nuclear capability, war would now be disastrous for both communists and capitalists;[59] therefore, peace could be achieved.

This was a radical break from orthodox, Stalinist thinking on the subject. Stalin had dictated that nuclear weapons made no difference to military affairs and that war was inevitable between the sides. During Stalin's lifetime, Soviet thinking had been paralysed by the domination of what were known as the 'permanently operating factors'. Even the explosion of the Soviet fission bomb in 1949 had made little visible impact upon this idea.[60] The permanently operating factors consisted of the stability of the home front; the morale of the armed forces; the quantity and quality of division; the armament of the armed forces and the ability of the commanders.[61] Stalinist military science maintained that other factors, such as surprise, were only a temporary influence upon the outcome of the war and could not be decisive. Capitalism, it was argued, was incapable of developing these five permanently operating factors, and, therefore, capitalist states could not, under any conditions, defeat the socialist bloc in a military contest. Even if a surprise nuclear attack was launched, Soviet military doctrine concentrated upon the ability to plan a counter-offensive which would destroy the enemy.[62]

Stalinist thinking about the international system also enshrined the Leninist notion of the law of the inevitability of war. The world, so Lenin and Stalin had held, was divided into two opposing blocs, which were doomed to conflict.[63] This meant that, in theory, it was impossible for capitalists and socialists to exist without war.

Immediately after Stalin's death, military theorists revised the mission of the Soviet armed forces to take account of the technological changes brought about by nuclear power. They now admitted that a military attack by a foreign power could paralyse the country before Stalin's permanently operating factors could come into action and a counter-offensive be staged.[64] In particular, the importance of 'surprise' as critical to military success became central.

In 1954, Malenkov reiterated and amplified the theme that some form of deterrence existed. He claimed that the Soviet explosion of the hydrogen bomb and the USSR's consequent military strength had brought about new conditions of peace.[65] He pointed out that a future war, because of 'modern' means of warfare, 'would entail the destruction of world civilisation'.[66] Malenkov was, therefore, claiming that a certain stabilisation had been attained between East and West. From this proposition he derived a further conclusion. This was that, because of the Soviet nuclear capability, Washington would be deterred from unleashing a further war. Hence, he argued, Soviet resources could be comfortably diverted away from defence spending to the consumer sector of the economy. In a speech to the Supreme Soviet, shortly after the successful Soviet test of a hydrogen bomb, Malenkov had remarked that

> Hitherto, we have not had the same opportunity to develop light industry and the food industry at the same rate as heavy industry. Now we can, and consequently we must accelerate the development of light industry in every way in the interests of securing a faster rise in the living standards and cultural levels of the people.[67]

So as far as Malenkov was concerned the external threat had been removed, or at least subdued for the immediate future.

This position had not been endorsed either by Khrushchev or by the military. Malenkov's opponent spoke rather of the critical nature of strengthening heavy industrial production. Khrushchev took the view that

> Only on the basis of further development of heavy industry will we be
> able successfully to promote all branches of the national economy, and
> to raise steadily the inviolability of the frontiers of the Soviet Union.[68]

In 1954, shortly after Malenkov had made the connection
between nuclear deterrence and cuts in heavy industry, he was forced
to retract his views. In a speech in April, he returned to the orthodox
view that although both capitalism and socialism would suffer in a
nuclear war, war would actually bring about the downfall of the
capitalist system.[69]

The Soviet service chiefs were forceful in their rejection of Malenkov's beliefs.[70] They did not share his view that the significance of
nuclear weapons was simply to act as a deterrent. Many of them
believed that it was imperative to incorporate nuclear power into
military planning. They reasoned that a future conflict with the West
would almost inevitably escalate into a nuclear confrontation; therefore, the armed forces had to be ready to meet this contingency.

The debate about defence continued throughout 1954–55, revolv-
ing around the issue of nuclear weapons and their impact on both
strategy and resource allocations. Malenkov's reluctance to
acquiesce in the views of his service chiefs engendered powerful
opposition against him.

Khrushchev seems to have backed the military in a pragmatic bid
to gain their support to oust Malenkov. On coming to power in
1955, his opinions changed on the issues of the external threat, and
he hi-jacked Malenkov's ideas on security. Khrushchev began to
propound the idea that a certain stability had been brought about by
nuclear power, and developed a theory of deterrence.

The theory of deterrence which developed under Khrushchev had
two central tenets. The first was a military-technical consideration
that, essentially, the military were correct in assuming that Soviet
armed forces had to be prepared to fight and win a nuclear war. The
second tenet was that a foreign policy programme had to be devised
to avert the risk of a confrontation in the first place. So Soviet
deterrence theory rested on the idea of armed forces tasked to win a
nuclear confrontation, and a political policy designed to avoid just
such a confrontation.[71]

These two aspects of deterrence theory are apparent in 1955. As
the Soviet armed forces prepared to 'win' the future conflict, and the

creation of the WTO was a preliminary step, Khrushchev sought ways of easing tensions with the West. He did this in two ways. The first was by demonstrating a willingness to negotiate on the outstanding issues of the peace settlement after World War II, and the second was by seeking arms control and disarmament agreements which would have harnessed US power.

Khrushchev felt that he was able to do this because the central front in Europe had been stabilised by the creation of the two blocs, and the strategic relationship had been stabilised through Soviet nuclear power. This latter idea was expressed at the Twentieth Party Congress in 1956, but in 1955, Khrushchev was able to display a much greater flexibility in European strategies.

Almost simultaneously with the creation of the Warsaw Treaty Organisation, the Austrian state treaty was signed. Moscow had indicated its willingness two months before to reopen talks on the settlement. The treaty established Austria as a neutral state, and it called for the withdrawal of foreign forces. Commentators have expressed surprise that Moscow was willing to withdraw its troops from a strategically important area of Central Europe, but it made some important gains from the settlement.

First, from a purely military point of view, it might be argued that Moscow gained space with the withdrawal of Western forces from a part of central Austria. Even if Austria had not been pulled into the Eastern bloc, it had been denied to the Western alliance. This had been a continuous concern for Moscow and, with the integration of West Germany into NATO, it must have been heightened. Better by far to have a neutral Austria than one aligned with NATO. Indeed, the neutrality of Austria actually provided a territorial barrier between the NATO allies, Italy and West Germany.

Second, the move on the Austrian question was a step towards the reduction of the probability of hostilities. The settlement, together with the division of Germany, paved the way for the first summit between the heads of government since Potsdam. The conference, held in Geneva during July, gave birth to the title of the Geneva Spirit, although little that was concrete was achieved.

Khrushchev, in his memoirs, states that he regarded this conference as a major test for his leadership.[72] He reveals that the Soviet leaders felt a deep sense of intimidation, despite the hydrogen bomb, in relation to US technology.[73] This was reminiscent of early Soviet worries about the United States and its economic and technical power, but, like Stalin, Khrushchev did not allow it to affect his negotiating tactics. The Soviet leader seemed determined to negotiate only from a position of apparent strength. He refused to allow the issue of international communism to be discussed; nor would he sanction debate on the control of Eastern Europe.

The main Soviet proposal at the conference returned to the theme of German unity. The Soviet delegation called for the mutual dissolution of NATO and the WTO, together with the gradual withdrawal of all foreign forces from the continent. This was to be followed by a pan-European security treaty. The offer is interesting. What it envisaged was that the two-bloc structure would oversee the transition away from an East–West cleavage[74] to a general security arrangement in which, it might be argued, after the withdrawal of US forces, the Soviet Union would be the dominant power. But it is quite clear that Moscow did not envisage giving up Eastern Germany. Both at the Geneva summit and again later in the year, Soviet leaders refused to countenance all-German elections; Khrushchev revealed that he did not believe that the East German working class would give up their 'socialist gains'.[75] Moscow would never allow them to be put to the test. Moscow remained adamant that genuinely free elections, as suggested by the British, would not be permitted. This points to concern over Soviet control in Eastern Europe generally and to a deeper anxiety about the prospects for the control of a unified Germany.

Moscow still appeared to be worried by the possibility of the Eastern zone of Germany being pulled into the Western camp. Adenauer visited Moscow in September 1955 for talks and offered financial assistance in return for unification. His terms amounted to an effort to 'buy' the Eastern zone from Moscow. Khrushchev was unwilling to accept such an offer: he believed that to do so would lead to the fragmentation of the Eastern bloc.[76] Internal control was critical in this period, as the events of 1956 in Hungary would reveal.

By the beginning of 1956, the stage was set for Khrushchev's denunciations of Stalin and Stalinist thinking about international relations. At the Twentieth Party Congress, Khrushchev declared that war was no longer fatalistically inevitable between the two systems and that peaceful coexistence was possible. This redefinition of Soviet thinking about the outside world had been made possible by the Soviet acquisition of nuclear power. The position had been partly stabilised with Washington, even though US technology was still much further advanced.

Stabilisation between East and West was also noticeable in Europe. Moscow had accepted a divided Europe with US troops as a permanent feature. However, there was a problem for Stalin's successors. Once US forces in Europe became nuclear-armed, they had a fundamental effect upon Soviet military-political planning. With the establishment of US bases around the periphery of Soviet-controlled territory, nuclear forces that could threaten the homeland were close to Soviet borders. The decision to give priority to the deployment of Soviet medium-range systems in the late 1950s arose, at least in part, from a consideration of this US nuclear presence in Western Europe.[77] The American nuclear presence also had an effect upon Soviet military doctrine. The mission of the Red Army was in the first instance to rebuff the enemy and once war started, to carry out offensive operations into Western Europe. This threat of a rapid Soviet offensive, it was hoped, would act as a deterrent against attack by the US Air Force.[78]

The increasing nuclear threat to the USSR from American forces in Europe during the mid- to late-1950s obviously complicated the Soviet view of a US troop presence. The benefits to be accrued from a military-political stranglehold on Germany had to be weighed against a European nuclear threat manipulated from Washington. This paradox continued to remain one of the fundamental problems for Soviet strategies in Europe throughout the post-war period. Did the stability offered by US troops outweigh any potential threat? On the whole the Kremlin believed that it could manage the US threat through diplomacy and arms control while using the stability of the bloc structure to maintain control in the east.

Conclusion

By 1956, the Cold War bloc structure had stabilised. American troops were installed in continental Europe in a system which would ensure that they would remain there. Germany was no longer a threat as a potential European superpower: it had been carved up between the Eastern and Western blocs. The remnant of the German threat, the Federal Republic, was occupied by United States forces and could not be expected to demonstrate any aggression beyond that which Washington might itself display. A *status quo* had been established; deterrence would maintain the new order.

The Eastern bloc was united under the WTO and was under Moscow's *de facto* control. In addition to offering a substantial military resource, the satellite states acted as a forward defensive buffer which could absorb, or at least postpone, territorial incursion.

Washington was regarded as a threat, but, because of the Soviet fusion capability, it was a threat that could be managed. The emasculation of Germany, and the Eastern bloc structure, meant that the old fear of German aggression had diminished, yet American troops appear still to have been regarded as a positive presence in Germany. The Soviet offer to join NATO and the strenuous efforts made to avoid the creation of an all-European defence league incorporating West Germany suggest that a US garrison, as a moderating influence, was still welcomed.

A powerful Western bloc incorporating the United States was also of some domestic value. It meant that the Kremlin could claim that its tight hold on the East European reins was justified as essential for defence. The maintenance of a military structure capable of 'winning' a future war was a criterion of successful deterrence and thus peace. This, in turn, created its own advantages and disadvantages. Large troop numbers allowed successful repression within those areas of the Soviet Union in which the potential for dissent existed. Soviet leaders would not have forgotten the numbers that had to be allocated to the Ukraine in the wake of the Second World War. The disadvantage was obvious in terms of cost, but it was a cost that the Kremlin was prepared to bear until 1990.

Notes

1 Anthony D'Agnostino, *Soviet Succession Struggles. Kreminology and the Russian Question from Lenin to Gorbachev* (Boston: Allen and Unwin, 1988).

2 See Decisions of 'Joint Meeting of the Plenary Session of the Central Committee of the Communist Party of the Soviet Union, USSR Council of Ministers and Presidium of the USSR, Supreme Soviet', *Pravda*, 7 March 1953, p. 1, quoted in *Current Digest of the Soviet Press*, Vol. V, no. 7, 1953, p. 6.

3 See L. Slepov, 'Collectivity is the Highest Principle in Party Leadership', *Pravda*, 16 April 1953, p. 2. Cited in *CDSP*, Vol. V, no. 13, 1953, p. 3.

4 *New York Times*, 12 May 1953.

5 In an editorial on President Eisenhower, *Pravda* was critical of Eisenhower's continuation of what they perceived as an anti-Soviet line, but

expressed Moscow's willingness to negotiate with the new administration. See 'On President Eisenhower's Speech', *Pravda*, 25 April 1953. Quoted in *CDSP*, Vol. V, no. 14, pp. 5–8.

6   'Statement by Chou En-lai, Minister of Foreign Affairs of Central People's Government of Chinese People's Republic', *Pravda*, 31 March 1953. Quoted in *CDSP*, Vol. V, no. 30, pp. 3–12 and p. 26.

7   H. A. Turner, *The Two Germanies since 1945* (New Haven and London: Yale University Press, 1987), p. 117.

8   *Neues Deutschland*, 11 June 1953, cited in W. Loth, *The Division of the World* (London: Routledge, 1988), p. 270.

9   Nicolaevsky claimed that Churchill's call for negotiation with the Soviet Union had been inspired by suggestions from Beria. See B. Nicolaevsky, 'Sovetsyaiya diktatura i germanskaia problema', *Sotsialisticheskii vestnik*, November 1955, pp. 209–10. Quoted in A. D'Agnostino, *Soviet Succession Struggles*, p. 183.

10   Speech of 8 March 1963, quoted in *Neues Deutschland*, 14 March 1963, cited in Loth, *Divison of the World*, p. 269.

11   See chapter 3.

12   See chapter 3 for Beria's association with Malenkov in the Eastern zones of Germany.

13   See note 9.

14   Andrei Gromyko, *Memoirs*, trans. Harols Shukman (London: Hutchinson, 1989), p. 316, quoted in Amy Knight, *Beria, Stalin's First Lieutenant* (Princeton: Princeton University Press, 1993), p. 316.

15   See J. M. Mackintosh, *Strategy and Tactics of Soviet Foreign Policy* (London: Oxford University Press, 1962), p. 77.

16   Ibid. See also Stephen S. Kaplan, *Diplomacy of Power. Soviet Armed Forces as a Political Instrument* (Washington, DC: Brookings Institution, 1981), pp. 72–5.

17   See Amy Knight's work, *Beria*.

18   *Pravda*, 4, 6, 7 April 1953. Quoted in Knight, *Beria*, p. 184.

19   For the origins of French thinking on the EDC, see chapter 5.

20   For a description of Adenauer's views see K. Adenauer, trans. by Beate Ruhm von Oppen, *Konrad Adenauer. Memoirs 1945–53* (London: Weidenfeld and Nicolson, 1965), pp. 311–12.

21   Ibid.

22   Hans-Jürgen Grabbe, 'Konrad Adenauer, John Foster Dulles, and West German-American Relations', in Richard H. Immerman, ed., *John Foster Dulles and the Diplomacy of the Cold War* (Princeton: Princeton University Press, 1990), pp. 109–32.

23   Ibid.

24   Ibid.

25   Ibid.

26   Moscow had consistently refused to contemplate free elections in

Germany. For an assessment of the situation, see Dean Acheson, *Present at the Creation. My Years in the State Department* (New York: Norton, 1969), pp. 622–50.

27 For an American perspective on the debate see Dean Acheson, *Present at the Creation*, pp. 622–50.

28 See Yu. Pavlov, 'In Defiance of Public Opinion', *Pravda*, 8 January 1954. Quoted in *CDSP*, Vol. 1, no. 1, p. 9.

29 See, for example, 'They have learned Nothing', *Pravda*, 2 January 1954. Quoted in *CDSP*, Vol. 1, no. 5, p. 10.

30 See V. Shumilin, 'Behind the Scenes of the Bonn Miracle', *Trud*, 12 January 1954, 12, 3. Quoted in *CDSP*, Vol. VI, no. 2, p. 19.

31 Draft Interim Status for Germany and Related Draft European Security Treaty, Proposed by the Soviet Delegation, 10 February 1954. Foreign Ministers' Meeting; Berlin Discussions, 25 January–18 February 1954. Department of State Publication, 5399, pp. 223–5.

32 Ibid.

33 Ibid.

34 See Yu. Zhukov and D. Kraminov, 'Berlin Conference', *Pravda*, 1 February 1954, p. 3. Quoted in *CDSP*, Vol. VI, no. 1, p. 5.

35 P. V. Curl, *Documents in American Foreign Relations,* Council on Foreign Relations, (New York: Harper, 1955), p. 62.

36 In his first national address as Secretary of State, Dulles had made his commitment to the EDC clear; he said that 'if France, Germany and England should go their separate ways . . . it would be necessary to give a little rethinking to America's own foreign policy in relation to Western Europe'. Dulles had threatened an agonising reappraisal of basic United States policy if the EDC was not ratified. Dulles to the North Atlantic Council Meeting, 13 December 1953, *FRUS*, 1952–54. Quoted in R. Steinberger, 'The EDC and the German Question', in Richard H. Immerman, *Dulles*, p. 86.

37 Department of State Memorandum, 740.5/10–2850. A memo for the Secretary of State noted that the French seemed determined that there should be no German army.

38 For a discussion of Franco-American disagreements over Indo-China, see Dwight D. Eisenhower, *The White House Years. Mandate for Change 1953–1956* (London: Heinemann, 1963), pp. 332–47.

39 Ibid.

40 For a short discussion of the Soviet role in ending the war in Indo-China see W. Loth, *The Division of the World 1941–1955* (London: Routledge, 1988), p. 277.

41 Throughout the post-war period, Moscow consistently targeted France as the country most opposed to Western defence integration. Successive Soviet leaders saw quite rightly that French leaders sought an independent foreign policy outside Western alliance politics. See N. Yuryev, 'Franco-American Discord', *International Affairs*, Moscow, No. 3, 1987,

pp. 51–5.

42   For the twists and turns in the internal politics of the French Communist Party in the early Cold War, see Marshall Shulman, *Stalin's Foreign Policy Reappraised* (Cambridge, Mass.: Harvard University Press, 1969), pp. 213–18.

43   See Wilfried Loth, *Division of the World*, p. 294.

44   See Soviet Note of 31 March 1954 to the US Government, Post-Berlin Conference Exchanges on the Questions of Germany, Austria and European Security. Quoted in P. V. Curl, *Documents in American Foreign Relations*, pp. 229–32.

45   For this interpretation of Soviet policy in the 1970s, see L. Freedman, 'The United States Factor', in G. Segal and E. Moreton, ed., *Soviet Strategy towards Western Europe* (London: Allen and Unwin, 1984), pp. 87–110.

46   It is interesting that the EDC is singled out as a been particularly dangerous for European security in this period. See, for example, Major-General V. Mokovsky, *Znamya*, no. 2, February 1955, pp. 115–25, quoted in *CDSP*, Vol VII, no. 18, pp. 7–8 and 14.

47   For the impact of Moscow's policies on the GDR, see D. Childs, *The GDR. Moscow's German Ally* (London: Unwin Hyman, 1988), Second Edition, pp. 44–5.

48   Anthony F. D'Agnostino, *Soviet Succession Struggles*, p. 185.

49   *Pravda*, 14 November 1954.

50   The Pact was formally modelled on the organisational arrangements of NATO. See R. Garthoff, *Soviet Military Policy. A Historical Analysis* (London: Faber and Faber, 1966), p. 149.

51   V. F. Maltsev, ed., *Organizatsiva Varshavskogo Dogovora 1955–1985* (Moscow: Izdatel'stvo Politicheskoi Literatury, 1986), p. 9.

52   Ibid.

53   'Establishment of a Joint Command of the Armed Forces of the Signatories to the Treaty of Friendship, Cooperation, and Mutual Assistance', *New Times*, no. 21, 21 May 1955, 68.

54   Robin Alison Remington, *The Warsaw Pact Case Studies in Communist Conflict Resolution* (Cambridge, Mass.: MIT Press, 1971), p. 20.

55   This is discussed later in the chapter.

56   See D. Childs, *The GDR*, p. 45.

57   This was critical because the United States had introduced tactical weapons into Europe in 1952. See D. Holloway, *The Soviet Union and the Arms Race* (New Haven and London: Yale University Press, 1983), p. 36.

58   See chapter 4 for Malenkov's views on this issue in 1949.

59   D'Agnostino, *Soviet Succession Struggles*, p. 184. It might be argued that Malenkov had been formulating this idea of deterrence for a considerable period of time. Already in a speech on 7 November 1949 he had said that if the imperialists decided to unleash a third world war, the war would be the graveyard not only of the imperialists but the whole system. *Pravda*, 7

November 1949. This of course raises the issue of Stalin's thinking on the subject. There is little evidence that Stalin himself supported this view in this period.

60   Stalin's view was that 'atomic bombs are only for those with weak nerves'. Quoted in David Holloway, *The Soviet Union*, p. 27.

61   See David Holloway, *The Soviet Union*, p. 36.

62   Ibid.

63   See J. Stalin, 'The Foundations of Leninism', Lectures delivered at the Sverdlov University, 1924, in Bruce Franklin, ed., *The Essential Stalin. Major Theoretical Writings 1902–52* (London: Croom Helm, 1973), p. 89.

64   See D. Holloway, *The Soviet Union*, p. 36.

65   *Pravda*, 13 March 1954.

66   Ibid.

67   *Pravda*, 9 August 1953.

68   *Pravda*, 28 December 1954.

69   *Pravda*, 27 April 1954.

70   For a discussion of the debates among the military see J. M. Mackintosh, *Strategy and Tactics*, p. 96.

71   For many in the West the so-called nuclear war fighting doctrine of the Soviet armed forces, actually served to undercut Soviet foreign policy initiatives. Khrushchev's continual inflation of the Soviet nuclear arsenal and his threats to 'win' a nuclear war rendered him unreliable not only in Western eyes but after the humiliation of the Cuban Missile Crisis in those of the Soviet elite.

72   E. Crankshaw, *Khrushchev Remembers* (Boston: Little Brown, 1971), p. 392.

73   Ibid.

74   See Soviet Proposal of a Collective Security Treaty in Europe, July 20 1955, in Paul E. Zinner, *Documents in American Foreign Relations 1955*, Council on Foreign Relations (New York: Harper Brothers, 1956), p. 210.

75   Quoted in David J. Dallin, *Soviet Foreign Policy after Stalin* (Philadelphia: Lippincott, 1961), pp. 283.

76   E. Crankshaw, *Khrushchev Remembers*, p. 358.

77   David Holloway, *The Soviet Union*, p. 67.

78   Michael McGwire, *Perestroika and Soviet National Security* (Washington: Brookings Institution, 1991), pp. 18–19.

Conclusion

Strategies of Soviet foreign policy

Moscow and the Cold War

This study began as an attempt to fill a gap in the Western Cold War literature. It raised the possibility, ignored in most of the existing literature, that the Kremlin saw some good arising from a US troop presence in Europe after 1943. This idea was not, necessarily, to support a revisionist interpretation: that Stalin was wholly inclined to cooperate with the United States, and that the Cold War arose out of the American refusal to deal with Moscow. The idea was, rather, to move away from the old debate about who was to blame for the Cold War, and instead to examine the nature of Soviet security requirements in Europe, and to see whether a US military presence hindered or helped them.

Although originally a revolutionary regime, dedicated to the ideals of Marx and Lenin, the Soviet government rapidly jettisoned the active pursuit of revolution. Civil war, external intervention and the unmitigated hostility of the Western powers meant that the dominant concern of the Soviet leadership was the security and survival of the new Soviet state. The demands of survival necessitated the adoption of the apparatus of a 'normal' state, such as strong armed forces, secure borders and acceptance by the international community. The revolution was postponed indefinitely, and the Soviet leadership set about the tasks of internal modernisation.

The combination of a revolutionary heritage and economic weakness placed the Soviet Union in a uniquely awkward position. The role of the Soviet leadership and indeed of the Soviet Union was premised upon the notion of revolution. It was this claim that denied the legitimacy of other non-Marxist–Leninist states and aroused their hostility. Yet to survive, because of its economic dependence upon the West, Moscow had to find accommodation with the very capitalist states it was dedicated to destroying.

The years between 1917 and 1943 were formative ones, when certain patterns of Soviet foreign policy behaviour emerged. Survival, self-sufficiency and internal reconstruction were the key concerns. Technological inferiority drove the Soviet leadership to dependence on foreign powers for new technologies and underlined the feelings of both economic and military vulnerability. There was a determination to stave off war by forming tactical alliances where necessary. From the beginning of the Soviet period, there remained an ideologically motivated belief in an ability to exploit the contradictions among the capitalist states.

Of the capitalist states, Moscow's central preoccupation was with Germany. The treatment of Germany at Versailles meant that, like the USSR, it was a state outside the usual workings of the European system. An uneasy alliance was formed through which Moscow gained access to technology and training. Yet this alliance also helped provide the Germans with the requirements that they needed to rebuild their own state and helped lead to the re-emergence of Germany as a major force. Throughout the 1920s and 1930s, Moscow sought to forge alliances with the capitalist states to prevent the renewal of German militarism. The timing of the German invasion of 1941 was a traumatic shock for the Soviet leadership, and this, combined with the massive losses during the war, engendered a desire to exact the harshest possible settlement on Germany after it had been defeated. Hatred and fear became the enduring legacies.

The war years were spent in a desperate battle for survival. After 1943, and with the launching of the second front, Stalin started to outline his requirements for the peace. First, he demanded space on the Soviet periphery, through the annexation or control of territory. Second, he demanded complete subjugation of German power. For the former aim he used Soviet troops to achieve a pattern of occupation, and, for the latter, he called upon the aid of the United States.

Through a combination of diplomacy and troop movements, Stalin operated a strategy of denial to British and American influence in Eastern Europe. He used the Red Army to occupy Eastern Europe and hence to ensure *de facto* control. He also attempted, through the use of diplomatic measures, to assert special rights in the east. While excluding American influence in one part of Europe, Stalin sought its long-term presence and aid in another, Germany. It was Stalin who suggested the American occupation of a zone in both Germany and Austria, it was Roosevelt who hesitated.

The Soviet ability to distinguish between capitalist states became clear during the war years. Stalin differentiated between British and American objectives in Europe. He perceived Churchill, quite accurately, as far more hostile to Soviet security requirements than either Roosevelt or, initially, Truman.

At the Potsdam conference, Soviet security requirements were changed by the news of the American atomic bomb. In this respect, historians of the revisionist school are correct: it was indeed a turning point. The victory which had been secured over Germany, at enormous cost, had not been rendered meaningless, but could no longer guarantee future Soviet security. Soviet technological inferiority had been dramatically underlined. Yet Stalin was determined not to let it matter in terms of external policy. The superficial lack of concern at the news concealed a grim determination to catch up.

The news of the atomic bomb did, however, cause a dilemma. It made the strategic necessity of controlling Eastern Europe even more acute, not least in terms of air defence. Yet Moscow did not want to provoke an increasingly adversarial Truman administration over the future of Eastern Europe. From the summer of 1945 until early 1946, Moscow still pursued a policy of cooperation. The troop withdrawals from Czechoslovakia demonstrated that Moscow still had a vested interest in working with Washington. Similarly, the Soviet withdrawal from northern Iran was dictated by a desire not to antagonise the United States.

Throughout the period 1945–47, Moscow pursued contradictory strategies in the Eastern zone of Germany. There were disagreements amongst the Soviet leadership about what course of action should be pursued, but no serious attempt was made to raise the issue of US troops in Germany.

During 1948, the Soviet leadership embarked upon strategies of consolidation, both in response to US actions and because of developments within the communist bloc itself. There was little doubt that signs of bloc cohesion in the West, in the form of the Marshall Plan, caused alarm. The Soviet response was to put its relations with the satellites in Eastern Europe on a firmer footing through the treaties of friendship and cooperation. Any latitude that might have existed over allowing countries such as Czechoslovakia to deviate from Moscow's *diktat* was firmly reduced. The Cominform meeting of 1947 signalled for many in the West a more aggressive foreign policy, but the activities of the Cominform were also aimed at promoting a stricter bloc line. In particular, it was intended to make Tito follow a more pro-Soviet line. Indeed, the entire Berlin crisis of 1948 arose out of a desire to 'shut down' and control the Eastern bloc. This miscalculation, again over American responses, led to the creation of NATO and an anti-Soviet alliance centred on West Germany.

The period of 1949–53 was marked by intense opposition by the Kremlin to moves in the West to integrate West Germany into European defence arrangements. A series of initiatives were launched to manipulate what the Kremlin saw as 'contradictions' between the capitalist states to prevent this.

Yet, alongside this attempt to dilute Western cohesion, Moscow encouraged communist activity in Asia which merely gave impetus to moves towards greater cooperation in the West. The attack by North Korea on South Korea marked a more militant phase of communist activity in the Far East. Again, Moscow had not intended to challenge or antagonise Washington and, indeed, tried to limit the consequences of its actions in this respect. Nevertheless, the Korean War provided the impetus in the West for the rearmament of Moscow's historic enemy, Germany, and the incorporation of another enemy, Japan, into the Western security system.

Towards the end of Stalin's life, initiatives were made to prohibit the re-establishment of German power. Moscow even held out the prospect that it would be willing to accept a neutralised and unified Germany. This would have meant the removal of US troops from Germany. In one fell swoop, it might be claimed, Moscow would have achieved the destruction of German military power and removed the backbone of NATO–US troops. The flaw in this interpretation is that it does not take account of Soviet fears of Germany. Soviet security polices were not simply determined by a desire to remove US troops; they were fundamentally concerned with German power.

The death of Stalin was a turning point for Soviet foreign policy in many ways. The new leaders adopted a policy of limited restructuring, both in domestic and in foreign affairs. The struggle for power between Malenkov and Khrushchev dominated the politics of the Kremlin, but both had a general commitment to an easing of tensions with the West. In part, this resulted from a feeling amongst the leadership, but most notably expressed by Malenkov, that because of the successful explosion of the hydrogen bomb, Moscow no longer had to fear being 'frozen' into a position of significant technological inferiority. He put forward the idea that a situation of deterrence existed that stabilised the relationship between East and West. Khrushchev, who, for tactical reasons, initially opposed such a view, eventually adopted this position. The result was that from 1953 to 1956 the Soviet leadership sought to defuse tension from a position of growing strength.

Throughout this period there were also the familiar attempts, characteristic of Soviet foreign policy, to manipulate what were perceived as tensions between the Western states, particularly over the issue of Germany. Once more the belief emerged that the Western bloc was not a cohesive, and there were attempts to separate French ambitions *vis-à-vis* Germany from those of Washington.

The issues of Germany and German power remained a central preoccupation. Moscow's ambition was to try to ensure that West Germany did not become the mainstay of a West European defence alliance or enter NATO. In the end it had no choice but to settle for a divided Germany with a powerful West Germany included within NATO.

This was not the worst possible outcome for Moscow. A divided Germany at least consolidated Soviet power in the east and undermined potential German revanchism. The creation of the Warsaw Pact, in effect, evidenced acceptance of the division of Germany and, indeed, in many respects legitimated, in Soviet eyes, at least, if not in those of the Eastern Europeans, Soviet control of the satellite states. Moscow thereby had the satisfaction of negotiating from what it saw as a position of formal equality with another pact. This of course did not remove the problem of US strategic and military power, but Moscow adopted new strategies of deterrence to try to minimise the US nuclear threat.

The academic debate

The academic literature on the Cold War is located firmly in time and place. The traditionalists, including people such as George Kennan, on the whole created their premises about the Soviet role in the Cold War at the height of the Cold War in the 1940s and 1950s. Kennan for example, was close to the debate within the Truman administration about Soviet power and American opposition. At this stage, the literature on the Cold War depicted Moscow, motivated by Marxist–Leninist ideology, as bent on the pursuit of expansionist, anti-democratic impulses both in Europe and globally. The Soviet leadership was seen as monolithic, aggressive and dedicated to challenging US strength both politically, through foreign Communist Parties, and militarily, through the use of its satellites.

The subsequent, revisionist school of thinking placed the blame for the Cold War on the shoulders of successive American administrations. It pointed to the use of American nuclear and economic superiority to bully Moscow, and some of it depicted US power as malevolent and geared to the destruction of the Soviet Union. For a period in the 1960s, some of the revisionists allowed the trauma of the US experience in Vietnam to raise hostile questions about aspects of recent American foreign policy.

The neo-revisionists, who first entered the academic debate during the period of detente with Moscow, have tried to balance the two extremes of interpretation. They have pointed far more to the ambiguities that the sudden acquisition of global power provided for Washington during the Cold War.[1] But they have also pointed to the geopolitical imperatives of the United States that made it inevitable that there would be a clash of interests with the Soviet Union.

It is said that historians often write the history that access to documents allows them to. This was certainly true of the neo-revisionists, who having acquired access to US diplomatic papers from the early Cold War period proceeded to pick over the evidence. They, on the whole, provided an invaluable service by pointing to US concerns. The debate was, however, lopsided and it is only and somewhat ironically since the very collapse of the Soviet Union that we can begin to fully understand the Soviet side of the story.

This book, too, is a product of its time. The Soviet Union has collapsed and scholars in the field are more aware than ever of the limits of the power that Moscow possessed. We are aware as never before of its economic fragility, its technological inferiority, and its tenuous grip upon empire. The events of 1989/90 showed that deep-seated concern about the nature of German power on the continent remained. The limitations of Soviet policy in Eastern Europe have also been painfully underlined. A fascinating tale is beginning to emerge from work in the East European archives that promises to reveal fully the nature of Soviet anxieties over the Eastern bloc and point to an immense preoccupation on the Soviet side with establishing and maintaining the empire in Eastern Europe.

This study has raised questions about the behaviour of the former Soviet Union during the Cold War that are similar to those which the neo-revisionists have raised in relation to Washington in the same period. Was there uncertainty and ambivalence in Soviet behaviour in Europe? Was there an attempt at cooperation with Washington? It has answered them in the affirmative. This book asserts that these concerns were present in the period under review and points to the dilemmas for Moscow in trying to subdue its historic enemy, Germany, with the aid of its new enemy, Washington. It points to a complex set of priorities in Moscow after World War II that are worthy of further research. As the Moscow archives continue to 'yield' secrets, we will learn much more of the Soviet 'side' of the Cold War. This book claims only to add to the beginning of a new debate. The time is ripe for 'revising neo-revisionism'[2] to include the Soviet side.

Notes

1 J. L. Gaddis, *The United States and the Origins of the Cold War 1941–1947* (New York: Columbia University Press, 1972).

2 I am grateful to Elizabeth Kane for this phrase.

Select bibliography

Documents

Papers of the National Archives of the United States, Washington DC.
Truman Papers.
Papers of the Department of State, Record Group 59.
The Records of the Joint Chiefs of Staff, Record Group 218.

Collections of documents

Documents on American Foreign Relations 1952, ed. C. W. Baier and R. P. Stebbins, Council on Foreign Relations (New York: Harper, 1953).
Documents on American Foreign Relations 1954, ed. P. V. Curt, Council on Foreign Relations (New York: Harper, 1955).
Documents on American Foreign Relations 1955, ed. Paul E. Zinner, Council on Foreign Relations (New York: Harper, 1956).
Documents of the National Security Council 1947–1977, ed. Paul Kesaris (Washington DC, 1981), Brotherton Library, Leeds University.
Records of the Joint Chiefs of Staff Part 2, *1946–1953, The Soviet Union*, ed. Paul Kesaris (Washington DC, 1979) Brotherton Library, Leeds University.
US Department of State, *Foreign Relations of the United States 1943–1955*. (*FRUS*. Referred to, in text, by year and by volume.)
US Department of State, *The Berlin Crisis. A Report on the Moscow Discussions* (Washington DC: Government Printing Office, 1948).
Sovetskiy Soyuz na mezhdunarodnykh konferentsiyakh perioda Velikoy Otechestovennoy voyny 1941–1945:
Berlinskaya (Postdamskaya) konferentsiya rukovoditeley trekh soyuznykh derzhav SSSR. SShA i Velikobritanii (Moscow: Izdatel'stvo politicheskoy literatury, 1980).
Tegeranskaya konferentsiya rukovoditeley trekh soyuznykh derzhav SSSR, SShA i Velikobritanii (Moscow: Izdatel'stvo politischeskoy literatury, 1984).

Krymskaya konferentsiya rukovoditeley trekh soyuznykh derzhav SSSR, SShA i Velikobritanii (Moscow: Izdatel'stvo politicheskoy literatury, 1984).

Otnosheniya Sovetskogo soyuza s narodnoy Koreey 1945–1980, dokumenty i materialy (Moscow: Nauka, 1981).

M. Carlyle, ed., *Documents on International Affairs 1947–1948* (London: Oxford University Press, 1952).

J. Degras, ed., *The Communist International 1919–1943*. Documents, Vol. 1, 1919–22 (London, New York and Toronto: Oxford University Press, 1956).

B. Franklin, ed., *The Essential Stalin. Major Theoretical Writings 1905–52* (London: Croom Helm, 1973).

V. I. Lenin, *Collected Works*, Vol. 26 (Moscow: Progress Publishers, 1964).

V. I. Lenin, *Collected Works*, Vol. 31 (Moscow: Progress Publishers, 1966).

V. M. Molotov, *Problems of Foreign Policy. Speeches and Statements, April 1945–November 1948* (Moscow: Foreign Languages Publishing House, 1949).

J. V. Stalin, *Works*, Vol. 7, 1925 (Moscow: Foreign Languages Publishing House, 1954).

Stalin's Correspondence with Churchill, Attlee, Roosevelt and Truman 1941–1945 (London: Lawrence and Wishart, 1958), originally published as *Correspondence between the Chairman of the Council of Ministers of the USSR and the Presidents of the USA and the Prime Ministers of Great Britain during the Great Patriotic War of 1941–1945*, 2 vols. (Moscow: Foreign Language Publishing House, 1957).

L. Woodward and R. Butler, eds., *Documents on British Foreign Policy 1919–1939*, Vol. 1 (London: HMSO, 1949), Document 122.

The Bolsheviks and the October Revolution: Central Commitee Minutes of the RSDLP, 1917–1918 (London: Penguin, 1966).

Published papers

James Richter, 'Reexamining Soviet Policy towards Germany during the Beria Interregnum'. Working Paper No. 3. Cold War International History Project, Woodrow Wilson Center for Scholars, June 1992.

Kathryn Weathersby, 'Soviet Aims in Korea and the Origins of the Korean War, 1945–1950. New Evidence from the Russian Archives'. Cold War International History Project, Woodrow Wilson International Center for Scholars, November 1993.

Unpublished papers

S. Kudryashov, 'The Central Committee of the All-Union Communist Party and Eastern Europe 1945–1953. New Documents', Keynote Lecture given at the British International History Group Annual Conference, 1992, University of Leeds.

V. L. Mal'Kov, 'Soviet–American Relations, 1917–1940'. Paper prepared for seminar on the Origins of the Cold War. Sponsored by the United States Institute for Peace and the Research Coordination Centre, Ministry of Foreign Affairs, USSR, June 1990.

Newspapers

Pravda
Izvestiya
Krasnaya Zvezda
New York Times
Current Digest of the Soviet Press

Journals

Bolshevik/Kommunist
Foreign Affairs
For a Lasting Peace For a People's Democracy
International Affairs (Moscow)
International Security
Soviet Studies
Voprosy Ekonomiki
Voprosy istorii
Voprosy Filosofii

Articles

P. A. Allum and D. Sassoon, 'Italy' in M. M. McCauley, ed., *Communist Power in Europe 1941–1949* (London: Macmillan, 1977), p. 178.

Gar Alperovitz, 'More on Atomic Diplomacy', *Bulletin of the Atomic Scientists*, Vol. 41, no. 11, December 1985.

Caroline Anstey, 'The Projection of British Socialism. Foreign Office Publicity and American Opinion, 1945–50', *Journal of Contemporary History*, Vol. 19, no. 3, 1984.

J. A. Armstrong, 'W. G. Hahn and Post-War Soviet Politics. The Fall of Zhdanov and the Defeat of Moderation', Book Review, *Soviet Studies*, Vol. XXXV, no. 3, 1983, pp. 418–19.

Victor Baras, 'Stalin's Foreign Policy after Stalin', *Slavic Review*, Vol. 37, no. 2, June 1978.

K. Booth, 'Soviet Defence Policy', in J. Baylis, K. Booth, J. Garnett and P. Williams, *Contemporary Strategy, Theories and Policies* (Beckenham, Kent, Croom Helm, 1975).

P. Chuikov, 'Uchenie Lenina–Stalina o voynakh spravedlivykh i nespravedlivykh', *Bolshevik*, no. 7–8, 1945.

Robin Edmonds, 'Yalta and Potsdam. Forty Years Afterwards', *International Affairs*, Vol. 62, no. 2, 1986.

J. Erickson, 'The Origins of the Red Army', in R. P. Pipes, ed., *The Russian Revolution* (Cambridge, Mass.: Harvard University Press, 1968).

M. Evangelista, 'Stalin's Post-War Army Reappraised', *International Security*, winter 1982–83.

P. Fedoseev, 'Marksizm–Leninizm ob istokakh i kharaktere voyn', *Bolshevik*, no. 16, 1945.

M. Steven Fish, 'After Stalin's Death. The Anglo-American Debate over a New Cold War', *Diplomatic History*, Vol. 10, fall 1986.

L. Freedman, 'The United States Factor' in E. Moreton and G. Segal, eds., *Soviet Strategy toward Western Europe* (London: Allen and Unwin, 1984).

J. L. Gaddis, 'Was the Truman Doctrine a Real Turning Point?' *Foreign Affairs*, Vol. 52, 1974 (January).

J. L. Gaddis, 'The Emerging Post-Revisionist Synthesis on the Origins of the Cold War', *Diplomatic History*, Vol. 7, no. 3, summer 1983.

Charles Gatti, 'The Stalinist Legacy in Soviet Foreign Policy', in Erick P. Hoffman and Frederick Flernon, Jr., eds., *The Conduct of Soviet Foreign Policy* (New York: Aldine, 1980).

H. W. Gatzke, 'Russo-German Military Collaboration during the Weimar Republic', *American Historical Review*, 63, 1957–1958.

Hans-Jürgen Grabbe, 'Konrad Adenauer, John Foster Dulles, and West German–American Relations', in R. H. Immerman, ed., *John Foster Dulles and the Diplomacy of the Cold War* (Princeton, New Jersey: Princeton University Press, 1990).

T. Harris, 'The Origins of the Conflicts between Malenkov and Zhdanov 1939–1941', *Slavonic Review*, Vol. 35, no. 2, June 1976.

G. Kennan ('X'), 'Sources of American Conduct', *Foreign Affairs*, July 1947.

Lothar Kettenacker, 'The Anglo-Soviet Alliance and the Problem of Germany, 1941–1945', *Journal of Contemporary History*, Vol. 17, no. 3, 1982.

B. Leont'ev, 'Anglo-amerikanskaya politika raskola Evropy', *Bolshevik*, no. 13, 1948.

W. Lerner, 'Attempting a Revolution from Without: Poland in 1920', in T. T. Hammond and R. Farrell, *The Anatomy of Communist Takeovers* (New Haven: Yale University Press, 1975).

M. McCauley, 'East Germany', in M. McCauley, ed., *Communist Power in Europe 1944–49* (London: Macmillan, 1977).

W. O. McCagg, Jr, 'Domestic Politics and Soviet Foreign Policy at the Cominform Conference in 1947', *Slavonic and Soviet Series*, Vol. 2, no. 1, spring 1977.

Philip E. Mosely, 'Dismemberment of Germany. The Allied Negotiations from Yalta to Potsdam', *Foreign Affairs*, Vol. 28, no. 4, 1950.

J. L. Richardson, 'Cold-War Revisionsim. A Critique', *World Politics*, Vol. 24, no. 4, July 1972.

Robert Slusser, 'Soviet Far Eastern Policy, 1945–1950. Stalin's Goals in Korea', in Yonosuke Nagai and Akira Iriye, eds., *The Origins of the Cold War in Asia* (Tokyo: University of Tokyo Press, 1977).

'Sozdanie amerikanskoy sistemy baz v gody vtoroy mirovoy voyny', *Voprosy istorii*, no. 9, 1984.

W. Stueck, 'The Soviet Union and the Origins of the Korean War', *World Politics*, Vol. 28, no. 4, July 1976, pp. 622–35.

R. Harrison Wagner, 'The Decision to Divide Germany and the Origins of the Cold War', *International Studies Quarterly*, Vol. 24, no. 2, 1980.

Geoffrey Warner, 'The Truman Doctrine and the Marshall Plan', *International Affairs*, Vol. 51, no. 1, 1975.

N. Yuryev, 'Franco–American Discord', *International Affairs*, no. 3, 1987.

Memoirs

Dean Acheson, *Present at the Creation. My Years at the State Department* (New York: Norton, 1969).

K. Adenauer, trans. B. Ruhm von Oppen, *Memoirs 1945–53* (London: Weidenfeld and Nicolson, 1965).

W. Bedell Smith, *Moscow Mission 1946–1949* (Kingswood, Surrey: Windmill Press, 1950).

Charles Bohlen, *Witness to History 1929–1969* (New York: W. W. Norton, 1973).

J. F. Byrnes, *Speaking Frankly* (London: Heinemann, 1947).

J. F. Byrnes, *All in One Lifetime* (New York: Harper, 1958).

W. S. Churchill, *The Second World War*, Vol. V, *Closing the Ring* (London: Cassell, 1952).

W. S. Churchill, *The Second World War*, Vol. VI, *Triumph and Tragedy* (London: Cassell, 1954).

E. Crankshaw, ed., *Khrushchev Remembers* (Boston: Little Brown, 1971).

J. E. Davies, *Mission to Moscow* (New York, 1941).

M. Djilas, *Conversations with Stalin* (New York: Harcourt Brace, 1962).

The Earl of Avon (Anthony Eden), *The Eden Memoirs*, Vol. 1, *Facing the Dictators* (London, Cassell, 1962).

Dwight D. Eisenhower, *The White House Years. Mandate for Change 1953–1956* (London: Heinemann, 1963).

R. H. Ferrell, ed., *The Eisenhower Diaries* (New York and London: W. W. Norton, 1981).

A. Gromyko, *Memoirs*, trans. Harold Shukman (London: Hutchinson, 1989).

A. Harriman and E. Abel, *Special Envoy to Churchill and Stalin 1941–1946* (London: Hutchinson, 1976).

H. L. Hopkins, *The White House Papers of Harry Hopkins*, ed. R. Sherwood (London: Eyre and Spottiswoode, 1949).

C. Hull, *The Memoirs of Cordell Hull* (London: Hodder and Stoughton, 1948).

G. F. Kennan, *Memoirs 1925–1950* (Boston, Mass.: Little Brown, 1967).

W. D. Leahy, *I was There* (New York: McGraw-Hill, 1950).

W. Millis, ed., *The Forrestal Diaries* (London: Cassell, 1952).

R. Sherwood, *The White House Papers of Harry L. Hopkins*, Vol. II, *January 1942–July 1945* (London: Eyre and Spottiswoode, 1949).

Z. Sheinis, *Maxim Litvinov* (Moscow: Progress Publishers, 1988).

J. F. Smith, *The Papers of Lucius D. Clay. Germany 1945–49*, Vol. I and Vol. II (Bloomington: Indiana University Press, 1974).

S. M. Shtemenko, *The Soviet General Staff at War* (Moscow: Progress Press, 1986).

L. Trotsky, *My Life* (New York: Scribner, 1930).

H. S. Truman, *Memoirs I, Year of Decisions 1945* (London: Hodder and Stoughton, 1955).

H. S. Truman, *Memoirs II, Years of Trial and Hope 1946–1953* (London: Hodder and Stoughton, 1956).

A. H. Vandenberg Jr, ed., *The Private Papers of Senator Vandenberg*, (Cambridge, Mass.: Riverside, 1952).

S. Welles, *The Time for Decision* (New York: Harper, 1944).

A. Werth, *Russia at War* (London: Barrie and Rockliffe, 1964).

G. K. Zhukov, *The Memoirs of Marshal Zhukov* (London: Jonathan Cape, 1971).

G. K. Zhukov, *Reminiscences and Reflections* (Moscow: Progress Publishers, 1985).

Books

H. Adomeit, *Soviet Risk-Taking and Crisis Behaviour* (London: Allen and Unwin, 1982).

G. Alperovitz, *Atomic Diplomacy. Hiroshima and Potsdam* (New York: Simon and Schuster, 1965).

Elisabeth Barker, *The British between the Superpowers 1945–1950* (London: Macmillan, 1983).

S. Bialer, *The Soviet Paradox: External Expansion, Internal Decline* (New York: Vintage Books, 1987).

S. Bialer, ed., *Stalin and his Generals* (New York: Pegasus, 1969).

A. Bullock, *Hitler and Stalin: Parallel Lives* (London: Harper Collins, 1991), p. 69.

E. H. Carr, *The Bolshevik Revolution 1917–1923*, Vol. 1 (London:

Macmillan, 1950).

E. H. Carr, *The Bolshevik Revolution 1917–1923*, Vol. 3 (London: Penguin).

D. Childs, *The GDR. Moscow's German Ally*, Second Edition (London: Unwin Hyman, 1988).

V. I. Chuikov, *The End of the Third Reich* (London: MacGibbon, 1950).

Diane S. Clemens, *Yalta* (New York: Oxford University Press, 1970).

R. Conquest, *Stalin: Breaker of Nations* (London: Weidenfeld and Nicolson, 1991).

D. J. Dallin, *Soviet Foreign Policy after Stalin* (London: Methuen, 1962).

J. R. Deane, *The Strange Alliance* (New York: Viking, 1947).

Anne Deighton, *The Impossible Peace. Britain, the Division of Germany, and the Origins of the Cold War* (Oxford: Clarendon Press, 1990).

Anthony D'Agnostino, *Soviet Succession Struggles. Kremlinology and the Russian Question from Lenin to Gorbachev* (Winchester, Mass.: Unwin Hyman, 1988).

L. E. Davis, *The Cold War Begins. Soviet–American Conflict over Eastern Europe* (Princeton, N.J.: Princeton University Press, 1974).

I. Deutscher, *Stalin* (London: Oxford University Press, 1949).

I. Deutscher, *Stalin* (London: Penguin, 1966).

Herbert S. Dinerstein, *War and the Soviet Union. Nuclear Weapons and the Revolution in Soviet Military and Political Thinking* (New York: Frederick A. Praeger, 1959).

Michael Dockrill and John W. Young, eds., *British Foreign Policy 1945–56* (London: Macmillan, 1989).

W. Eagleton Jr, *The Kurdish Republic of 1946* (London: Oxford University Press, 1963).

Robin Edmonds, *Setting the Mould. The United States and Britain 1945–1950* (Oxford: Clarendon Press, 1986).

J. Erickson, L. Hasen and W. Schneider, *Soviet Ground Forces* (Colorado: Westview, 1986).

Herbert Feis, *Churchill, Roosevelt, Stalin. The War they Waged and the Peace they Sought* (London: Oxford University Press, 1957).

Herbert Feis, *Between War and Peace. The Potsdam Conference* (Princeton: Princeton University Press, 1960).

Herbert Feis, *The Atomic Bomb and the End of World War II* (Princeton: Princeton University Press, 1966).

R. Fischer, *Stalin and German Communism* (Cambridge, Mass.: Harvard University Press, 1948).

D. F. Fleming, *The Cold War and its Origins 1917–1960* (New York: Garden City, 1961).

Rosemary Foot, *The Wrong War. American Foreign Policy and the Dimensions of the Korean Conflict, 1950–1953* (Ithaca: Cornell University Press, 1985).

Richard M. Freeland, *The Truman Doctrine and the Origins of McCarthyism* (New York: New York University Press, 1985).

J. L. Gaddis, *The United States and the Origins of the Cold War 1941–1947* (New York: Columbia University Press, 1972).

J. L. Gaddis, *The Long Peace* (New York: Oxford University Press, 1987).

J. L. Gaddis, *Russia, the Soviet Union and the United States. An Interpretive History*, Second Edition (New York: McGraw-Hill, 1990).

G. Galli, 'Italian Communism', in W. E. Griffiths, ed., *Communism in Europe* (Oxford: Pergamon, 1964).

R. L. Garthoff, *Soviet Strategy in the Nuclear Age* (New York: Frederick A. Praeger, 1958).

John Gimbel, *The American Occupation of Germany; Politics and the Military, 1945–1949* (Stanford: Stanford University Press, 1968).

E. Gnedin, *Iz istorii otnosheniy mezhdu SSSR i fashistkoy Germaniey* (New York: Khronika, 1977).

W. Hahn, *The Fall of Zhdanov and the Defeat of Moderation 1946–53* (New York: Cornell University Press, 1982).

L. B. Halle, *The Cold War as History* (New York: Harper and Row, 1967).

T. T. Hammond and R. Farrell, *The Anatomy of the Communist Revolution* (New Haven: Yale University Press, 1975).

Fraser J. Harbutt, *The Iron Curtain; Churchill, America, and the Origins of the Cold War* (New York: Oxford University Press, 1986).

C. R. S. Harris, *Allied Military Administration of Italy 1943–1945* (London: HMSO, 1957).

J. Haslam, *The Soviet Union and the Struggle for Collective Security in Europe 1933–1939* (New York: St Martin's, 1984).

G. C. Herring Jr, *Aid to Russia 1941–1946. Strategy Diplomacy. The Origins of the Cold War* (New York: Columbia University Press, 1973).

D. A. Holloway, *The Soviet Union and the Arms Race* (New Haven and London: Yale University Press, 1983).

J. W. Hulse, *The Forming of the Communist International* (Stanford: Stanford University Press, 1959).

Carl G. Jacobsen, ed., *Strategic Power USA/USSR* (Basingstoke: Macmillan Press, 1990).

Stephen S. Kaplan, *Diplomacy of Power. Soviet Armed Forces as a Political Instrument* (Washington: The Brookings Institution, 1981).

C. Keeble, ed., *The Soviet State. The Domestic Roots of Soviet Foreign Policy* (Aldershot: Gower, 1985).

C. Keeble, *Britain and the Soviet Union, 1917–89* (Basingstoke: Macmillan, 1990).

G. F. Kennan, *Russia and the West under Lenin and Stalin* (Boston, Toronto: Little Brown, 1960).

R. A. Kilmarx, *A History of Soviet Air Power* (London: Faber and Faber, 1962).

Amy Knight, *Beria. Stalin's First Lieutenant* (Princeton: Princeton University Press, 1993).

Bruce Kuklick, *American Policy and the Division of Germany. The Clash with Russia over Reparations* (Ithaca: Cornell University Press, 1972).

W. Lacqueur, *Russia and Germany. A Century of Conflict* (New Brunswick and London: Transaction Publishers, 1990. Originally published in 1965 by Little Brown).

V. I. Lenin, *The Essentials of Lenin*, Vol. 11 (London: 1947).

M. Light, *The Soviet Theory of International Relations* (Brighton: Wheatsheaf, 1988).

W. Loth, *The Division of the World 1941–1955* (London: Routledge, 1988).

J. M. Mackintosh, *Strategy and Tactics of Soviet Foreign Policy,* (London: Oxford University Press, 1962).

Malcolm Mackintosh, *Juggernaut: A History of the Soviet Armed Forces* (London: Secker and Warburg, 1967).

V. Mastny, *Russia's Road to the Cold War: Diplomacy, Warfare and the Politics of Communism* (New York: Columbia University Press, 1979).

David Mayers, *George Kennan and the Dilemmas of US Foreign Policy* (New York: Oxford University Press, 1988).

W. O. McCagg Jr, *Stalin Embattled, 1943–1948* (Detroit: Wayne State University Press, 1978).

M. McGwire, *Perestroika and Soviet National Security* (Washington: The Brookings Institution, 1991).

W. H. McNeill, *America, Britain and Russia. Their Co-operation and Conflict 1941–46* (London: Oxford University Press, 1953).

R. Medvedev, *Krushchev*, English Translation (Oxford: Basil Blackwell, 1982).

Robert S. Messer, *The End of an Alliance. James F. Byrnes, Roosevelt, Truman and the Origins of the Cold War* (Chapel Hill: The University of North Carolina Press, 1982).

S. Mikolajczck, *The Pattern of Soviet Domination* (London: Sampson Low, 1948).

J. P. Nettl, *The Eastern Zone and Soviet Policy in Germany, 1945–1950* (London: Oxford University Press, 1951).

Thomas G. Paterson, *Soviet–American Confrontation. Post-War Reconstruction and the Origins of the Cold War* (Baltimore: Johns Hopkins University Press, 1973).

Henry Pelling, *Britain and the Marshall Plan* (New York: St Martin's Press, 1988).

R. P. Pipes, ed., *The Russian Revolution* (Cambridge, Mass.: Harvard University Press, 1968).

H. B. Price, *The Marshall Plan and its Meaning* (Ithaca: Cornell University Press, 1955).

G. D. Ra'anon, *International Policy Formation in the USSR. Factional Debates during the Zhdanovshine* (Hamden, Conn.: Archon, 1983).

R. K. Ramazani, *Iran's Foreign Policy 1941–1973* (Charlottesville: University of Virginia Press, 1975).

W. W. Rostow, *Europe after Stalin. Eisenhower's Three Decisions of March 11, 1953* (Austin: University of Texas Press, 1982).

H. B. Ryan, *The Vision of Anglo-America. The US–UK Alliance and the Emerging Cold War 1943–1946* (Cambridge: Cambridge University Press, 1987).

Gregory W. Sandford, *From Hitler to Ulbricht. The Communist Reconstruction of East Germany, 1945–46* (Princeton: Princeton University Press, 1983).

T. Sharpe, *The Wartime Alliance and the Zonal Division of Germany* (London: Oxford University Press, 1975).

Martin J. Sherwin, *A World Destroyed. Hiroshima and the Origins of the Arms Race* (New York: Vintage, 1987).

R. E. Sherwood, *Roosevelt and Hopkins. An Intimate History* (London: Eyre and Spottiswoode, 1948–49).

Avi Shlaim, *The United States and the Berlin Blockade 1948–1949: A Study in Crisis Decision Making* (Berkeley: University of California Press, 1983).

Marshall D. Shulman, *Stalin's Foreign Policy Reappraised* (Cambridge, Mass.: Harvard University Press, 1963).

R. Slusser, *Soviet Economic Policy in Post-War Germany* (New York: Research Programme on the USSR, 1953).

Rolf Stieninger, *The German Question. The Stalin Note of 1952 and the Problem of Unification* (New York: Columbia University Press, 1990).

H. R. Swearer, *The Politics of Succession in the USSR. Materials on Khrushchev's Rise to Leadership* (Boston: Little Brown, 1964).

W. Taubman, *Stalin's American Policy. From Entente to Detente to Cold War* (New York and London: Norton, 1982).

R. Tucker, *Stalin as Revolutionary 1879–1929. A Study in History and Personality* (London: Chatto and Windus, 1974).

V. G. Turkhanovsky and N. K. Kapitonova, *Sovetsko-angliyskie otnoshenia 1945–1978* (Moscow: Mezhdunarodnye otnosheniya, 1979).

H. A. Turner, *The Two Germanies since 1945* (New Haven: Yale University Press, 1987).

A. Ulam, *Stalin* (London: Allen Lane, 1973).

A. Ulam, *Expansion and Coexistence. Soviet Foreign Policy 1917–73*, Second Edition (New York: Praeger, 1974).

A. Ulam, *The Communists. The Story of Power and Lost Illusions 1948–1991* (New York and Toronto: Charles Scribner's Sons, 1992).

D. Volkogonov, *Triumf i tragediya. Politicheskiy portret*, kniga 1 (Moscow: Izdatelstvo agenstva politicki, novostii, 1989).

D. Volkogonov, trans. H. Shuckman, *Stalin. Triumph and Tragedy* (London: Weidenfeld and Nicolson, 1900).

William A. Williams, *The Tragedy of American Diplomacy*, Revised Edition (New York: World Publishing, 1962).

T. Wolfe, *Soviet Power and Europe 1945–1970* (Baltimore: Johns Hopkins Press, 1970).

Daniel Yergin, *Shattered Peace. The Origins of the Cold War and the National Security State* (Boston: Houghton Mifflin, 1977).

John W. Young, *France, the Cold War and the Western Alliance 1944–1949* (Leicester: Leicester University Press, 1990).

Harold Zink, *The United States in Germany 1944–1955* (Princeton: Van Nostrand, 1957).

Index

Note: 'n.' after a page reference indicates the number of a note on that page.

DATE DUE